'LOUISE BOGAN;

A Reference Source

by

CLAIRE E. KNOX

Scarecrow Author Bibliographies, No. 86

The Scarecrow Press, Inc.
Metuchen, N.J., & London
1990

<u>Frontispiece:</u> Photo of Louise Bogan courtesy of Ruth Limmer.
Photo by Sylvie Pasche.

British Library Cataloguing-in-Publication data available

Library of Congress Cataloging-in-Publication Data

Knox, Claire E., 1936-
    Louise Bogan : a reference source / by Claire E. Knox.
      p.   cm. -- (Scarecrow author bibliographies ; no. 86)
    Includes indexes.
    ISBN 0-8108-2379-9 (alk. paper)
    1. Bogan, Louise, 1897-1970--Bibliography. I. Title. II. Series.
Z8106.37.K58 1990
[PS3503.0195]
016.811'52--dc20   90-47804

To Jim

"Some things I overlooked, and some I could not
find.
Let the crystal clasp them
When you drink your wine, in autumn."

CONTENTS

PREFACE

This book came into being because I went to a concert in Boston several years ago and heard a chorale sing Louise Bogan's poem, "To Be Sung on the Water," which was put to music by Samuel Barber. I recognized this poet because I vaguely remembered two widely-anthologized poems by Bogan, "Women" and "Cartology," but I knew little about her. The words of "To Be Sung on the Water" affected me so strongly that I decided to find out just who Louise Bogan was and what other wonderful poems she had written. At that time I was pursuing an advanced graduate degree in English, specializing in modern American poetry, so Bogan's work fit into my field perfectly. I began my Bogan study with a linguistic analysis of "To Be Sung on the Water" and continued researching her life and work for other courses. My final project was a ten-year annotated Bogan bibliography, which began where Jane Couchman's 1976 bibliography, published in The Bulletin of Bibliography, left off. This publication grew out of that project.

Incorporated in this book are both Couchman's bibliography and the bibliography compiled by the Library of Congress staff members and published with William Jay Smith's memorial lecture, "Louise Bogan: A Woman's Words." My comprehensive annotated bibliography contains all the items from both those works, along with many additional important references. Bogan's New Yorker reviews comprise the largest section of the book. Although many of these reviews were first collected in Selected Criticism and later incorporated in A Poet's Alphabet, I have included almost 60 pages of additional reviews that have not been collected anywhere. Many were published anonymously in the New Yorker "Briefly Noted" section. Along with these reviews, I have noted all short stories, essays, and poems listed in The New Yorker's library files.

In addition to using <u>The New Yorker</u>'s files, I
also researched additional Bogan materials in the
Widener and Houghton Libraries at Harvard
University, the Berg Collection at the New York
Public Library, the Library of Congress, and
Amherst College Library.

This bibliography is divided into two major
sections, "Part I: Works by Louise Bogan," and
"Part II: Works About Louise Bogan." The entries,
all of which I have seen except for those few so
noted, cover the period from 1915 to 1989. Most
of the longer sections in Parts I and II are
arranged chronologically, while the shorter
sections are arranged alphabetically. The poems
collected in the books of poetry are numbered
consecutively in the order they appeared in the
books. Bogan divided each book of poetry, except
her first, into sections headed by Roman
numerals, which I have kept here. I have used
the <u>Chicago Manual of Style</u> citation format.

Many people encouraged me to continue with this
labor of love. Jane Nelson, retired faculty
member of the Northeastern University English
Department, started me on the project. Irene
Fairley kept me going, while Guy Rotella and Jim
Nagle encouraged me. Kinley Robey, Chair of the
Department, allowed me six months' leave of
absence to research the material. My research
load was considerably lightened by Martha Collins'
generous sharing of her files. The text was
lovingly proofread by Gwen Bindas. Alice Quinn,
Poetry Editor of <u>The New Yorker</u>, arranged for my
use of the magazine's files. Most importantly, my
husband, Jim Knox, performed the hardest job of
all, putting the work on the computer, with all
the problems that entailed. I thank you all and
apologize to the many others who had to put up
with my obsession with Louise Bogan.

Claire E. Knox
Northeastern University

INTRODUCTION

Since Louise Bogan's death in New York City on February 4, 1970, the feminist literary movement has revived her poetry, giving her work more support after her death than it received during her life. The 1977 paperback reissue of her final poetry collection, The Blue Estuaries, and the January 30, 1978, New Yorker issue containing her memoirs and musings, "From the Journals of a Poet," illustrate how this feminist interest resurrected her writings for a general audience who did not read women's literary journals. Although Bogan, an independent woman, provided for herself and her daughter on the money she earned from her work, ironically she helped few of her women poet contemporaries with their writing. She criticized them more severely than male poets, especially those she called "surrealists." For example she judged Muriel Rukeyser's ideological poetry more harshly than Archibald MacLeish's political polemics. She asserted that men write from their intellect, while women write from their feelings. And she neglected May Sarton's work in her New Yorker poetry reviews, despite their long friendship. Yet Bogan's early poetry shows influences from important women poets of the 1920s, especially Edna St. Vincent Millay and Sara Teasdale. Her reviews of both poets' later works were mixed.

Bogan's ambivalent feelings towards women stem from her stormy relationship with her mother, a passionate woman of Irish descent. Bogan was born in Livermore Falls, Maine, on August 11, 1897, the second child of Mary Shields Bogan and Daniel Bogan. Her early home life in New England towns and later Boston, as the family moved because of her father's railroad jobs, was disorganized. This transient life disturbed the young girl who longed for the peace and order she saw in other people's homes. Her classical education at Girls' Latin High School in Boston provided her with an excellent background for her writing career and was the one bright spot in her unhappy

ix

adolescence. Her poetry, short stories, and
essays were published in The Jabberwocky, the
school publication.

Her mother's affairs most likely contributed to
Bogan's own tempestuous relations with men
throughout her adult life. Much of her inability
to develop a satisfactory romantic relationship
stemmed from her extreme jealousy of the men in
her life.

These problems contributed to Bogan's severe
bouts of depression and subsequent hospitalization
for psychiatric care. But her anxieties also
helped produce her poetry, for she wrote most of
her best poems between 1920 and 1940, the years
when she was most depressed. Her method of
delving into the unconscious for poetic material
helped stir up the old conflicts between her
mother and herself.

Her 1916 marriage to a dashing military man,
Curt Alexander, after her first year at Boston
University, where she published several poems in
the school's literary review, The Beacon, seemed
to provide her with a means of escape from her
tumultuous home life. But this marriage failed
shortly after the birth of her daughter Maidie on
Oct. 19, 1917. Bogan and her baby returned home
from the Panama Canal Zone, where Alexander had
been stationed. After an unsuccessful attempt at
reconciliation in 1918, the same year that her
brother was killed fighting in France, Bogan
separated from her husband, who died two years
later. Many of Bogan's early openly biographical
poems such as "The Young Wife" and "Others" came
from this time, but Bogan left these poems out of
her poetry collections once she decided not to
expose the harsh reality of her life in her work.
She hid personal experiences behind myth and
symbol in her later poems.

After the failure of her marriage, Bogan left
Maidie with her mother and was free to pursue her
career. She returned to Greenwich Village, where
she and Alexander had lived briefly, and joined
the Bohemian literary group of the 1920s. She
worked at several different branches of the New
York Public Library and in Brentano's bookstore.
She was living in Vienna for six months in 1922,
when five of her poems were published in Poetry by

Harriet Monroe under the title "Beginning and
End." Her first book of poetry, <u>Body of This
Death</u>, was published in 1923. This book's
reception, which set the pattern for all of
Bogan's subsequent poetry collections, was one of
critical acclaim for the poetry's formality,
music, and beauty, but little popular acceptance
because of its perceived difficulty. In 1925
Bogan married Raymond Holden, a writer and editor
at <u>The New Yorker</u>, and Maidie moved in with them.

Her second book of poetry, <u>Dark Summer</u>, came
out in 1929. In December of the following year
the farmhouse in Hillsdale, New York, where Bogan,
Maidie, and Holden had moved, burned down,
destroying all their belongings, including their
papers. The family returned to live in New York
City where Bogan had her first breakdown in 1931.
In 1933 she again traveled to Europe, this time on
a Guggenheim fellowship, and went to Italy and
France, returning to New York to find Holden
living with another woman, a vindication of her
jealous fears. She divorced Holden in 1937, after
suffering another breakdown, but she recovered to
publish her third book of poetry, <u>The Sleeping
Fury</u>, the same year. Her other romantic liaisons
included a brief fling with Theodore Roethke,
which matured into a lifelong friendship in which
Bogan acted as a mentor to Roethke. Her long
affair with the never-identified electrician she
met on the boat trip back from Ireland where she
had gone in 1937 to complete her unfinished
Guggenheim fellowship, seems to have been her only
happy relationship with a man. Much of her poetry
shows the unhappiness of male-female love, with
the woman trying to escape her sexual passion for
an unworthy man.

It seemed that the more mental stability she
attained, the less poetry she wrote. She tried to
still her insistent muse, but it broke through her
silence (upon the urging of her various editors)
for a few new poems which were published in three
more collections of poetry, each of which
contained a majority of republished poems. These
books are: <u>Poems and New Poems</u>, published in
1941; <u>Collected Poems 1923-1954</u> in 1955; and her
final collection, <u>The Blue Estuaries: Poems 1923-
1968</u> in 1968.

Beginning in the 1940s, Bogan concentrated on

her criticism, her other major interest, although
she had also written short stories and essays.
She had begun to write poetry criticism for The
New Yorker in 1931 and continued as poetry critic
for almost 38 years until her retirement in 1968.
Many of these reviews were collected in Selected
Criticism - Poetry and Prose, published in 1955,
and the posthumous publication, A Poet's Alphabet:
Reflections on the Literary Art and Vocation, in
1970. Her other works include Achievement in
American Poetry 1900-1950 and translations of
European literature, as well as a collaboration on
a children's anthology, The Golden Journey.

Bogan received many awards for her poetry,
beginning with the John Reed Memorial Prize given
by Poetry in 1930, including the Harriet Monroe
Award from the University of Chicago in 1948, and
the sharing of the Bollingen prize with Léonie
Adams in 1955. Although she never received the
major American literary prizes, she was given
several awards from the National Institute of Arts
and Letters, the Academy of American Poets, and
the National Endowment for the Arts. Her literary
honors started with her appointment as the Poetry
Consultant for the Library of Congress in 1945,
continued with her election to the National
Institute of Arts and Letters in 1952, and ended
with her election to the American Academy of Arts
and Letters in 1969, just a year before her death.

She began her teaching career at the University
of Washington during the summer of 1948 at
Roethke's request. She also taught at the
University of Chicago, New York University evening
school, the New York YMHA (where Marianne Moore
attended her classes), the University of Arkansas,
and Brandeis University. She lectured at the
Salzburg Seminar of American Studies in 1958.

Bogan is best known for her poetry, which has
been added to the canon by her feminist
revivalists. As interest in her poetry continues,
more books are written about her life and work.
Ruth Limmer, her literary executor, published
Bogan's letters in What the Woman Lived: Selected
Letters of Louise Bogan, 1920-1970 in 1973 and
Bogan's journal musings, Journey Around My Room:
The Autobiography of Louise, A Mosaic, in 1980.
Bogan studies continued to move forward with
Martha Collins' 1984 collection of critical

articles, <u>Critical Essays on Louise Bogan</u>, and
Elizabeth (Perlmutter) Frank's 1985 biography,
<u>Louise Bogan: A Portrait</u>. Gloria Bowles' book of
literary criticism on Bogan's lack of poetic
output, <u>Louise Bogan's Aesthetic of Limitation</u>,
was published in 1988. The many doctoral
dissertations written since 1974 focus on Bogan's
poetry and compare her work to the writings of
other women poets.

Louise Bogan's place in American literature
grows with the passage of time. The best source
of collected critical material on Bogan is
Collins' book, which reprints major essays and
reviews of Bogan's poetry from the 1920s through
the 1980s, and includes six new articles by Bogan
scholars, several of whom have written their
dissertations on Bogan. It is clear, however,
that there is much left for scholars to do,
especially in studies of Bogan's criticism and her
short stories. Recent articles in reference books
still concentrate on Bogan's poetry, while simply
mentioning her contribution to criticism.

Bogan's poetry criticism in <u>The New Yorker</u> set
the standard for reviewers. She has not been
replaced in the 22 years since she left the
publication, according to Donald Hall in his 1989
article in <u>Harper's</u>. Much could be written about
the contrast between Bogan's criticism and the
academic schools of criticism, beginning with the
New Criticism of John Crowe Ransom, which Bogan
despised. It is interesting to speculate what she
would have said about the Marxist,
Deconstructionist, Lancanian, and Freudian
schools. Although feminists have championed her
poetry, they have ignored her criticism because it
does not fit their ideology.   Little critical
analysis of Bogan's short stories and essays has
been published, except for a discussion centering
on their autobiographical aspects in Elizabeth
Frank's <u>Portrait</u> and autobiographical excerpts
reprinted in Ruth Limmer's <u>Journey Around My Room</u>.
I hope this annotated bibliography will help
future Bogan scholars in their studies.

ABBREVIATIONS

BD   Body of This Death

DS   Dark Summer

SF   Sleeping Fury

PNP   Poems and New Poems

CP   Collected Poems 1923-1953

BE   Blue Estuaries: Poems 1923-1968

SC   Selected Criticism

APA   A Poet's Alphabet

PART I

WORKS BY LOUISE BOGAN

A. BOOKS

POETRY COLLECTIONS

Included here are Louise Bogan's six books of
poetry. The title and publication facts of the
book are given first. Then the individual poems
in the collection are listed as they appear in the
book, with initial place of publication given.
Inclusion in subsequent collections is also noted
in the first entry of a poem. When these poems
reappear in sections of Bogan's later books of
poetry, they are simply listed by name. Reprints
of the poem in other sources are mentioned only
when it is the major focus of an article.

1. BODY OF THIS DEATH. New York: Robert M.
    McBride & Company, 1923.

2. "A Tale." New Republic 28 (19 Oct. 1921):
    214. Reprinted in Bookman (22 Jan. 1922):
    475. Also in PNP, CP, BE.

3. "Decoration." New Republic 27 (24 Aug. 1921):
    357. No further publication.

4. "Medusa." New Republic 29 (21 Dec. 1921):
    101. Also in DS, PNP, CP, BE.

5. "Sub Contra." First published in BD. Also
    in DS, PNP, CP, BE.

6. "A Letter." First and only publication in BD.

1

7.   "The Frightened Man." _Measure_ 24 (Feb.
      1923): 13. Also in PNP, CP, BE.

8.   "Betrothed." _Others_ 4 (Dec. 1917): 10. Also
      in PNP, CP, BE.

9.   "Words for Departure." _Measure_ 2 (Apr. 1921):
      8-9. No further publication.

10.   "Ad Castitatem." First published in BD.   Also
      in DS, PNP, CP, BE.

11.   "Knowledge." Published with title "Beginning
      and End," in _Poetry_ 22, No. 5 (Aug. 1922):
      249. Reprinted in _Current Opinions_ 76 (Feb.
      1924): 223. Also in PNP, CP, BE.

12.   "Portrait." _Liberator_ 5, No. 4 (Apr. 1922):
      27. Also in DS, PNP, CP, BE. Reprinted in
      May Days, ed. Genevieve Taggard. New York:
      Boni and Liveright, 1925. p. 85.

13.   "The Romantic." _Measure_ 24 (Feb. 1923): 13.
      Also in DS, PNP, CP, BE.

14.   "My Voice Not Being Proud." _Liberator_ 6, No.
      2 (Jan. 1923): 18. Also in PNP, CP, BE.
      Reprinted _May Days_, ed. Genevieve Taggard.
      New York: Boni and Liveright, 1925. p. 175.

15.   "Statue and Birds." _New Republic_ 30 (12 Apr.
      1922): 197. Also in PNP, CP, BE.

16.   "Epitaph for a Romantic Woman." First
      publication unknown. No further publication.

17.   "The Alchemist." _New Republic_ 29 (22 Feb.
      1922): 370. Also in DS, PNP, CP, BE.

18.   "Men Loved Wholly Beyond Wisdom." _Literary_

Review of the New York Evening Post 3, No. 33
(22 Apr. 1923): 617. Also in DS, PNP, CP,
BE.

19. "The Crows." Literary Review of the New York
Evening Post 2, No. 32 (15 Apr. 1922): 577.
Also in PNP, CP, BE.

20. "Memory." New Republic 30 (10 May 1922):
311.

21. "Women." Measure 12 (Feb. 1922): 14.
Printed for Miss Bogan's private distribution
by Ward Ritchie, Pasadena, 1929. Also in
PNP, CP, BE. Reprinted in Bookman 55 (May
1922): 259, with comments by Stanley
Braithwaite.

22. "Last Hill in a Vista." Measure 21 (Nov.
1922): 14. Also in PNP, CP, BE. Reprinted
in The Independent 3 (10 Nov. 1923): 216.

23. "Song." First line "Love me because I am
lost." First publication unknown.
Reprinted in Voices 146 (Sept.-Dec. 1951):
8-9.

24. "Stanza." Measure 21 (Nov. 1922): 14.
Also in DS, PNP, CP, BE.

25. "The Changed Woman." Rhythmus 2, No. 1
(Jun-Jul. 1923): 47. Also in DS, PNP, CP,
BE.

26. "Chanson un peu naïve." First published in
Vanity Fair, July 1923, 47. Also in DS, PNP,
CP, BE as "Chanson Un Peu Naïve." Reprinted
in Bookman 58, No. 2 (Oct. 1923): 197-198,
with comments by Genevieve Taggard.

27. "Fifteenth Farewell." Vanity Fair, Aug. 1923,
39. Also in DS, PNP, CP, BE.

28. "Sonnet." Title of poem first published in
     BD. First line, "Since you would claim the
     sources of my thought," used as title in DS.
     Also in PNP, CP, BE. (Entry 29)

29. "Since You Would Claim the Sources of My
     Thought." Title of "Sonnet" in DS. (Entry
     28)

30. DARK SUMMER. New York: Charles Scribner's
     Sons, 1929.

                        Section I

31. "Winter Swan." "Books." New York Herald
     Tribune, 1926. Day, month, and page
     unknown. Also in PNP, CP, BE. (Not
     seen by bibliographer.)

32. "If We Take All Gold." Nation 121 (21 Oct.
     1925): 464.

33. "The Dream." First published in DS.
     Reprinted in Nation 146 (12 Feb. 1938): 187.
     Also in PNP, CP, BE.

34. "The Drum." New Republic 50 (30 Mar. 1927):
     167. Also in PNP, CP, BE.

35. "Division." First published in DS. Also in
     PNP, CP, BE.

36. "Cassandra." Nation 119 (3 Dec. 1924): 599.
     Also in PNP, CP, BE.

37. "The Cupola." New Republic 52 (Sept. 1927):
     142. Also in PNP, CP, BE.

38. "A Girl to Juan." Original title of "Girl's
     Song." Measure 39 (May 1924): 10.
     Original first lines, "Winter, that is a
     roofless room/Tavern to rain, was our love's

home." (Entry 39)

39. "Girl's Song." Title of "A Girl to Juan" in
    BD. First lines, "Winter that is a fireless
    room/In a locked house, was our love's home."
    Also in PNP, CP, BE. (Entry 38)

40. "Feurnacht." New Republic 51 (June 1927):
    72. Also in PNP, CP, BE as "Feur-Nacht."

41. "Second Song." Nation 123 (15 Sept.1926):
    246. Also in PNP, CP, BE.

42. "The Mark." New Republic 58 (9 Jan. 1929):
    214. Also in PNP, CP, BE.

43. "Late." Nation 125 (7 Sept. 1927): 230. Also
    in PNP, CP, BE.

44. "Simple Autumnal." New Republic 49 (1 Dec.
    1926): 44. Also in PNP, CP, BE.

                    Section II

45. "The Flume." Measure 52 (June 1925): 3-10.
    No further publication.

                    Section III

Poems in this section originally collected in BD.

"Medusa"
"Sub Contra"
"Ad Castitatem"
"Portrait"
"The Romantic"
"The Alchemist"
"Men Loved Wholly Beyond Wisdom"
"Stanza"
"Chanson Un Peu Naïve"
"Fifteenth Farewell"
"Since You Would Claim the Sources of My Thought"

Section IV

46. "Dark Summer." <u>Nation</u> 123 (13 Oct. 1926):
    359. Also in PNP, CP, BE. Reprinted in
    <u>America</u> 153 (31 Aug.-7 Sept. 1985): 107 with
    biographical notes by Virginia Spencer Carr.

47. "For a Marriage." First published in DS.
    Also in PNP, CP, BE.

48. "Didactic Piece." <u>Poetry</u> 31, No. 6 (Mar.
    1928): 314-15. Also in PNP, CP, BE.

49. "Tears in Sleep." <u>Nation</u> 125 (7 Sept. 1927):
    230. Also in PNP, CP, BE.

50. "Song for a Slight Voice." <u>Century</u> 109, No. 1
    (Nov. 1924): 14. Also in DS, PNP, CP,BE.

51. "The Crossed Apple." First published in DS.
    Reprinted in <u>Poetry</u> 37, No. 2 (Nov. 1930):
    111-12. Also in PNP, CP, BE.

52. "Sonnet." First line "Dark, underground, is
    furnished with the bone." First published in
    DS. Also in PNP, CP, BE.

53. "Fiend's Weather." First published in DS.
    Also in PNP, CP, BE.

54. "I Saw Eternity." First published in DS.
    Also in PNP, CP, BE.

55. "Song." Original title of "Come, Break with
    Time." <u>New Republic</u> 53 (1 Feb. 1928): 290.
    (Entry 56)

56. "Come, Break with Time." Title of "Song"
    in DS. Reprinted in <u>Poetry</u> 37, No. 2 (Nov.
    1930): 112. Also in PNP, CP, BE. (Entry
    55)

57. "Old Countryside." <u>Scribner's Magazine</u> 86,
     No. 2 (Aug. 1929): 219. Also in PNP, CP,
     BE.

                      Section V

58. "Summer Wish." First published in DS. Also
     in PNP, CP, BE.

59. <u>THE SLEEPING FURY: POEMS</u>. New York and
     London: Charles Scribner's Sons, 1937.

                      Section I

60. "Song." First line "It is not now I learn."
     <u>Scribner's Magazine</u> 87, No. 5 (May 1930):
     527. Also in PNP, CP, BE.

61. "Henceforth, From the Mind." <u>New Republic</u> 65
     (121 Jan. 1931): 270. Also in PNP, CP, BE.

62. "Homunculus." <u>New Yorker</u> 6 (8 Mar. 1930): 16.
     Reprinted in <u>New Yorker Book of Verse 1925-
     1935</u>. New York: Harcourt, Brace, 1935. p.
     60. Also in PNP, CP, BE.

63. "Single Sonnet." <u>Scribner's Magazine</u> 99, No.
     3 (Mar. 1936): 160. Also in PNP, CP, BE.

64. "Exhortation." <u>Scribner's Magazine</u> 93, No. 3
     (Mar. 1933): 1939. Also in PNP, CP, BE.

65. "Hypocrite Swift." <u>Poetry</u> 39, No. 1 (Oct.
     1931): 12-13. Also in PNP, CP, BE.

66. "At a Party." <u>New Yorker</u> 8 (11 Feb. 1933):
     24. Also in PNP, CP, BE.

                      Section II

67. "To Wine." <u>Scribner's Magazine</u> 46, No. 1
     (Jul. 1934): 45. Also in PNP, CP, BE.

68. "Poem in Prose." Scribner's Magazine 47, No.
     1 (Jan. 1935): 18. Also in PNP, CP, BE.

69. "Short Summary." New Yorker 10 (4 Aug.
     1934): 18. Also in PNP, CP, BE.

70. "Italian Morning." Scribner's Magazine 93,
     No. 2 (Aug. 1935): 104. Also in PNP, CP, BE.

71. "Man Alone." New Yorker 10 (3 Nov. 1934):
     22. Also in PNP, CP, BE.

Section III

72. "Baroque Comment." New Republic 84 (23 Oct.
     1935): 292 (under title "Eight Women Poets").
     Also in PNP, CP, BE.

73. "To My Brother." New Yorker 11 (26 Oct.
     1935): 31. Misprint in stanza 4 "All things
     indeed" corrected in SF to "All things
     remain." Also in PNP, CP, BE.

74. "Roman Fountain." New Yorker 11 (14 Sept.
     1935): 13. Also in PNP, CP, BE.

75. "The Sleeping Fury." Poetry 49, No. 3 (Dec.
     1936): 119-21 (under title "Three Poems").
     Also in PNP, CP, BE.

76. "Rhyme." New Yorker 11 (June 1935): 26.
     Also in PNP, CP, BE.

77. "M., Singing." Poetry 49, No. 3 (Dec. 1936):
     121 (under title "Three Poems"). Also in
     PNP, CP, BE.

78. "Evening Star." Scribner's Magazine 48, No.
     4 (Oct. 1935): 199. Line left out of poem
     "Big in the cirrus sky, at evening:." (Entry
     79)

79. "Evening-Star."   Title in SF. "Big
    in the cirrus sky, at evening" changed to
    "Held in the cirrus sky, at evening:." Also
    in PNP, CP, BE. (Entry 78)

Section IV

80. "Spirit's Song." New Yorker 12 (12 Dec.
    1936): 34. Also in PNP, CP, BE.

81. "Putting to Sea." Poetry 49, No. 3 (Dec.
    1936): 122-23 (under title "Three Poems").
    Also in PNP, CP, BE.

82. "Kept." First published in SF. Also in PNP,
    CP, BE.

83. "Heard by a Girl." First published in SF.
    Also in PNP, CP, BE.

84. "Packet of Letters." New Yorker 12 (2 Jan.
    1937): 21. Also in PNP, CP, BE.

85. "Song for a Lyre." Poetry 49, No. 5 (Feb.
    1937): 245. Also in PNP, CP, BE.

86. POEMS AND NEW POEMS. New York: Charles
    Scribner's Sons, 1941.

Section I

Poems in this section originally published in BD
except for "Juan's Song."

"A Tale"
"Medusa"
"Sub Contra"
"The Frightened Man"
"Bethrothed"
"Ad Castitatem"
"Knowledge"

87. "Juan's Song." New Yorker 6 (24 May 1930):
    28. Reprinted in The New Yorker Book of

Verse (1925-1935). New York: Harcourt,
Brace, 1935. p. 119.

"Portrait"
"The Romantic"
"My Voice Not Being Proud"
"Statue and Birds"
"The Alchemist"
"Men Loved Wholly Beyond Wisdom"
"The Crows"
"Memory"
"Women"
"Last Hill in a Vista"
"Stanza"
"The Changed Woman"
"Chanson Un Peu Naïve"
"Fifteenth Farewell"
"Sonnet"

Section II

Poems in this section originally published in DS.

"Winter Swan"
"If We Take All Gold"
"The Drum"
"Division"
"Cassandra"
"The Cupola"
"Girl's Song"
"Fuer-Nacht"
"Second Song"
"The Mark"
"Late"
"Simple Autumnal"
"Dark Summer"
"For a Marriage"
"Didactic Piece"
"Tears in Sleep"
"Song for a Slight Voice"
"The Crossed Apple"
"Sonnet"
"Fiend's Weather"
"I Saw Eternity"
"Come, Break with Time"
"Old Countryside"
"Summer Wish"

Section III

Poems in this section originally published in SF.

"Song"
"Henceforth from the Mind"
"Homunculus"
"Single Sonnet"
"Exhortation"
"Hypocrite Swift"
"At a Party"
"To Wine"
"Poem in Prose"
"Short Summary"
"Italian Morning"
"Man Alone"
"Baroque Comment"
"To My Brother"
"Roman Fountain"
"The Sleeping Fury"
"Rhyme"
"M., Singing"
"Evening-Star"
"Spirit's Song"
"Putting to Sea"
"Kept"
"Heard by a Girl"
"Packet of Letters"
"Song for a Lyre"

Section IV

88. "Several Voices Out of a Cloud." <u>Partisan Review</u> 5, No. 1 (Fall 1938): 19. Also in CP, BE.

89. "Animal, Vegetable and Mineral." <u>New Republic</u> 103 (9 Dec. 1940): 803-4. Also in CP, BE.

90. "Question in a Field." <u>New Yorker</u> 13 (31 Jul. 1937): 19. Also in CP, BE.

91. "Solitary Observation Brought Back from a Sojourn in Hell." <u>New Yorker</u> 7 (30 May 1931): 17. Reprinted in <u>The New Yorker Book of Verse (1925-1935)</u>. New York: Harcourt, Brace, 1935. p. 278. Also in CP, BE.

92. "Variation on a Sentence." <u>New Yorker</u> 12 (12 Sept. 1936): 16. Also in CP, BE.

Section V

"The Dream." Originally published in DS.

93. "To an Artist, to Take Heart." <u>New Yorker</u> 13
     (3 July 1937): 15. Also in CP, BE.

94. "To Be Sung on the Water." <u>New Yorker</u> 13 (21
     Aug. 1937): 26. Also in CP, BE.

95. "Musician." First published in PNP. Also in
     CP, BE.

96. "Cartography." <u>New Yorker</u> 14 (23 July 1938):
     15. Also in CP, BE.

97. "'Come, Sleep....'" <u>Nation 148</u> (1 Apr. 1939):
     379.

98. "Zone." First published in PNP. Also in CP,
     BE. Included in <u>Poet's Choice</u>. Ed. Paul
     Engle and Joseph Langland. New York: Dial
     Press, 1962. pp. 33-34. Comment by Bogan on
     choice of poem. Also in CP, BE. (Entry 695)

99. "Kapuzinerberg (Salzburg)." <u>New Republic</u>
     103 (18 Nov. 1940): 699. Also in CP, BE.
     (Entry 718)

100. "From Heine." First published in PNP. Also
     in CP, BE.

101. "Evening in the Sanitarium." <u>Nation</u> 147 (10
     Dec. 1938): 625 (under title "Five Parodies"
     with subtitle "Imitated from Auden"). Also
     in CP, BE.

102. "The Daemon." <u>New Yorker</u> 14 (2 Apr. 1938):
     25. Also in CP, BE.

103. <u>COLLECTED POEMS 1923-53</u>. New York: Noonday
     Press, 1954; and London: Peter Owen Limited,
     1956.

Section I

Same as Section I in PNP.

Section II

Same as Section II in PNP, except that "The
Crossed Apple" precedes "Song for a Slight Voice."

Section III

Same as Section III in PNP.

Section IV

Same as Section IV in PNP.

Section V

Similar to Section V in PNP, except "Evening in
the Sanitarium" precedes "From Heine" and the
following poems are added:

104. "After the Persian." <u>New Yorker</u> 27 (3 Nov.
     1951): 36. Reprinted in <u>Poetry</u> 81, No. 1
     (Oct. 1952): 14-15 (under the title "After
     the Persian 1, 2, 3, 4"). Also in BE.

105. "After the Persian II, III." <u>New Yorker</u>
     27 (3 Nov. 1951): 36. Reprinted in <u>Poetry</u>
     81, No. 1 (Oct. 1952): 14-15 (under the title
     "After the Persian 1, 2, 3, 4"). Also in BE.

106. "After the Persian IV, V." <u>New Yorker</u> 27
     (3 Nov. 1951): 36. Reprinted in <u>Poetry</u> 81,
     No. 1 (Oct. 1952): 14-15 (under the title
     "After the Persian 1, 2, 3, 4"). Also in BE.

107. "Train Tune." <u>New Yorker</u> 27 (14 July 1951):
     24. Also in BE.

108. "Song for the Last Act." <u>New Yorker</u> 25 (15

Oct. 1949): 34. Also in BE.

109. THE BLUE ESTUARIES: POEMS 1923-1968.   New
York: Farrar, Straus & Giroux, 1968.
Paperback reprint New York: The Ecco Press,
1977.

Sections I, II, III, IV same as CP. Section V
same except "After the Persian" is changed to
"After the Persian I."

Section VI

110. "The Dragonfly." Poetry in Crystal. Steuben
Glass, New York: Spiral Press, 1963, p. 18.
Poem interpreted in engraved glass by George
Thompson and Bruce Moore.

111. "St. Christopher." Art News 57 (Sept. 1958):
24 (under title "Poets on Paintings 5").

112. "The Sorcerer's Daughter." Times Literary
Supplement (6 Nov. 1959) in special number,
"The American Imagination," 24.

113. "The Young Mage." Times Literary Supplement
(6 Nov. 1959) in special number, "The
American Imagination," 24.

114. "March Twilight." New Yorker 33 (23 Mar.
1957): 32.

115. "July Dawn." Poems in Folio: San Francisco,
1957. Edition of 1150 broadsides with 150
copies signed by Bogan and other poets.
Bogan includes a brief discussion on the
lyric gift with her poem.

116. "The Meeting." New Yorker 32 (9 Feb. 1957):
36.

117. "Night." Poetry 101, Nos. 1 and 2 (Oct.-Nov.
1962): 12.

118. "Morning." <u>Poetry</u> 101, Nos. 1 and 2 (Oct.-
     Nov. 1962): 13.

THREE SONGS

119. "Little Lobelia's Song." <u>New Yorker</u> 43 (1
     Apr. 1967): 45 (under title "Three Songs").

120. "Psychiatrist's Song." <u>New Yorker</u> 43 (1 Apr.
     1967): 45 (under title "Three Songs").

121. "Masked Woman's Song." <u>New Yorker</u> 43 (1
     Apr. 1967): 45 (under title "Three Songs").

CRITICISM

In this section are Bogan's three books of
criticism. <u>Achievement in American Poetry</u> is a
survey of fifty years of important events in
poetry in America. <u>Selected Criticism</u> and <u>A
Poet's Alphabet</u> are collections of Bogan's book
reviews and longer critical pieces first published
elsewhere, principally in <u>The New Yorker</u>. These
reviews are numbered and listed individually with
the original publication noted, along with any
subsequent reprinting. All of the entries
published in <u>Selected Criticism</u> were reprinted in
the later book <u>A Poet's Alphabet</u>.

122. <u>ACHIEVEMENT IN AMERICAN POETRY 1900-1950</u>
     (1951)
     Chicago: Henry Regnery Company, 1951 (first
     edition).

Bogan discusses the major work and literary
significance of every important American poet who
published from 1900-1950. She includes a history
of American criticism as well. The book is
divided into periods, beginning at the turn of the
century when American poetry was judged by "a set
of moralistic and materialistic values." European
impressionism broke through these bourgeois
standards and was accepted first by newspaper
critics such as Theodore Dreiser and urban
Bohemian poets. Edwin Arlington Robinson's <u>The</u>

<u>Children of the Night</u> helped turn American poetry
toward "psychological truth,"   while Emily
Dickinson's work was rediscovered. Little
magazines, including Harriet Monroe's <u>Poetry</u>,
which first published Pound and the Imagists,
greatly influenced American poetry. Midwesterners
Vachel Lindsay, Edgar Lee Masters, and Carl
Sandburg expanded American poetry, while New
Englander Robert Frost's early poems in <u>North of
Boston</u> "promised more tragic power than was ever
realized" in his later works. Three major talents
in the experimental field were Wallace Stevens
whose "dramatic sense saved him from affectation,"
Marianne Moore, who "combined attributes of
naturalist with philosophic moralist," and William
Carlos Williams, who had an "infallible instinct
toward the heart of the commonplace."

After the First World War, America broke away from
"oppressive and outmoded ideas. . . and hampering
provincial taboos," led by Pound, who "was forced
to discover modernity". . . and Eliot who "was
modern from the beginning." Eliot's <u>The Sacred
Wood</u>, a "landmark in modern literary criticism"
returned to prominence Jonson, Blake, Dante, Donne
and Baudelaire, as well as beginning the new
school of criticism, by focusing attention on the
poetry, not the poet. Eliot's poem, <u>The Waste
Land</u>, began the emphasis on spiritual malaise.
Women poets such as Sara Teasdale, Edna St.
Vincent Millay, and Elinor Wylie renewed "a
feminine vein of lyricism."

A period of relative creative quiet followed the
turbulence of the twenties, when many poets,
including Archibald MacLeish and Muriel Rukeyser,
became "overwhelmingly influenced by Marxist
ideology." Others followed religious tendencies,
as seen in Eliot's Anglican theology in his
poetry. In critical works, Edmund Wilson's <u>Axel's
Castle</u> (1931) related twentieth-century poetic
style to nineteenth-century French origins. The
Surrealist School also began.

Other European influences such as Lorca, Rilke,
and Gide appeared at midcentury, and there was an
awakened interest in Henry James. The new poets
who emerged during the forties, who brought back
form to modern style, included Randall Jarrell,
Delmore Schwartz, Karl Shapiro, Elizabeth Bishop,
Robert Lowell, Peter Viereck, Richard Wilbur,

Richard Eberhart and Theodore Roethke. Poets, who
had performed the "function of the look-out aboard
ship," especially during the cultural revolution
of 1912 to 1927, led in the development of
American arts and culture in this fifty-year
period.

123. SELECTED CRITICISM: POETRY AND PROSE (1955)
     New York: The Noonday Press, 1955 (first
     edition).

Bogan's sixty-nine reviews and essays on current
poetry and prose, most of which first appeared in
The New Yorker, are arranged in rough
chronological order, after an introductory essay
on modernism in American literature. Several of
the original titles, not reflective of the
contents, are clarified in A Poet's Alphabet,
which contains all the selections from this book.
American and British poets make up the majority of
the writers criticized, although several
translations from Rilke and Goethe are included.
The book also contains reviews on contemporary
novels, many taken from The New Republic. Bogan's
criticism is fair and eminently readable. She
also gives explicit suggestions on the art of
writing.

Each selection is numbered and annotated below,
with the original place and date of its
publication noted, if available.

124. "Modernism in American Literature." 3-20.
     American Quarterly 2, No. 2 (Summer 1950):
     99-111.

Flaubert and Baudelaire in Madame Bovary and Les
Fleurs du Mal "charted the direction of modern
prose and poetry." The Symbolist revolt brought
into modern literature "a permanent avant-
gardism," in "a state of "permanent revolution."
After World War I, the air was cleared, although
American realism had broken through earlier with
Dreiser's Sister Carrie and E. A. Robinson's The
Children of the Night. European influences were
felt in Bohemian gatherings and described in
little magazines. Post-impressionism in American
painting influenced music and poetry, especially
Imagism.

Eliot's "Prufrock," with its irony, and Pound's
poetic methods of combining form with everyday
material helped shape a modern poetry that is a
"commodious and flexible carrier of complicated
thought and sensibility." Surrealism can be
dangerous, although it is a tremendous
accomplishment with inexhaustible motifs. Poetry
now needs to interpret the modern environment.
Although the novel has enormous possibilities,
poetry has come to the end of its "explorative and
experimental side."

125. "Laughter in a Switchback World." 21-23.
     Review of Troy Park by Edith Sitwell. New
     Republic 45 (23 Dec. 1925): 142 (titled
     "Laughter and a Switchback World").

This work compares with Sitwell's Bucolic Comedies
and The Sleeping Beauty in that it contains the
same fairy tales with "hard surfaces and
sophisticated implications." However reality has
entered these more recent poems in the form of the
human voice which has cracked Sitwell's carrousel
world "crying out with mature horror and despair."

126. "Satirist to Sybil." 24-26.
     Review of A Song of the Cold by Edith
     Sitwell. New Yorker 24 (25 Dec. 1948):
     56-57.

Bogan traces Sitwell's progress from her early
poetry before World War I in which she was the
master puppeteer manipulating her "artificial
universe" and satirizing the English upper class.
Her later poems in the twenties, including Gold
Coast Customs, tell of her absolute rejection of
the real world in a Swiftian manner, using
materialistic symbols, including money and blood.
The poems in the book show her prophesying with
biblical symbols that mankind will bring about a
revelation. Here she rejects satire and humor.

127. "Cold Print." 26-27.
     Review of Gardeners and Astronomers by Edith
     Sitwell. New Yorker 30 (27 Feb. 1954): 113-
     15.

In cold print Sitwell's "verbal incantations" do

not read as well as they sound when spoken aloud.
Her dazzling verbal skills may not lead to
spiritual intensity, but these fifteen poems will
delight her admirers.

128. "Colette." 28-32.
     Review of <u>Cheri</u>, trans. Janet Flanner; and
     <u>Mitsou</u>, trans. Jane Terry. <u>New Republic</u> 63
     (13 Apr. 1930): 375.

Colette's first two novels to be published in this
country are reviewed in this 1930 essay. The
novels are based on Colette's experiences of life
and "what her sharp senses and hearty nature have
told her as the truth." The first book traces the
relationship between an aging woman and a young
man, and the second describes the ordinary life of
a little singer in a music hall. Overall Colette
has produced a "solid body of work that owes
little to masculine attitudes," coming solely from
her feminine sensibilities.

129. "Flowering Judas." 33-35.
     Review of <u>Flowering Judas</u> by Katherine
     Porter. <u>New Republic</u> 64 (22 Oct. 1930):
     277-78.

The stories in this work "can claim kinship with
the order of writing wherein nothing is
fortuitous, where all details grow from the matter
at hand simply and in order." The title story is
the best, with "Rope" the next remarkable one.

130. "The Ladies and Gentlemen." 36-39.
     Review of <u>Three Guineas</u> by Virginia Woolf.
     <u>New Republic</u> 96 (14 Sept. 1938): 164-165.

This work may be Virginia Woolf's answer to the
question "How can war be avoided?" However Woolf
hardly answers it in this 1930 review when she
suggests that upper-class women could simply
organize themselves into an "Outsiders' Society"
which would shun both the evil patriarchal and the
nasty professional systems. The reader should
"check Mrs. Woolf continuously in her
conclusions."

131. "Hart Crane." 40-41.
     Review of <u>Collected Poems</u>. <u>New Yorker</u> 9 (15
     Jul. 1933): 46-48.

Waldo Frank's introduction to <u>Collected Poems</u> is
"rather puzzling and misleadingly spiritually
attributed." Bogan contradicts his interpretation
of "The Bridge" and explains that "Crane's quarrel
with himself was far more grievous than his
quarrel with the world." Crane's immediate
influences came from modern French writing. He
was "a poet of genius whose untimely death was a
certain loss to American literature."

132. Review of <u>The Letters of Gerard Manley
     Hopkins to Robert Bridges</u> and <u>Correspondence
     of Gerard Manley Hopkins and Richard Watson
     Dixon</u>. Ed. C. C. Abbott. 42-43. <u>New Yorker</u>
     11 (4 May 1935): 81.

These letters are "the most important recent
addition to the annals of English poetry." In them
Hopkins brillantly discusses the great figures of
the nineteenth century and the "progress of his
own poetic martyrdom."

133. Review of <u>Further Letters of Gerard Manley
     Hopkins, Including His Correspondence with
     Coventry Patmore</u>. Ed. C. C. Abbott. 43-47.
     <u>Nation</u> 147 (30 July 1938): 111-12.

Hopkins' second collection includes the underlying
scholarly discussion of his time, his unfailing
curiosity about the natural world, and his
interest in music and literature, as well as his
poetic insight. The Patmore correspondence
illustrates Hopkins' severe but fair critcism of
Patmore's poetry. The letters also show Hopkins'
obsessions, which may have arisen from the
conflict between his rich nature with its delicate
sensibilities and the severity of the Jesuit life.

134. "Feats on the Fjord." 48-51.
     Review of <u>Letters from Iceland</u> by W. H.
     Auden and Louis MacNeice. <u>Nation</u> 145 (11
     Dec. 1937): 658.

Auden, with MacNeice as collaborator, has written

a travel book with "moments of insight." Five
chapters are written as a "Letter to Lord Byron"
in the Byronic stanza form. Some of MacNeice's
lighter contributions are "extravagantly funny."
They have included the standard guidebook
information, with excellent photographs. "Even
though they sometimes sound a tiresome schoolboy
note, they are constantly amusing and frequently
brilliant."

135. "The Oxford Book of Modern Verse." 52-54.
     Review of The Oxford Book of Modern Verse
     1892-1935). Ed. W. B. Yeats. New Yorker 11
     (14 Nov. 1936): 115-7.

W. B. Yeats has chosen this somewhat idiosyncratic
selection of modern poets from Tennyson to those
writing in the thirties. He is optimistic about
the current state of poetry. His preface is a
masterpiece in which he states, "I think England
has more good poets since 1900 to the present than
during any period of the same length since the
early seventeenth century."

136. "From Despair to Faith." 55-56.
     Review of Collected Poems by T. S. Eliot.
     New Yorker 12 (23 May, 1936): 98-100.

This is "a work of poetic regeneration," in which
the reader can trace Eliot's progress from despair
in "Gerontion" to faith in "Burnt Norton." "Eliot
brought back into English poetry the salt and
range of which it had long been deprived."

137. "The Religious Encounter." 56-58.
     Review of The Family Reunion by T. S. Eliot.
     New Yorker 15 (15 Apr. 1939): 83-85.

Eliot "brings off a Christian . . . theme of
reconciliation with the conscience . . . and
exposes . . . the hollow convention of the
[English] upper class." The spectacle of master
and servant "riding off to spiritual liberty in a
well-kept car is the play's one faintly ridiculous
effect." This play is the first incontrovertible
evidence that Eliot has experienced the value of
religious experience.

138. "From Form to Content." 58-61.
     Review of <u>The Four Quartets</u> by T. S. Eliot.
     source unknown.

<u>The Four Quartets</u> show Eliot's acceptance of the
Anglican religion. His unifying devices include
the basic construction of each quartet into five
sections, with a lyric in its second section,
followed by a meditation and a second lyric in the
fourth section, similar to the sonata form. The
other device is his use of place names as titles
to the poems in which Eliot weaves back and forth
between his native America and adopted Britain.
The <u>Quartets</u> are a journey to faith, from deep
depression in "Burnt Norton" to bitterness in
"East Coker," through reconcilation of many of
Eliot's themes in the "Dry Salvages" and "Little
Gidding."

139. "Euripides in Modern Dress." 62-63.
     Review of <u>Ion</u>. Trans. Hilda Dolittle. <u>New</u>
     <u>Yorker</u> 13 (8 May 1937): 70.

H. D.'s translation of <u>Ion</u> brings Euripides into
an Imagist play which "produces some perfectly
beautiful poetry, but reduces the play to
nonsense," by removing the irony and leaving only
a shell of the work.

140. "The People, Yes and No." 64-66.
     Review of <u>The People, Yes</u> by Carl Sandburg
     and <u>The Mediterranean and Other Poems</u> by
     Allen Tate. <u>New Yorker</u> 12 (22 Aug. 1936):
     59-62.

Carl Sandburg loves the American people. His new
book is filled with memoranda of their speech and
folklore. He feels that "as long as the people
continue to talk and laugh with style and humor,
there is no need to despair." In contrast is
Allen Tate's book, which contains "much mature
writing," but also "romantic wishful-thinking and
bitterness" for a lost romantic world of special
Southern values.

141. "Landscape with Jeffers." 67-69.
     Review of <u>Such Counsels You Gave to Me and</u>
     <u>Other Poems</u> by Robinson Jeffers. <u>New Yorker</u>

13 (2 Oct. 1937): 68.

Jeffers "latest set-piece of human savagery
contains a hero who has "abetted his mother's
incestuous passion for himself and stood by at his
father's murder." The hero, who expiates his
mother's guilt, arouses little sympathy in the
reader. The mother seems simple-minded. The poet
"tends towards the state of God himself." His
lyrics are "now vitiated by pronouncements."

142. Review of <u>Requiem and Other Poems</u> by Rainer
     Maria Rilke. Trans. J. B. Leishman. 70-78.
     <u>Poetry</u> 50, No. 1 (Apr. 1937): 34-42.

This collection contains versions of poems from
the <u>Neue Gedichte</u> (1907) "wherein the great and
mature Rilke first came into view." Poems from
<u>Malte Laurids Brigge</u> (1910) translated by Leishman
in the 1931 <u>Poems</u> show that Rilke's study of the
streets of Paris and its people, as well as its
terrors, granted him "access to that 'inscape'
which Hopkins and the great mystics have felt to
be present in all objects in literature." In <u>The
Sonnets to Orpheus</u>, "containing some of the
profoundest poems of our time," the original
German is printed opposite the English versions.
His work "is one of the strongest antidotes to the
powers of darkness that our time has produced."

143. Review of <u>Duino Elegies</u> by Rainer Maria
     Rilke. Trans. J. B. Leishman and Stephen
     Spender. 78-80. <u>New Yorker</u> 15 (24 June
     1939): 70-71.

The <u>Duino Elegies</u>, along with the <u>Sonnets to
Orpheus</u> "mark the summit of [Rilke's] career."
Leishman has contributed an illuminating preface
and many notes, but his and Spender's translation
does not work because it has not "carried over in
any way . . . the underlying emotional pulse of
the poetry." In the <u>Elegies</u> Rilke traces "the
ills of our time back to their source . . . the
spiritual infection of a world without values."

144. "Asian Exoticism." 81-82.
     Review of <u>Anabase</u> by St. John Perse. Trans.
     T. S. Eliot. <u>New Yorker</u> 14 (12 Mar. 1938):
     63-64.

T. S. Eliot's translation is "sometimes flattened
and deadened" from the original French "sonority
and ecstasy." "Perse's poem is filled with that
special Asian exoticism of which our time
approves."

145. "The Decoration of Novels." 83-85.
     Review of <u>The Buccaneers</u> by Edith Wharton.
     <u>Nation</u> 147 (22 Oct. 1938): 418-19.

Wharton, in this, her last unfinished novel,
arranges her characters to fit the exigencies of
her preconceived plot with neat coincidences. Her
descriptions fill in the background with "great
color and accuracy," leading the way to a
contemporary "women's-magazine dream of suburban
smartness." Her characters and "mildly ironic
descriptions of life in the great English houses"
can be compared to Henry James' "true dissection"
of the same subject.

146. "William Butler Yeats." 86-104. <u>Atlantic
     Monthly</u> 161 (May 1938): 637-44.

Bogan traces Yeats' life and work from his
beginning in Sligo and the poems written about
Irish legends of that area to his old age when his
literary powers still remained strong. She begins
with his youth in Dublin and moves to his becoming
a Nationalist, his newspaper career and mystical
stirrings in London. She describes his return to
Ireland and emergence in the Irish Literary
Revival with Lady Gregory, his plays and support
for the Irish Dramatic Movement and the Abbey
Theatre and his mature period as an Irish
statesman and renowned literary figure. In his
old age his works continued strong as ever. Among
the works quoted to illustrate Yeats' artistic
development are parts of "The Wild Swans at
Coole," "September 1913," and two selections from
his plays. Yeats' "desire of artistic perfection"
has given the world "the greatest poet writing in
English today."

147. "Light and Adult."   105-6.
     Review of The Oxford Book of Light Verse. Ed.
     W. H. Auden. New Yorker 14 (24 Dec. 1938):
     50-52.

Auden's reasons for the decline of light poetry
given in the preface are the Industrial
Revolution's breaking up of agricultural society
and the formation of middle classes. Simple
working people produce folk songs and the leisure
society writes verses with high skill. The poems
Auden chooses, however, should be irresistible to
all. The poetry in this collection is casual in
content, popular and unpretentious in form, and
easily understood.

148. "Heads Will Roll."   108-110.
     Review of Trial of a Judge by Stephen
     Spender. New Yorker 14 (1 Oct. 1938): 64-65.

This work is "straight post 1935-Party-line
liberal scaring." "It marks a new low in Mr.
Spender's career, is frightful poetry and,
academically speaking, no tragedy at all."

149. "Ruins and Visions."   110-11.
     Review of Ruins and Visions by Stephen
     Spender. New Yorker 18 (10 Oct. 1942):
     72-73.

Spender's style is "clogged with rhetoric and
adolescent emotion and has a strong strain of
nineteenth century hope and hero worship."
However in this collection "reality has moved in
on the poet" and "real majesty and sensitiveness
of phrase become more conscious and controlled" as
the book goes on.

150. "James on a Revolutionary Theme."   112-21.
     Review of The Princess Casamassima by Henry
     James. Nation 146 (23 Apr. 1938): 471, 471,
     474. Reprinted in Literary Opinion in
     America. Ed. Morton D. Zabel, 351-56. New
     York: Harper, 1951.

In an essay that helped initiate the James
revival, Bogan evaluates the book as one of James'
best, in spite of negative contemporary criticism

and misreadings. She closely describes the hero,
the lower class Hyacinth, the revolutionary
Muniment, and the upper class Princess, who wants
to help the movement. Bogan narrates the story so
that the reader understands James' intention of
bringing to light the conflicts between these
three who are symbols of their respective social
levels. James paints superb portraits of the
characters, after the first three rather overblown
chapters.

151. "Country Things." 122-24.
      Review of Collected Poems: 1939 by Robert
      Frost. New Yorker 15 (4 Mar. 1939): 68-70.

This collection of six of Frost's books, begins
with A Boy's Will, which let into "literary
parlors," the "freshness of new hay." It continues
with North of Boston, which "put New England
speech into literature" and ends with Further
Range. Some of Frost's popularity "can be put
down to the fact that he has always expressed
American nostalgia for a lately abandoned rural
background." However Frost's poetry has not grown
throughout his work, and "carping and
conservatism" have appeared.

152. "The Pure in Heart." 125-28.
      Review of The Death of the Heart by Elizabeth
      Bowen. Nation 148 (28 Jan. 1939): 123-24.

In the plot of this novel a sixteen-year-old
adopted girl exposes the lack of human feeling in
a smart London household. Bowen's depiction of
the reaction of sensitive children to their
environment also illustrates women writers'
ability to discuss unsuitable people falling in
love. But her writing lacks humility in this
novel of "the horrors experienced by open
innocence up against a closed world."

153. "Poet in Spite of Himself." 129-32.
      Review of Valery's essays trans. by William
      Aspenwall Bradley. Nation 148 (7 Jan. 1939):
      38-39.

This uninspired translation and editing of
Valery's miscellaneous essays contains several

"distinguished pieces of analytical appreciation
in the essays on Stendhal and Baudelaire." But
Valéry's "sad views of the breakdown of the human
spirit in the modern world . . . sound feeble and
complaining." Valéry's dialogues and
reminiscences of Mallarmé and Dégas should be
translated to show his "connoisseurship in the
minor arts."

154. "On the Death of William Butler Yeats."
     133-37. Nation 148 (25 Feb. 1939): 234-35
     (titled "Cutting of an Agate.")

Yeats gave up his attempt to "satisify middle
class ideals of [the] arts" around 1909. From
then on his work came from either the highest or
lowest ends of the scale of artistic expression,
represented respectively by his Noh plays with
their difficult subtleties and his "Crazy Jane"
songs with their bawdiness. His poems, plays, and
prose writings achieved an eloquence and
simplicity in his old age.

155. "Make It New." 138-41.
     Review of Guide to Culture (Kulcher) by Ezra
     Pound. Nation 148 (29 Apr. 1939): 505-5.

Pound's reactions to "careful well-bred opinions
on the subject of the arts" are contained in these
"diatribes against the canned reverence accorded
literature." The English edition spells it
"Kulcher," which "perfectly sets the tone of the
book." "Pound walks into the field [of academic
rigmaroles] armed with stink bombs." In the
beginning of his career "he determined to exhume
poetry . . . from the grave into which scholars
and moralists have lowered it." He has recently
become a "soldier of an Economic Faith Militant,"
with his passionate beliefs in the theories of
Major Douglas and Mussolini's planned economy.
The alert reader needs to pick his or her way
through the minefield of stink bombs.

156. "Proteus, or Vico's Road." 142-48.
     Review of Finnegans Wake by James Joyce.
     Nation 148 (6 May 1939): 533-35.

In spite of "Joyce's miraculous virtuosity with

language," Bogan finds that the themes and
language are as retrogressive as the style which
regresses back to the conundrum. The most
frightening thing about the book is "the feeling .
. . . that Joyce himself does not know what he is
doing." Joyce brings into the book music's
structure and masterful parodies of every written
or oral style known to man. The title of the
essay refers to Vico's speculation on recurrent
cycles in human progress according to universal
laws as used by Joyce and to the Protean changing
of the phantasmagoric figures in the book.

157. "Approaching Ur."   149-53.
     Review of A Skeleton Key to Finnegan's Wake
     by Joseph Campbell and Henry Morton Robinson.
     Nation 159 (19 Aug. 1944): 214-15.

It is doubtful that Finnegan's Wake is the complex
masterpiece of a master artist. This first
attempt at translating Joyce's work "brings up new
problems with every step of ground it clears."
Was Joyce a compulsive neurotic or a controlled
writer? Bogan wonders if "the whole book is a
masked attempt at the fullest apologia pro vita
sua that Joyce has yet given us, in which the
exiled Joyce returns to Dublin to raze it "with
the fires of his love and hatred."

158. "Unofficial Feminine Laureate."   154-56.
     Review of Huntsman, What Quarry by Edna
     Millay. New Yorker 15 (20 May 1939): 80-82.

This book "is a strange mixture of maturity and
unresolved youth." Millay, hampered by the
"sometimes destructive role of the unofficial
feminine laureate" continues to write poems on
subjects unsuitable for a woman poet in the middle
of her career. Her development from rebellious
girl to maturely contemplative woman, begun in her
previous publication Wine from These Grapes, does
not appear to have continued here.

159. "The Poetry of Paul Eluard."   157-70.
     Partisan Review 6, No. 5 (Fall 1939): 76-89.

Bogan's longstanding dislike for surrealism is
apparent in this outline of the history of

Surrealism and Paul Eluard's place in the
movement, beginning with the French Symbolists'
revolt against Dadaism. In the beginning of the
essay she quotes from Marcel Raymond's De
Baudelaire à Surrealisme's descriptions of the
writings of Apollinaire. In the second part she
quotes several of Eluard's poems and proverbs in
French. Two poems, "Upon What Wall Am I Engraved"
and "Painted Woods," are not reprinted from the
Partisan Review article. Translations in English
appear at the end of the article. Bogan makes an
analogy between the functioning of Surrealism and
the mechanisms of a person suffering from
psychosis. Eluard is too timid and rigid for this
poetry with its loose form and continually
changing imagery. His only emotional effect is
pathos.

160. "America Was Promises."   171-174.
     Review of American was Promises by Archibald
     MacLeish and A Turning Wind by Muriel
     Rukeyser. New Yorker 155 (16 Dec. 1939):
     100-1.

Archibald MacLeish's political poetry in this
collection is his "saddest and most conglomerate
attempt at public speech." He has buried his
gifts of lyric poetry in his role as official
poet. Muriel Rikeyser is a highly gifted poet who
is deficient in a sense of human life. Her world
is static and literary, filled with "chaste and
noble proletarian myths." She should "mix some
loud laughs with her high scorn."

161. "Utilitarianism Disguised." 175-77.
     Review of The Enjoyment of Poetry. Ed. Max
     Eastman. New Yorker 15 (28 Oct. 1939):
     68-69.

Eastman insists that "because modern poets cannot
easily be understood, they are to be distrusted."
The poems in this anthology were chosen because
they are "general and clear," not according to
"taste." Poetry has advanced beyond his values,
especially in the "unintelligible poetry which can
extend consciousness."

162. Review of Cantos LII-LXXI by Ezra Pound.

178-80. <u>New Yorker</u> 16 (9 Nov. 1940): 76-78.

"Faced with these new Cantos, one's warmest
charity is certainly called into play . . . ."
"The dullness and brutishness of the Ming and
Manchu rulers . . . are equalled only by the
fustiness and mustiness of John Adams' notations
on life and business conditions." If Pound's
early Cantos are structured on Dante's <u>Commedia</u>,
these are his <u>Purgatorio</u>.

163. Review of <u>The Pisan Cantos</u> and <u>The Cantos</u> by
     Ezra Pound. 181-83. <u>New Yorker</u> 24 (30 Oct.
     1948): 107-9.

Pound began publishing his Cantos in 1925 when his
reputation was at its height. In the beginning
this work exhibited his full range of genius,
including his scholarship in medieval Romantic
literature, his interest in the Italian and French
Renaissance, Greek literature and Chinese poetry,
as well as his episodic and disjunct style and
inclusion of languages that need transliteration.
At first Pound impressed his reader with his
magical powers, but then his obsessions turned him
into a fanatic who gave the reader "nothing but
deadly repetition." Pound's imprisonment in Pisa
brought him back to art and life and gave him a
new sense of proportion seen in <u>The Pisan Cantos</u>.
Perhaps the "stresses that beset" this most
influential American poet will be understood and
he will be honored for his contribution to modern
poetry sometime in the future.

164. "The Poet in New York and Elsewhere." 184-5.
     Review of <u>The Poet in New York</u> by Frederico
     Garcia Lorca. Trans. Rolfe Humphries. <u>New
     Yorker</u> 16 (1 June 1940): 73-75.

Lorca's Surrealism, seen in the poems in the first
section of the book, came from the Spanish
literary tradition. He also had access to a
living folk tradition, included in his earlier
poems in <u>Gypsy Ballads</u>, and found in the second
part of this book.

165. "Katherine Mansfield." 186-88.
     Review of <u>The Scrapebook of Katherine</u>

Mansfield. Ed. John Middleton Murry. New
Republic 102 (25 Mar. 1940): 415.

This collection of miscellanea "adds little to the
Mansfield canon." Her love of childhood helped to
give her finest stories their purity, but she
later failed to escape from its neurotic hold.
Her English sensibility, seen in the journals,
make her nearer to Lawrence and Joyce than she
cared to admit.

166. "I. Compton-Burnett." 189-90.
     Review of Darkness and Day by Ivy Compton-
     Burnett. Source unknown.

This novel describes the Victorian world of three
antagonistic interacting groups: masters, servants
and children. Compton-Burnett's "great gifts of
intelligence and style" alleviate her fixation on
childhood's emotional level. Her irony shows her
to be a "female Swift of our day."

167. "Sensibility and Luggage." 191-94.
     Review of The Expense of Greatness by R. P.
     Blackmur. Nation 151 (7 Dec. 1940): 572-74.

"As with all sensitive critics, [Blackmur's]
reactions are at bottom instinctive." Although he
knows the difference between serious and folk art,
his critical vocabulary baffles the reader and his
courage in making judgments often wavers. The
best essay is on D. H. Lawrence. He needs more
reading and experience to be a first class critic.

168. "The Wartime Letters." 195-98.
     Review of Rilke's Wartime Letters.
     Nation 151 (5 Oct. 1940): 305-6.

These letters "cover the most unproductive period
of Rilke's life," the years from 1914 to 1921, to
his last great poems. The course of his
development, which was achieved through
reconciliation between "narcissism and
objectivity," leads ultimately to his "triumph in
art" and "reconciliation with himself."

169. Review of Letters of Rainer Maria Rilke.

Trans. Jane Bannard Greene and M. D. Herter
Norton. 199-201. <u>New Yorker</u> 21 (15 Sept.
1945): 83-84.

This book contains selections from Rilke's
correspondence between 1892 and 1910. The letters
show Rilke's tendency to emphasize the worth of
his work, his horror of "the little official
post," and his solicitations from wealthy patrons
for money or a place to write in. Bogan
apologizes for Rilke's ability to advocate a
simple life while working in the great castle of a
friendly sponsor. He had a "kind of religious
hunger" that appeals to contemporary poets and
seekers.

170. Review of <u>Last Poems and Plays</u> by W. B.
    Yeats. 202-3. <u>New Yorker</u> 16 (1 June 1940):
    74-75.

The poems are "the most naked and terrible he ever
wrote." Yeats in his old age is an example "of
what kind of spirit poetry demands."

171. Review of <u>The Collected Poems of W. B. Yeats</u>.
    204-6. <u>New Yorker</u> 27 (20 Oct. 1951): 152.

This final edition of Yeats' poetry "adds to the
earlier work the poetry written . . . from about
1935 to 1939, the year of his death." "This
additional material embodies [his] last
preoccupation as well as his last stylistic
development." Yeats'"increasing bitterness and
irritability" appear in his final works. Bogan
traces Yeats' spiritual inventions, his alienation
from the Irish middle class, and his political
fortunes. His renewal of power was expressed in
the "coarse human vitality" of the "Crazy Jane"
poems and the "lofty style" of his last poems
which celebrate human greatness.

172. "The Gothic South." 207-9.
    Review of <u>A Curtain of Green</u> by Eudora Welty.
    <u>Nation</u> 153 (6 Dec. 1941): 572.

Miss Welty's stories resemble in their oblique
humor those of Gogol. Her descriptions are
eminently suitable for her eccentric southern

characters who could have come from "some broken-
down Medieval scene" or Russian landscape.

173. "A Revolution in European Poetry." 210-15.
     Review of A Revolution in European Poetry:
     1660-1900 by Emery Neff. Nation 152 (12 Apr.
     1941): 441-44.

This "valuable book which should serve as a
rational point of reference" traces the "enormous
influence of French literary taste during the
reign of Louis XIV" upon the countries of Europe
and of Baudelaire, Rimbaud, and Verlaine upon
modern poetry. Poetry in the United States in the
thirties has lost contact with its European roots.
Neff's account of the historic background of
poetry is thorough, although he does not deal with
its ironic qualities. Neff could have included
the influential works of Vico, the English Gothic
Revival, Horace Walpole, and William Beckford.
Madame de Staël is noticeably missing, as well as
other important French poets.

174. "War Poetry." 216-18.
     Review of Awake! and Other Wartime Poems by
     W. R. Rodgers. New Yorker 18 (4 Apr. 1942):
     64-66.

The young Ulsterman's war poems are written in a
"firm, rugged Ulster idiom," which includes many
unexpected details of his battle observations.
War poems no longer can be only the classic battle
cry and elegy, nor can they be written by
noncombatants. They must be written by soldier
poets such as Rodgers.

175. "Wise After the Event." 219-222.
     Review of Modern American Poetry: A Critical
     Anthology, ed. Louis Untermeyer; and Modern
     British Poetry: A Critical Anthology, ed.
     Louis Untermeyer. New Yorker 18 (4 July
     1942): 54-56.

The sixth revision of Modern American Poetry
contains "all the interesting and feasible
information pertaining to poem and poet" from Walt
Whitman to Delmore Schwartz, in a charming but
rather unwieldy format of 712 pages. Modern

British Poetry in its fifth revision begins with
Thomas Hardy and closes with Dylan Thomas. These
anthologies "stand right at the heart of poetry
appreciation in America." Untermeyer, for all his
faults, "remains true to the lyric cry and simple-
heartedness" in choosing poets.

176. "Sentimental Education Today." 223-30.
     Review of L'Education Sentimentale by Gustave
     Flaubert. Trans. Goldsmith. Nation 55 (3
     Oct. 1942): 301-2.

This is the "first intelligent English
translation of Flaubert's misunderstood book." It
deals not with realism or romance, but with satire
of a "high but hidden order." Bogan provides a
historical background of the social and political
upheavals in France. The plot includes a
description of the hero's adventures in Paris with
the newly-created middle class to illustrate
social upheaval against bourgeois rule. This book
reveals the "modern split between emotion and
reason."

177. "Isak Dinesen." 231-34.
     Review of Winter's Tales. Nation 156
     (26 June 1943): 894-95.

The stories in this collection are compared to her
earlier works, Gothic Tales and Out of Africa.
These stories are parables in which the "lines of
meaning are not pulled tight." "They show the
simplicity and background . . . of folk art."
They are "written in the European tradition
without any middle-class materialism, by a person
"whose sources were in some manner attached to the
feudal tradition."

178. "Stephan George." 235-37.
     Review of Poems. Trans. Ernst Morwitz and
     Carol North Valhope. New Yorker 29 (17 Apr.
     1943): 68-70.

"Anyone interested in comparative literature . . .
should try to understand George while trying to
enjoy him." The translators chose these poems
from seven volumes of George's work. English and
French readers show little interest in George,

compared with Rilke. His physical strangeness and
"high-priest act" may have put readers off, but
his "magnificent language combined with his simple
heart . . . saved him in the end."

179. "Some Notes on Popular and Unpopular Art."
     238-51. <u>Partisan Review</u> 10, No. 5
     (Sept./Oct. 1943): 391-104. Discussion of
     contemporary American poetry given as Hopwood
     Lecture University of Michigan in 1944.
     Reprinted in <u>The Writer and His Craft</u> under
     the title, "Popular and Unpopular Poetry in
     America." Ed. Roy M. Crowden. Ann Arbor,
     Michigan: University of Michigan Press, 1954.
     pp. 173-90. (Entry 734)

"Formal art does not need to search out the folk
for refreshment." Yeat's Irish peasant tales and
Lorca's Spanish flamenco tradition are examples of
folk art used by formal artists at the
"improvisatory stage and of an audience creatively
involved." But America's present attempts to
return to folk art in order to be saved from
"creative and moral aridity" stem from "the sense
of profound nostalgia for an already disappearing
non-urban way of life." Folk tradition has
become "thoroughly bourgeoisified" in the United
States.

Similar to the earlier music hall urban folk music
in England and France is the vigorous American
"hot jazz," especially improvisation. Folk art
crosses formal art when "it has reached a moment
of comparative breadth and elegance" and "when
formal art has become easy and secular enough to
realize just where folk lies."

Middle-class American intellectuals, the "fine
nervous flower[s] of the bourgeoisie," have
produced their own literature judged by middle-
class critics. Bogan suggests that the remedy for
middle-class art is satire. It should take its
cue from Rilke: "to love everything and take
everything into itself."

180. Review of <u>Nevertheless</u> by Marianne Moore.
     252-54. <u>New Yorker</u> 20 (11 Nov. 1944): 88-89.

This collection is "the best" of Moore's poetry

because it is more "musical and openly warm
hearted" than her former collections. Her "love
of animals, fruit, flowers and beautiful artifacts
. . . touches her subjects with a subdued but
penetrating light." Moore is "now our most
distinguished contemporary American poet."

181. Discussion of Marianne Moore's artistic
     lineage. 254-57. Quarterly Review of
     Literature 4, No. 2 (1948): 150-52.

Marianne Moore "is at once a contemporary
American, a seventeenth century survivor, and a
native of . . . timeless and pure spiritual
regions." She is an example of a Renaissance
scholar for whom "man was the measure of all," a
"gentle moralist, and a stern technician." Her
passion for miscellany leads her to "imaginatively
correlate the world's goods," while "her
Protestant inheritance" makes her poems into
little sermons.

182. "The Time of the Assassins." 258-63.
     Development of the detective novel. Nation
     158 (22 Apr. 1944): 475-76, 478. (Entry 755)

The detective story developed from the early
nineteenth century French roman policier, moving
from Poe's tale of ratiocination to Simenon's
Maigret. The modern detective story, with its
death and violence, "openly accommodates fear and
aggression" in these "dramas of sin and
retribution. Graham Greene's thrillers are the
best examples of archetypal subconscious themes."
Although the detective novel falls outside of
conventional literary standards, it should not be
ignored because it contains "every rejected and
denied human impulse."

183. "The Silver Clue." 264-68.
     Review of Henry James: The Later Phase by F.
     O. Matthiessen. Nation 159 (23 Dec. 1944):
     775-76.

Bogan hopes this "intelligent study of James's
later period . . . presages other criticism
directed toward [James's] works." Previously
"middle-class-minded" readers and critics have

attacked and misinterpreted James's books.
Matthiessen deals with the novels The Ambassadors,
The Wings of the Dove, and The Golden Bowl. He
underestimates the last book in which James
recognizes a new American type, the
multimillionaire Adam Verver. The later works of
James should be read as music, "following the
development of the theme."

184. "Yvor Winters." 269-71.
     Review of The Giant Weapon. New Yorker 20
     (22 Jul. 1944): 57-58.

This collection of poems shows Winters'
"continuing conservative tendency [which is]
unpopular in this age." His general tone and form
could be called "neo-classic," but his poetry
stays on "the side of life and joy," instead of
"dead formality and generalized emptiness."

185. "The Prophet Job, Yankee Style." 272-74.
     Review of A Masque of Reason by Robert Frost.
     New Yorker 21 (7 Apr. 1945): 83-84, 86.

Frost, in this short verse play, makes Job a dry
cracker-box Yankee philosopher. But this "little
divertissement" reduces God and Satan to bickering
opponents who finally consent to having their
picture taken by Mrs. Job.

186. Review of The Dog Beneath the Skin, or,
     Where Is Francis? by W . H. Auden, with
     Christopher Isherwood. 275-77. New Yorker
     11 (9 Nov. 1935): 84-87.

The play is a "long, highly amusing revue" of a
"noble youth who descends from his class to give
humanity in general a hard and unprejudiced
stare." It is Auden's first successful work,
unhampered by the private associations which
appeared in his earlier works.

187. Review of The Double Man by W. H. Auden.
     278-79. New Yorker 17 (12 Apr. 1941): 82-85.

In his new book, Auden "returns to the nice,
crisp, open beat of four-stress iambic line to the

couplets in rhyme and . . . to the simple
proposition that man is not perfect . . . ." The
"New Year Letter" to Elizabeth Mayer, "a running
comment upon the world and one's soul," is
followed by more notes than the lines in the poem.
"The Quest," chiefly a group of sonnets "sounds
a little composed."

188. Review of For the Time Being by W. H. Auden.
     280-82. New Yorker 20 (23 Sept. 1944):
     77-78.

The general effect of the two long poems "The Sea
and the Mirror: a Commentary on Shakespeare's The
Tempest" and the title poem which is a Christmas
oratorio is "one of restlessness under control, of
talent steadied and enlarged." The poems
"constitute the most minute dissection of modern
spiritual illness that any poet . . . has given
us."

189. Review of The Collected Poetry of W. H.
     Auden. 282-85. New Yorker 21 (14 Apr. 1945):
     86, 89.

Bogan compares Eliot and Auden and states "Auden
... has succeeded Eliot as the strongest influence
in American and British poetry." Auden is "more
exuberant, restless, sanguine and unselfconscious"
and is "a [more] natural dramatist." Eliot's
"sensitivity and melancholy foreboding [sensed]
the general tragedy of his period." Auden is "not
afraid or ashamed to laugh or weep." The poems in
this collection have a tone of "composure and
simplicity."

190. Review of The Age of Anxiety by W. H. Auden.
     285-88. New Yorker 23 (26 Jul. 1947): 64-66

Auden has not let middle age keep him from
attempting new forms. His semi-dramatic structure
in this work, subtitled "A Baroque Eclogue,"
differs from classical eclogues in that it is set
in a city instead of the country. Moreover, Auden
experiments with language in the characters'
conversations. This comic poem surveys
"contemporary manners and morals on the basis of
. . . Christian [ideals].

191. "The Summers of Hesperides Are Long."
     289-94. Review of _Ancestors' Brocades: The
     Literary Debut of Emily Dickinson_ by
     Millicent Todd Bingham and _Bolts of Melody_ by
     Emily Dickinson. _New Yorker_ 21 (21 Apr.
     1945): 84-86.

The biography by Bingham is "a full account of the
circumstances" of the publication of Dickinson's
first three books of poems and the letters edited
by Mrs. Todd, Bingham's mother. Bogan traces the
history of publication of the poems and discusses
the development of the poems themselves, beginning
with the "early sentimental and experimental
poems," followed by the "middle ground of
technical and spiritual control," leading "to the
great period of compressed, direct force."
Dickinson's two personalities appear in the poems:
the poet of the final period in her "massive and
imperturbable maturity;" and Emily "the child in
her father's shadow." Her influence on Auden, if
not Eliot, "is inestimable" and "her work stands
beside the poetry of the great masters."

The _New Yorker_ article includes a comment not
reprinted in this review on the difference between
the poems edited by Mabel Loomis Todd and Martha
Dickinson Bianchi, whose work Bogan calls
"careless and haphazard," both in her editing of
the poems and in her biography of Dickinson.

192. "The Portrait of New England." 295-301.
     Review of _The Bostonians_ by Henry James.
     Nation 161 (1 Dec. 1945): 582-86.

This 1886 novel by James has finally been
reprinted in an American edition. The characters
move in "the New England social, spiritual and
physical scene as it has never been rendered,
before or since."

193. "The Modern Syndrome." 302-304.
     Review of _Medea: Freely Adapted from the
     Medea of Euripides_ by Robinson Jeffers. _New
     Yorker_ 22 (11 May 1946): 94, 96-97.

Jeffers' "romantic-Nihilist attitude toward life
and his overblown rhetorical tendencies" appear in
his adaptation of Euripides' tragedy. This

hysterical version is more relevant to our present
situation. His Medea is a "creature so obsessed
by jealousy, pride and paranoid fear of ridicule
that she passes . . . into the realms of
insanity."

194. "The Secular Hell." 305-315.
     Discussion of the Hero in modern literature.
     Chimera 4, No. 3 (Spring 1946): 12-20.

This is an unusually difficult, dense discussion
of modern man's turning the classic myth of the
Hero, with its many labors, taboos and assumption
of guilt, inward. The religious ritual, derived
from the mythical since the breakup of the
Catholic Church during the Reformation, becomes
absorbed in literature. Examples are the Gothic
exploration of the "nightside of nature" and the
Romantic emphasis upon an "outmoded, demonic,
fatal, insatiable hero." Currently dread and
terrible events appear in ordinary surroundings to
ordinary people. Bogan begins and ends the essay
with two brief quotations from Goethe in German,
neither of which are translated.

195. "Satire and Sentimentality." 316-18.
     Comparison of Poems 1930-1945 by Robert
     Graves and The Big Road by Norman Rosten.
     New Yorker 22 (6 July 1946): 57-59.

Rosten writes for a general audience, while Graves
professes to write poetry for other poets and
prose for people in general. Roster gives the
public "romantic braggadocio" in his poem of
building the Alcan Highway during the Second World
War, while Graves "merely uses a trained ear and
eye and a mature set of emotions to note certain
striking features . . . set down in musical
language . . . [by] a sardonic mind."

196. Review of Imaginary Interviews by André Gide.
     Trans. Malcolm Cowley. 319-24. Nation 159
     (28 Oct. 1944): 526, 528, 530.

This, the first book to come out of France since
the beginning of the Second World War, was written
by Gide in his seventies. It is final proof of
his belief in "Christianity without dogma."

American readers will not be able to grasp the
foundation for this work unless they can read
French. Cowley's translation lacks annotations.
Gide's crucial thought in this work is "the fact
of each man's personal responsibility for evil."

197. Review of The Journals of André Gide: 1889-
     1939, Vol. 1. 324-28. Nation 165 (18 Oct.
     1947): 412-13 (under title "As Much Humanity
     as Possible").

The first book of Gide's Journals: 1889-1939
"draws Gide's other work into focus" and provides
a basis for "judgment of his character and place
in letters." They are based on sincerity of
feeling. "He brought emotion over into the moral
realm and claimed that spiritual values would . .
. operate outside of the rituals of religion."

198. Review of Journals: 1914-1927, Vol. 2.
     328-31. Nation 166 (5 June 1948): 636 (under
     title "Midway the Journey . . . ").

Gide continues his "search for equilibrium in
highly organized modern man." His important
decisions, shown in his three journals, were to
reject orthodox religion, to put down his
childhood recollections frankly, and to publish
his study of homosexuality.

199. "Baudelaire Revisited." 332-34.
     Review of Flowers of Evil by Baudelaire.
     Trans. Geoffrey Wagner. New Yorker 23 (3 May
     1947): 114-16.

This new translation is a great disappointment
because of its "elemental blunders in choice, in
tone, and in detail." Furthermore, fundamental
aids to the reader have been omitted, including
pagination, table of contents, notes, and index.
The value of the book lies in Enid Starkie's
introduction and the French text of the poems by
Baudelaire, who was the first poet to write about
"urban man's bitter loneliness and spiritual
isolation."

200. "The Heart and the Lyre." 335-45.

Discussion of American women poets.
<u>Mademoiselle</u>, May 1947, 184-85, 278-81.

This essay considers "the rise and development of
female poetic talent . . . and the worth and scope
of women's poetic gifts." At first women poets
were paid for "grim, pious and lachrymose" poems.
Later poems by "female songstresses" became more
"ardent and airy." Emily Dickinson represented
"the final flowering of a long Puritan tradition."
H. D., Gertrude Stein, and Marianne Moore
"experimented boldly with form and language in the
early twentieth century." After 1918 women lyric
poets such as Sara Teasdale and Edna Millay
restored "genuine and frank feeling" to the
contemporary "genteel, artificial and dry literary
scene." In spite of Virginia Woolf's lament that
there will never be a female Shakespeare, women
"are capable of perfect and poignant song."

201. "John Betjeman." 343-45.
      Review of <u>Slick But Not Streamlined</u> by John
      Betjeman. Ed. W. H. Auden. <u>New Yorker</u> (13
      Sept. 1947): 118-19.

Betjeman's skill as satirist shows first in these
poems, underlined by pathos concerning British
middle-class mores. His interests are "basically
topographical and architectural" with concrete
symbols of middle-class pretension in these poems
which are "written in perfect replicas of
nineteenth century verse forms."

202. "The Poet Lawrence." 346-49.
      Review of <u>Selected Poems</u> by D. H. Lawrence.
      Ed. Kenneth Rexroth. <u>New Yorker</u> 24 (20 Mar.
      1948): 110-14.

The poems show Lawrence's rapid development from
the constriction of his early work to the
disappearance of this conformity with the
anguished poems resulting from his mother's death.
Nature then becomes Lawrence's subject of poetic
reality, followed by the difficult love
relationship, and finally the prophecy of modern
Europe in ruins. Readers must be aware of
Lawrence's duality: "a writer in command of his
gifts and the victim of his obsessions." In his
<u>Last Poems</u> he was finding "a new voice of grandeur

and dignity."

203. "The Creative Experiment."   350-53.
     Review of The Creative Experiment by C. M.
     Bowra. New Yorker (27 Aug. 1949): 63-65.

This new volume of essays on modern poetry written
in the first half of the twentieth century by a
sympathetic scholar with broad knowledge of
European literature, includes such fruitful
innovators as Guillaume Apollinaire and Boris
Pasternak. Bowra, a good critic, says that the
aim of modern poetry is simply to present, not to
teach or exhort. His exegesis of The Waste Land
is the "most nearly complete and rewarding of any
. . . by Eliot's contemporaries."

204. "Goethe Two Hundred Years After."   354-59.
     Discussion of Goethe's works in English
     translation on the occasion of the
     two-hundredth anniversary of his birth. New
     Yorker 30 (17 Sept. 1949): 100, 102-3.

The best critical work in English is Barker
Fairley's A Study of Goethe. Goethe's
interpretative imagination underlies all of his
work. The reader finds it difficult to reach
Goethe's meanings in his poetry because of
translation problems and the barrier of two
hundred years. Goethe's writing epitomized the
classical ideal, which was overturned by the
Romantic Age. The best introduction to Goethe's
lyric poetry is Beethoven's and Shubert's songs.

205. "Post-War British Poets."   360-62.
     Review of The New British Poets: An
     Anthology. Ed. Kenneth Rexroth. New Yorker
     25 (26 Mar. 1949): 109-11.

In this detailed survey of current British thought
and feeling, Bogan finds the poetry shifts from
"Audenesque wit and semi-realism" to "new
Romanticism." The poetry ranges from London to
remote districts of England. Poets who are not
major, well-known talents, seem "fairly washed out
and feeble."
206. "The Auroras of Autumn."   363-64.
     Review of The Auroras of Autumn by Wallace

Stevens. New Yorker 26 (28 Oct. 1950):
129-30.

Steven's later more explicit, logical poetry has
"weakened or destroyed a good deal of his original
'magic.'" His natural world is peopled with
"bloodless symbols," although "no one can describe
the simplicities of [this] natural world with more
direct skill."

The New Yorker review also contains a discussion
of The Shaping Spirit: A Study of Wallace Steven
by William Van O'Connor, "the first long, detailed
analysis of Steven's work," which is omitted here.

207. "The Skirting of Passion." 365-69.
Review of The Captain's Death Bed by Virginia
Woolf. New Republic 122 (29 May 1950):
18-19.

Bogan asserts "Mrs. Woolf is frequently
intellectually pretentious and always emotionally
immature." The high point of this posthumously
published collected works is the essay "Memoir of
a Working Woman's Guide" in which Woolf
"transcends her prejudices even as she states
them." The selections range from the interior
monologue "Reading" to her impressionist criticism
in which she "never let go of the classical
rhetorical devices."

208. "From Chaucer to Yeats." 371-73.
Review of Poets of the English Language.
Eds. W. H. Auden and Norman Holmes Pearson.
New Yorker 27 (17 Mar. 1951): 126-28.

This five-volume work on poetry is a "pioneer
effort to place poetry in the midst of history and
life, and to connect it to other arts with which
it shares a common creative source." The
relationship of English poetry to European,
British, and American history over six centuries
has been shown by comparing the poetry with major
events. Many complete long works appear in these
volumes, as well as difficult and neglected works.
Their inclusion makes the volumes "a peculiarly
modern achievement," since the study of English
literature is comparatively new.

209. "The Later Dylan Thomas."   374-76.
     Review of In Country Sleep by Dylan Thomas.
     New Yorker 28 (2 Aug. 1952): 65.

Thomas incorporates the formal techniques of the
folk ballad into this collection. His move beyond
Surrealism into more sense is accompanied by his
usual joy and exuberance for life, in contrast to
the "emotional blankness and inertia [which]
pervade poetry in general." He also directly
celebrates sexual themes.

210. "The Fable and the Song."   377-80.
     Review of The Fables of La Fontaine, trans.
     by Marianne Moore; and Poems: A Selection by
     Leonie Adams. New Yorker 30 (4 Sept. 1954):
     304-6.

Moore's style, humor, intelligence, wit and taste,
similar to those of La Fontaine, contribute to her
success in catching the underlying tone in the
fables. She has given her readers "La Fontaine in
a modern English idiom."

Adams' poems are an "indication of a poetic
endowment as deep as it is rare." Her major
themes include the "entrapment of the spirit in
the flesh and the shadow cast by eternity." The
difficulty of reading her work comes from the
"tension and complication of her initial poetic
impulse."

211. "The Minor Shudder." 381-84.
     Review of Selected Poems by Horace Gregory,
     The Seven-League Crutches by Randall Jarrell,
     Selected Poems by Richard Eberhart, and
     Praise to the End! by Theodore Roethke. New
     Yorker 27 (16 Feb. 1952): 96-98.

These four poets attempt to "project feelings of
mystery and awe" by four different methods. In
Gregory's work the backgrounds are real, the
characters ghostly and his use of the "mask has
come to disguise [his] face only too well."
Jarrell is obsessed with problems of reality and
non-reality in his dealings with creatures who
revolve in a "bloodless limbo of pain and fear."
The poems in Eberhart's collection are successful
because he possesses "the innocent unself-

consciousness of one to whom the spirit is a
reality." Roethke has invented a symbolism of
terror in his poems, which concern "the journey
from the child's primordial subconscious world,
through the regions of adult terror, guilt and
despair, toward a final release into the freedom
of the conscious being."

212. Review of <u>Selected Poems, 1923-1943</u> by Robert
     Penn Warren and <u>A Wreath for the Sea</u> by
     Robert Fitzgerald. 385-88. <u>New Yorker</u> 20
     (22 Apr. 1944): 76-78.

The new formal English style of poetry, derived
from Eliot and Pound and their sources, as well as
the satirical style of the thirties, appears in
these two books. Warren handles language
beautifully with "the courage of his convictions."
Fitgerald's "observation is delicate, but
precise," and his "grasp of classic resonance and
balance brings him out always on the side of
simplicity."

213. Review of <u>North and South</u> by Elizabeth
     Bishop. 388-89. <u>New Yorker</u> 22 (5 Oct.
     1946): 121-23.

Miss Bishop's poems combine "an unforced ironic
humor with a naturalist's accuracy of
observation." She writes descriptions of New
England and Florida landscapes from her own
unmistakable point of view, taking a central idea
and expanding it into a metaphor, as in the
"Imaginary Iceberg."

214. Review of <u>Lord Weary's Castle</u> by Robert
     Lowell. 389-91. <u>New Yorker</u> 22 (30 Nov.
     1946): 137-40.

The poems in this book mirror Lowell's desperation
with modern materialism. In spite of his
conversion to the Roman Catholic Church from New
England Calvinism, his work still "bears some
relationship to Herman Melville's, [who] had
Puritan Hell-fire in his bones." Lowell's overall
technical competence is remarkable. "Lowell may
be the first of the post-war generation who will
write in dead earnest . . . attempting to find a

basis for faith."

215. Review of <u>The Beautiful Changes</u> by Richard
     Wilbur. Brief mention of <u>Poems</u> by William J.
     Smith and <u>Other Skies</u> by John Ciardi.
     391-93. <u>New Yorker</u> 23 (15 Nov. 1947): 130,
     133-34.

"Wilbur surpasses the majority of his
contemporaries in range of imagination and depth
of feeling." These poems are romantic, emotional,
and derivative, especially of Marianne Moore,
Eliot, Rilke, and Hopkins. "Fidelity to nature
underlies every word." Smith is "often able to
write a true lyric often edged with effective
satire." Ciardi's work, which covers his war
experiences, "brings out many overlooked sides of
aerial warfare . . . and includes warm and direct
elegies to dead friends."

The original <u>New Yorker</u> review also mentioned
Howard Nemerov's book, <u>The Image and the Law</u>,
which is "completely lacking in sensuous responses
to reality," and Karl Shapiro's <u>Trial of a Poet</u>,
which is "occupied more with character and motive
than scene."

216. Review of <u>A Mask for Janus</u> by W. S. Merwin
     and <u>The First Morning</u> by Peter Viereck.
     393-96. <u>New Yorker</u> 28 (31 Jan. 1953):
     75-76.

Merwin's first volume contains poems which are
technically proficient, which is unusual in this
era. His use of mythological material "makes a
promise for the future." He has a "warm
affection for the infinitely various possibilities
of English rhyme and meter." Viereck's work,
however, shows that "a return to form has its
hazards as well as its rewards." His third book
has not lived up to his early promise of
vanquishing the moderns. "He now appears to be a
writer of verse that is fundamentally not
serious."

217. Review of <u>Poems, 1940-1953</u> by Karl Shapiro.
     396-97. <u>New Yorker</u> 30 (5 Jun. 1954):
     118-19.

Shapiro, spokesman for his generation, has written
"a remarkably full chronicle of a troubled and
tragic era." His war elegies are "distinguished
for their rightness of tone," but his later work
"seems to have become rather embittered."

218.   Review of In the Cold Country by Barbara
       Howes. 397-98. New Yorker 30 (5 June
       1954): 119-20.

Her second volume "announces the most accomplished
woman poet of her generation." She is working
with tradition to form a new reconciliation with
"modern attitudes and techniques."

219.   A POET'S ALPHABET (1970)
       Edited by Robert Phelps and Ruth Limmer.
       New York: McGraw-Hill Book Company, 1970
       (first edition). (Entry 1018)

This posthumously-published collection contains
all of the material from Bogan's 1955 Selected
Criticism, as well as most of her later essays,
and several other works not previously collected.
Her obituary from The New Yorker serves as an
introduction and states, "The exactness and
lucidity of her criticism suggested that she was
attempting to create a new kind of lyric poetry
out of statements about poetry." Included are 177
of her essays and reviews arranged in alphabetical
order. Many reviews group several poets together
and a few are brief notices from her reviews in
The New Yorker. All selections are numbered and
annotated below, with the original place of
publication noted, except for those that were
first collected in Selected Criticism. For these
only their titles and page numbers in both
Selected Criticism and A Poet's Alphabet are
given.

"American Literature at Mid-Century (1950)." 1-
14.   Titled "Modernism in American Literature" in
SC.   3-20.   (Entry 124)

220. "Pro-Tem (1967)." 14-15. First publication.

The present state of poetry is one in which a
great deal of questionable work is privately
published in little presses. In the academies
"critical industries thrive on close explications
and biographical material of major figures."
Avant-garde poetry is tediously Existential. It
is necessary to remember and to trust "pleasures
in those formalities that language has built up
over . . . time."

"Anthology for the Enjoyment of Poetry, edited by
Max Eastman (1939)." 16-18. Titled
"Utilitarianism Disguised" in SC. 175-77. (Entry
161)

"Modern American Poetry: A Critical Anthology and
Modern British Poetry: A Critical Anthology,
edited by Louis Untermeyer (1942)." 18-20.
Titled "Wise After the Event" in SC. 219-22.
(Entry 175)

"The New British Poets: An Anthology, edited by
Kenneth Rexroth (1949)." 20-22. Titled "Post-War
British Poets" in SC. 360-62. (Entry 205)

221. "New Poets of England and America, edited by
      Donald Hall, Robert Pack, and Louis Simpson
      (1958)." 22-24. New Yorker 34 (29 Mar.
      1958): 122-24.

The volume has a "delightfully shrewd
introduction" by Robert Frost, followed by mainly
lyric poems, written on the whole in verse on
conventional poetic themes of love and death.
"Myth seems to give way to actual history." The
collection contains much liveliness and
achievement even though the poets are associated
with academics, popularly thought to dry up
inspiration.

222. "The New American Poetry 1945-1960, edited by
      Donald M. Allen." 24-26. New Yorker 36 (8
      Oct. 1960): 199-200.

Bogan questions these new poets, "Is this a true
avant-garde manifestation . . .?" and obliquely

answers, or "Is it . . . a late and peculiarly
American development of the post-Symbolist revolt
. . . ?" She wonders, "What degree of anarchy can
be projected in poetry?"

223. "American Poetry, edited by G. W. Allen,
     W. B. Rideout, and J. K. Robinson
     (1966)." 26-29. New Yorker 42 (1 Oct.
     1966): 221-23.

This anthology, written to be used as a textbook,
is useful in its description of convention,
attitudes and style. The editors deal briskly
with the poetry of the Colonial period, the
nineteenth century and the first forty years of
the twentieth. Here Bogan finds the disappearance
of great American poets such as Edgar Lee Masters
disturbing, but commends the selections from
Robert Lowell and Theodore Roethke.

"W. A. Auden: The Dog Beneath the Skin (1935)."
30-32. Titled "The Quest of W. H. Auden" in SC.
275-77. (Entry 186)

"W. A. Auden: Letters from Iceland (1937)." 32-
35. Titled "Feats on the Fjord" in SC. 48-51.
(Entry 134)

"The Oxford Book of Light Verse [ed. W. A. Auden]
(1938)." 35-36. Titled "Light and Adult" in SC.
105-7. (Entry 147)

"W. A. Auden: The Double Man (1941)." 36-38.
Titled "The Quest of W. H. Auden 2" in SC. 278-
79. (Entry 187)

"W. A. Auden: For the Time Being (1944)." 38-40.
Titled "The Quest of W. H. Auden 3" in SC. 280-
82. (Entry 188)

"The Collected Poetry of W. H. Auden (1945)." 40-
42. Titled "The Quest of W. H. Auden 4" in SC.
282-85. (Entry 189)

"W. H. Auden: "<u>The Age of Anxiety</u> (1947)."   42-44.
Titled "The Quest of W. H. Auden 5" in SC.   285-
87.   (Entry 190)

"<u>Poets of the English Language</u> [ed. W. A. Auden]
(1951)."   44-47.   Titled "From Chaucer to Yeats in
SC."   371-73.   (Entry 208)

224. "W. A. Auden: <u>The Shield of Achilles</u> (1955)."
      47-48.   <u>New Yorker</u> 31 (30 Apr. 1955): 116-18.

Auden's poems on modern dilemmas show his incisive
wit.   His "emphasis has shifted from political to
moral and spiritual areas."   His "Bucolics" are a
modern occasional poem and his religious side
appears in "Horae Canonical."   Auden has
successfully shifted "his diction and conceits
close to the mainstream of American humor."

225. "<u>The Criterion Book of Modern American Verse</u>
      (1957)."   48-49.   <u>New Yorker</u> 33 (2 Mar.
      1957): 111-12.

Auden has chosen poets for their sincerity and
intensity in this anthology of the last fifty
years of American poetry, beginning with E. A.
Robinson and ending with Anthony Hecht, leaving
out himself and Eliot.   He contrasts American
poets with their European counterparts, finding
that Americans can break more easily with
tradition.   Now that modern American poetry has
been accepted officially, it has become stiff and
orthodox.

226. "<u>Homage to Clio</u> (1960)."   49-50.   <u>New Yorker</u>
      36 (8 Oct. 1960): 197-99.

Although Auden is the acknowledged leader of the
international poetic movement, he has not allowed
himself to be "egged on to performances that are
not natural to his gifts."   His new poems are
written in "the simplest and most seemingly
artless of forms."   He shows his talent in the
light and occasional verse and his authority in
the poems on dark and difficult themes.

"Charles Baudelaire (1947)."   51-52. Titled
"Baudelaire Revisited" in SC.   332-34. (Entry
199)

227. "John Berryman (1964)."   53-54.
      Review of 77 Dream Songs.   New Yorker 40
      (7 Nov. 1964): 242-43.

"A more exasperating collection of verse has
probably never been written." Bogan compares
Berryman's "method of escaping any touch or taint
of the sublime" with Karl Shapiro's "recent
dislocations and disguises." Berryman and "his
whole group of alter egos . . . sound sort of
tired and resigned."

"Slick but Not Streamlined [on John Betjeman],
edited by W. H. Auden (1947)."   55-56. Titled
"John Betjeman" in SC.   343-45. (Entry 201)

228. "John Betjeman: Collected Poems, edited
      by Lord Birkenhead (1959)."   56-58. New
      Yorker 35 (18 Apr. 1959): 169-70.

Betjeman's light verse shows his love for
Englishness, his nostalgia for middle-class
virtues, and admiration for English eccentricity.
"However light his means, his purpose is never
trivial." Although his verse forms reproduce
Victorian techniques, the sentiment in his poems
"becomes . . . acceptable to our modern
sensibilities."

"R. P. Blackmur (1940)."   59-61. Titled
"Sensibility and Luggage" in SC.   191-94.
(Entry 167)

"Elizabeth Bowen (1939)."   62-65. Titled "The
Pure in Heart" in SC.   125-28. (Entry 152)

"C. M. Bowra (1949)."   66-68. Titled "The
Creative Experiment" in SC.   350-53. (Entry 203)

229. "Lawrence Durrell (1960)."   69.

Review of <u>Collected Poems</u>. <u>New Yorker</u> 37
(11 Mar. 1961): 172.

Durrell's Romanticism appears in these poems on
the Mediterranean coastal region. While most of
the poems "evoke with full poignance ancient and
modern moments of time and spirits of place,"
sometimes he sounds like a "highly suggestible and
articulate lotus-eater."

230. "Roy Fuller (1958)." 69-70.
Review of <u>Brutus's Orchard</u>. <u>New Yorker</u> 34
(13 Sept. 1958): 162-63.

This is a book of the "utmost technical
distinction" by a poet "with a firm sense of
life's tragic ironies." The poet tells the truth
about the modern world with "no disguised
trivialities."

231. "Elizabeth Jennings (1956)." 70-71.
Review of <u>A Way of Looking</u>. <u>New Yorker</u> 32
(6 Oct. 1956): 178-79.

Although these first poems by Jennings to appear
in America may be only slightly connected to the
real world, a second reading will bring out their
musical quality and meaning.

232. "James Kirkup (1954)." 71.
Review of <u>A Spring Journey and Other Poems</u>.
<u>New Yorker</u> 30 (16 Oct. 1954): 161.

Kirkup writes "in form with ease, with no sign of
[contemporary] spiritual strain." He has the
ability to "transmute the ordinary into the
extraordinary."

233. "The Movement: John Wain and Kingsley Amis
(1958)." 71-73.
Review of <u>A Word Carved on a Sill</u> by John
Wain and <u>A Case of Samples: Poems 1946-1956</u>
by Kingsley Amis. <u>New Yorker</u> 34 (13 Sept.
1958): 158, 161-63.

These two members of the fifties "Movement" in
Great Britain show its limitations in their

collections. The qualities of the "Movement"
include stress on intellectual virtues at the
expense of human feeling and distrust of all large
systems of thought. Wain bypasses romantic
subjects in poems written in terza rima. Amis is
also "bitterly unromantic" in his collection which
is "edged with penetrating cynicism."

234. "William Plomer (1956)." 73.
     Review of <u>Borderline Ballads</u>. <u>New Yorker</u> 30
     (4 Feb. 1956): 98, 101-2.

Plomer shows his heritage in Swiftian satire. He
is savage, but also terribly funny in his
rollicking verse, shocking diction and exposure of
British pretentiousness.

235. "Kathleen Raine (1954)." 73-74.
     Review of <u>The Year One</u>. <u>New Yorker</u> 30
     (27 Feb. 1954): 113-15.

Raine has the ability to be in nature in a
mystical identification with the Scottish hills
and sea. Her poems "fuse spirit and substance in
a remarkable way."

236. "Vernon Watkins (1960)." 74.
     Review of <u>Cypress and Acacia</u>. <u>New Yorker</u> 36
     (26 Mar. 1960): 146, 154.

Watkins' delightful poetry is "completely free of
ambiguity, irony, and skepticism." Although he
has been called neo-Romantic, under the surface "a
modern sensibility is at work."

"Colette (1930)." 75. Titled "Colette" in SC.
28-32. (Entry 128)

"Ivy Compton-Burnett (1951)." Titled "Childhood's
False Eden, No. 2., I. Compton-Burnett" in SC.
189-90. (Entry 166)

"Hart Crane (1938)." 81-82. Titled "Hart Crane"
in SC. 40-41. (Entry 131)

"Detective Novels (1944)." 83-87. Titled "The
Time of the Assassins" in SC. 258-63. (Entry
182)

"Life and Letters [of Emily Dickinson] (1945)."
88-92. Titled "The Summers of the Hesperides are
Long" in SC. 289-94. (Entry 191)

237. "The Poems (1955)." 92-94. Review of <u>The</u>
      <u>Poems of Emily Dickinson</u>. Ed. Thomas A.
      Johnson. <u>New Yorker</u> 31 (8 Oct. 1955):
      178-79 (titled "The Poet Dickinson Comes to
      Life").

Johnson's introduction clarifies several major
Dickinson enigmas. He shows that Dickinson
followed the "usual progress of a lyric poet who
does not force or falsify his gifts." He gives
statistical proof in the volume of the poems
produced of Dickinson's greatest emotional
experience, her love for Reverend Charles
Wadsworth. He suggests that her chosen seclusion
was "based partly on her desire to have some
control over her life." She was "a self-
determined woman who made choices, rather than the
pathetic recluse of the legend." This new edition
shows Dickinson's poems in their original
idiosyncratic form, "undiluted and unadulterated
by former editors."

238. "A Mystical Poet (1959)." 94-103.
      Talk given at bicentennial celebration of
      Amherst, Massachusetts, on Oct. 23, 1959.
      Published in <u>Emily Dickinson: Three Views</u>.
      Amherst: Amherst College Press: 1960. pp.
      27-34.

Dickinson's power is the "power of the seer."
"The progress of the mystic toward illumination
and of the poet toward the full depth and richness
of his insight, is much alike." Bogan compares
Dickinson with the English romantic poets Blake,
Wordsworth, Coleridge, Shelley, and Keats who
"fought against the eighteenth century's cold
logic and mechanical point of view, as she
rebelled against religious dogma." Bogan explores
the resemblances between the life and works of

Emily Brontë, Blake, and Dickinson. However, "at
the highest summit of her art, she resembles no
one." This high period is when she can describe
"with clinical precision the actual emotional
event." Bogan calls "My life had stood--a loaded
gun" an example of a poem "whose reverberations
are infinite, as in great music . . . ."

"Isak Dinesen (1943)." 104-106. Titled "Isak
Dinesen" in SC. 231-34. (Entry 177)

"T. S. Eliot: Collected Poems (1936)." 107-9.
Titled "The Progress of T. S. Eliot, From Despair
to Faith" in SC. 55-56. (Entry 136)

"T. S. Eliot: The Family Reunion (1939)." 108-9.
Titled "The Religious Encounter" in SC. 56-58.
(Entry 137)

"T. S. Eliot: Four Quartets (1943)." 109-11.
Titled "From Form to Content" in SC. 58-61.
(Entry 138)

"Paul Eluard (1939)." 112-22. Titled "The Poetry
of Paul Eluard" in SC. 157-70. (Entry 159)

"European Poetry (1941)." 123-27. Titled "A
Revolution in European Poetry [by Emery Neff]" in
SC. 210-215. (Entry 173)

239. "Experimentalists of a New Generation
     (1957)." 128-30. New Yorker 33 (13 Apr.
     1957): 172-74.

This is a general discussion on the new generation
of experimentalists whose work, published by small
presses, is against the formal and academic.
Bogan warns these poets that they cannot shock in
their form or content because Rimbaud, Pound,
Eliot, and Gertrude Stein have beaten them to it.
These new poets are striving for large poetic
forms, like those of W. C. Williams' Paterson and
Pound's Cantos. They want spontaneity similar to
improvisation in cool jazz in their spoken poetry

on records and before live audiences. Readers
should read these new poets' works for their humor
and excitement.

"Gustave Flaubert (1942)." 131-36. Titled
"Sentimental Education Today" in SC. 223-30.
(Entry 176)

"Folk Art (1943)." 137-47. Titled "Some Notes on
Popular and Unpopular Art" in SC. 238-51. (Entry
179)

240. "Formal Poetry (1953): The Pleasures of
     Formal Poetry." 148-159. Paper presented at
     Bard College Conference, Nov. 5-6, 1948,
     (titled "Experimental and Formal Verse").
     Published in Quarterly Review of Literature
     7, No. 3 (1959): 176-185. Reprinted in
     Quarterly Review of Literature Thirtieth
     Anniversary Poetry Retrospective 19, Nos. 1-2
     (1974). Also reprinted in The Poet's Work.
     Ed. Reginald Gibbons. Boston: Houghton
     Mifflin, 1979. pp. 203-213.

In this essay, an excellent introduction to poetic
form, Bogan links form to human function. She
traces the history of the avoidance of form from
the precursors of the modern poets such as
Baudelaire and Rimbaud to present-day young poets
who cannot write sonnets or verse with regular
stress and who "avoid form as they would some
stupid or reprehensible action." She shows how
wrong they are and how form became out of favor
because of the anti-Romantic reaction in France
and the outdated Victorian tradition in England.
Pound and Eliot, however, have performed "miracles
of deflation and revivification of modern poetry."

Bogan defines formal poetry as poetry written in
meter and rhyme. She describes meter as rhythm as
experienced in marching and rowing, as well as the
reiterative pattern of a drum beat. "Rhyme
becomes necessary when rhythm weakens." Rhyme
took hold when "vulgar" languages displaced Latin
and Greek. She quotes Gilbert Murray on the
subject of MOLPE and the tragic pattern and Eliot
on vers libre and originality in poetry. Even
though today poets are "frightened of emotion and

of the Sublime," formal art "is still alive. . .
as modern as this moment and as ancient as the
farthest antiquity."

This reprint of her speech omits her agreement
with W. C. Williams' statement, "If a poem has
measure it is a poem." Williams was the other
main speaker at the conference and gave a paper
entitled "Some Hints Toward the Enjoyment of
Modern Verse."

"Robert Frost: Collected Poems (1939)." 160--162.
Titled "Country Things" in SC. 122-24. (Entry
151)

"Robert Frost: A Masque of Reason (1945)." 162-
63. Titled "The Prophet Job, Yankee Style" in SC.
272-74. (Entry 185)

240. "A Lifework (1962)." Biography of Robert
     Frost. 163-83. Major Writers of America.
     Vol. 2, Ed. Perry Miller. New York:
     Harcourt, Brace & World, Inc., 1962. pp.
     643-69 (titled "Robert Frost 1874-1963").

Frost's life and works are described in this
lengthy essay, divided into eight parts, beginning
with his Yankee countryman and Scottish crofter
inheritance, and ending with Frost's apotheosis in
his middle eighties "as an unofficial American
poet-laureate." In the second section Bogan
discusses Frost's difficult youth and patchwork
education, his devotion to his mother and
courtship of his wife-to-be, as well as his early
publications. The young Frost family's
unsuccessful farm in New Hampshire and his more
successful teaching at Plymouth, while continually
writing poetry, make up the next section. The
fourth section concentrates on Frost's ventures to
England to find a publisher for his first volume,
A Boy's Will, and his short-lived friendship with
Ezra Pound. Section five traces the family's farm
life in Herefordshire, England, and their
subsequent return to New England, as well as the
enthusiastic reception of the American publication
of Frost's first books.
Bogan then turns to a critical examination of
Frost's work and a discussion of the reasons for

his popularity. She finds a lack of close
critical examination of his poetry and proceeds to
give her own interpretation, including his
remarkable mastery of formal poetics, his
flexible, musical, and completely natural style.
She considers Frost's influences to be E. A.
Robinson's crusty New Englanders and Browning's
dramatic monologues. In the next section she
mentions Frost's fear of machinery and his
conservatism. She concludes this part with a
comparison of Frost's later works with those of
Yeats and Eliot and finds Frost's _Masques_ "seem
extremely light in weight compared to [their later
poems]."

"Stephan George (1943)." 184-85. Titled "Stephan
George" in SC. 235-37. (Entry 178)

"André Gide: _Imaginary Interviews_ (1944)."
187-91. Titled "The Head and the Heart" in SC.
319-24. (Entry 196)

"André Gide: _Journals_ (1947)." 191-94. Titled
"The Head and the Heart 2" in SC. 324-28. (Entry
197)

"André Gide: _Journals_ (1948)." 194-96. Titled
"The Head and the Heart 3" in SC. 328-31. (Entry
198)

"Goethe (1949)." 197-201. Titled "Goethe Two
Hundred Years After" in SC. 354-59. (Entry 204)

"Robert Graves: _Poems_ (1946)." 202-4. Titled
"Satire and Sentimentality" in SC. 316-18.
(Entry 195)

242. "New Poems (1964)." 204-5.
     Review of _New Poems_ by Robert Graves. _New
     Yorker_ 40 (11 Apr. 1964): 178, 180.

Robert Graves writes brilliant formal poetry even
in his old age. His tone in these memorable
lyrics "frequently slides over into the

incantatory and his gods and demons are recurrent
and slightly obsessive."

243. "Nathaniel Hawthorne (1960)." 206-210.
     Foreword to The Scarlet Letter: A Romance.
     New York: Libra, 1960. pp. ix-xiv.
     (Entry 747)

The importance of this novel in American
literature in general and its influence on Henry
James in particular are emphasized in this review.
Hawthorne's Puritan forebears may have provided
background and motivation for ths novel, but it is
written about real humans. Bogan includes
Hawthorne's Salem upbringing, his isolated period,
his education and his early hardships taking care
of his family. She calls this novel "a perfect
balance of good and evil." The figure of Hester
Prynne is "the first portrayal in American fiction
of woman's nature in all its complication and
contradiction."

244. "Heine (1956)." 211-12.
     Review of reissue of Antonina Vallentin's
     Heine: Poet in Exile. New Yorker 32 (7 Apr.
     1956): 157-59.

The only American notation of the centenary of
Heine's death is the reissue of this book.
Heine's influence on English poetry shows in the
work of A. E. Housman, Auden, MacNeice, and
Betjeman. Heine was Germany's first satirist,
"cruelly caustic, intensely skeptical."

"Letters [of Gerard Manley Hopkins] (1935)." 213-
14. Titled "The Letters of Gerard Manley Hopkins
1" in SC. 42-43. (Entry 132)

"Further Letters [of Gerard Manley Hopkins]
(1938)." 214-17. Titled ""The Letters of Gerard
Manley Hopkins 2" in SC. 43-47. (Entry 133)

"Leonie Adams (1954)." 218-29. Titled "The Fable
and the Song" in SC. 379-80. (Entry 210)

"Elizabeth Bishop (1946)." 219-20. Titled "Young

Poets 2" in SC. 388-89. (Entry 213)

245. "Abbie Huston Evans (1961)." 220-21.
     Review of <u>Fact of Crystal</u>. <u>New Yorker</u> 37
     (1 Apr. 1961): 130-31.

In opposition to prevailing contemporary poetical
practices of limiting feeling to "violence, guilt,
anxiety and fear," Evans shows a "mystic
apprehension." Her New England perceptions and
sense of "inscape" can be "set against Hopkins'
and Dickinson's."

246. "Jean Garrigue (1960)." 221-22.
     Review of <u>A Water Walk by the Villa d'Este</u>.
     <u>New Yorker</u> 36 (26 Mar. 1960): 154, 157.

Garrigue's fourth book of poetry contains poems
about extremes in nature, from Alpine landscapes
to Italian fountains, which succeed when she
brings her "high and glittering subjects into
relation with each other and with ordinary
existence."

247. "Anthony Hecht (1954)." 222-23.
     Review of <u>Summoning of Stones</u>. <u>New Yorker</u> 30
     (5 June 1954): 119.

The influence of Dylan Thomas, war experiences,
and a writing fellowship to the American Academy
at Rome can all be seen in Hecht's first book.
Bogan maintains "the shimmer of a virtuoso
technique cannot entirely obscure the fact that
the poems have very little content, emotional or
otherwise."

"Barbara Howes (1954)." 223-24. Titled "Young
Poets 7" in SC. 397-8. (Entry 218)

248. "Galway Kinnell (1961)." 224.
     Review of <u>What a Kingdom It Was</u>. <u>New Yorker</u>
     37 (1 Apr. 1961): 130.

In his first book Kinnell is concerned about the
"enigmatic significance of nature and man" in city
or country.

249. "Kenneth Koch (1963)." 224-24.
     Review of Thank You and Other Poems. New
     Yorker 39 (12 Oct. 1963): 210-12.

The poems in his second book are "chiefly
occasional, with a slight leaning. . . towards
lyricism." Surrealism mixes with farce and his
comic inventiveness seldom fails.

250. "Stanley Kunitz (1958)." 225-26.
     Review of Selected Poems: 1928-1958. New
     Yorker 34 (6 Dec. 1958): 236-38.

Kunitz, a formalist and dramatic lyricist, "seems
to be trapped in . . . an area of almost
unrelieved shadow."

251. "Josephine Mills (1956)." 226.
     Review of Prefabrications. New Yorker 32
     (7 Apr. 1956): 158.

Miss Mills writes about everyday life in
California, including the parking lot, motel, and
Los Angeles high school, using both her heart and
intellect.

252. "Marcia Nardi (1956)." 226-27.
     Review of Poems. New Yorker 33 (4 May 1957):
     167.

Miss Nardi is so directly involved with her work
that "she often seems to be not so much writing
poems as having them write her."

253. "Howard Nemerov (1961)." 227.
     Review of New and Selected Poems. New Yorker
     38 (1 Apr. 1961): 129-30.

Nemerov's work, termed "academic," is the "formal
poetry of a young middle generation at its best."

254. "Louise Townsend Nicholl (1954, 1959)."
     227-28. Review of The World's One Clock and
     Collected Poems. New Yorker 30 (27 Feb.
     1954): 114-15 and New Yorker 35 (28 Nov.
     1959) 236, 238, 240.

Nicholl's mystic and religious poetry has not
received enough critical recognition. The World's
One Clock shows off her mystic gift and Collected
Poems her "rare double vision" in religious poetry
that "touches the sacred in man and nature."

255. "Ned O'Gorman and W. D. Snodgrass (1959).
     228-29. Review of The Night of the Hammer
     and Heart's Needle. New Yorker 35 (24 Oct.
     1959): 194-96.

O'Gorman's poetry in The Night of the Hammer "has
the kind of vitality that an active belief
sometimes sets in motion." Heart's Needle by
Snodgrass shows the same kind of technical
expertise, with "an eye for telling detail."

"Muriel Rukeyser (1939)." 229-30. Titled
"America Was Promises" in SC. 173-74. (Entry
160)

256. "Frederick Seidel (1963)." 230-31.
     Review of Final Solutions. New Yorker 39
     (12 Oct. 1963): 210-12.

Seidel rages against the "basic stupidities and
depravities of mankind itself." His satirical
poems, written in strictly controlled meter with
difficult rhymes, are set in scenes of this world.

257. "William Jay Smith (1958)." 231.
     Review of Poems 1947-1957. New Yorker 34
     (29 Mar. 1958) 124.

Smith's book is a collection of lyrics wherein
"serious poems filled with fresh observation and
direct emotion" and light verse which "sparkles
and flies free" are about evenly balanced."

258. "May Swenson (1958)." 231-32.
     Review of A Cage of Spines. New Yorker 34
     (6 Dec. 1958): 326-38.

Although Swenson's poems are "lively, ingenious
and fanciful," sometimes she writes with "too
continuous a sparkle."

259. "John Updike (1959)." 232.
     Review of The Carpentered Hen and Other Tame
     Creatures. New Yorker 35 (18 Apr. 1959):
     170.

Updike's first poetry collection "exhibits all the
surface characteristics of verse at its tightest"
and he is "wildly original and charmingly
perceptive."

"Peter Viereck (1953)." 232-34. Titled "Young
Poets 5" in SC. 394-96. (Entry 216)

260. "Edmund Wilson (1962)." 233-34.
     Review of Wilson's Night Thoughts. New
     Yorker 37 (20 Jan. 1962): 118, 120.

Wilson is a "true man of letters" as shown in his
collection of critical prose and serious and light
verse collected since 1917.

"Henry James: The Princess Casamassima 1936)."
234-42. Titled "James on a Revolutionary Theme" in
SC. 112-21. (Entry 150)

"Henry James: The Bostonians (1945)." Titled "The
Portrait of New England" in SC. 295-301. (Entry
192)

"The Later Phase [of Henry James] (1944)." 247-
250. Titled "The Silver Clue" in SC. 264-68.
(Entry 183)

"Such Counsels You Gave to Me [on Robinson
Jeffers] (1937). " 251-53. Titled "Landscapes
with Jeffers" in SC. 67-69. (Entry 141)

"Robinson Jeffers: Medea (1946)." 253-55. Titled
"The Modern Syndrome" in SC. 302-4. (Entry 193)

261. "Juan Ramón Jiménez (1958)." 256-59.
     Review of Selected Writings of Juan Ramón
     Jiménez. Trans. H. R. Hays. New Yorker 33

(8 Feb. 1958): 130, 132-33 (titled "Steel and Quicksilver").

Although the preface by Eugenio Florit gives a most sympathetic account of Jiménez's critical powers, the translation loses "nearly all the savor and point of the poetry," while the prose comes through rather blunted. Jiménez, who received the 1956 Nobel Prize, influenced the other Spanish poets Machado and Lorca. He resembles Yeats in his special power and language and his origin in a "backward country's most primitive region."

262. "David Jones (1963)." 260-61.
     Review of <u>The Anathemata</u>. <u>New Yorker</u> 39
     (17 Aug.): 95-96.

The American publication of Jones' book of "fragments of an attempted writing" reveals his "ardent desire to uncover and restore sacred signs and symbols to . . . a society [which has] lost the sense of living myth through negation and neglect." In spite of its impenetrability, "certain passages of haunting beauty and power come through."

"James Joyce: Proteus, or Vico's Road." 262-67.
Titled "<u>Finnegan's Wake</u> 1 Proteus, or Vico's Road" in SC. 142-48. (Entry 156)

"James Joyce: Approaching Ur (1944)." Titled "2 Approaching Ur" in SC. 149-53. (Entry 157)

263. "Patrick Kavanagh (1965)." 271-72.
     Review of <u>Collected Poems</u>. <u>New Yorker</u> 41
     (10 Apr. 1965): 194, 196.

This Irish poet, standing outside the "solemn post-Yeatsians," continually breaks boundaries in his work. He goes from recounting the life of the agricultural laborer in his early poems to describing Dublin's literary and political life in his later work. Both situations fill him with disillusion and his satire spares nothing and no one.

264. "Philip Larkin: <u>The Less Deceived</u> (1958)."
     273. <u>New Yorker</u> 34 (13 Sept. 1958): 158,
     161-63.

Larkin "considered the most gifted poet of his
generation . . . recognizes limits . . . but also
apprehends depths" in these poems. His manner can
be compared to Hardy's. "He has completely
escaped the dry and flippant excesses of some of
his contemporaries" in the British Movement.

265. "Philip Larkin: <u>The Whitsun Weddings</u> (1965)."
     273-275. <u>New Yorker</u> 41 (10 Apr. 1965):
     193-94, 196.

In his fifth book of poetry Larkin assumes a
British sense of class. He restricts his poetry
to the present and professes little regard for
form, but "possesses formal gifts that are not
only perfectly controlled and strongly sustained,
but capable of wide and interesting variation."

266. "D. H. Lawrence: <u>Birds, Beasts and Flowers</u>
     (1923)." 276-79. <u>New Republic</u> 49 (9 Jul.
     1924): 190-91.

In her first critical review, Bogan finds that
Lawrence changes his poetry to reflect his
changing views. His belief in the salvation of
physical passion turns to belief in absolute
isolation in this collection, in which only poems
such as "The Snake" are successful.

"D. H. Lawrence: <u>Selected Poems</u> 1948." 279-82.
Titled "The Poet Lawrence in SC. 346-49. (Entry
202)

"Federico García Lorca (1937, 1940)." 283-84.
Titled "The Poet in New York and Elsewhere" in SC.
184-85. (Entry 164)

"Robert Lowell: <u>Lord Weary's Castle</u> (1946)." 285-
87. Titled "Young Poets: 1944-54, 3" in SC. 389-
91. (Entry 214)

267. "Robert Lowell: <u>Life Studies</u> (1959)."
    287-88. <u>New Yorker</u> 35 (24 Oct. 1959):
    194-96.

"These poems . . . gain much of their power and
interest from the fact that they are almost
entirely autobiographical." Lowell succeeds in
this difficult task by his "balance, detachment,
and consistent moral courage."

268. "Robert Lowell: <u>For the Union Dead</u> (1965)."
    288-89. <u>New Yorker</u> 41 (10 Apr. 1965): 194.

Lowell's latest book is "largely a collection of
personal memories . . . with much bitterness
eliminated by the passage of time." Lowell is now
the "official poet of his generation."

269. "Robert Lowell: <u>Near the Ocean</u> (1967)." 289.
    <u>New Yorker</u> 43 (20 May 1967): 179-80.

Lowell has become the leader of the confessional
school, but these poems "exhibit a certain
coldness and theatricality that often seem to
spring from a will toward pure shock." This is
"an interim work in every respect."

270. "Hugh MacDiarmid (1967)." 290-91.
    Review of <u>Collected Poems of Hugh MacDiarmid</u>.
    <u>New Yorker</u> 38 (17 Nov. 1962): 238, 241.

At seventy his collected poems are a "frank if
frequently shocking portrait" of a Scot, whose
enthusiasm for political and patriotic poems
resembles that of Pablo Neruda. MacDiarmid's
early lyrics attempt a revival of a Scottish
dialect and his later poems are long and
discursive.

"Archibald MacLeish (1939)." 292-93. Titled
"America Was Promises" in SC. 171-73. (Entry
160)

271. "Louis MacNeice (1940)." 294.
    Review of <u>Collected Poems 1925-48</u>. <u>New
    Yorker</u> 40 (11 Apr. 1964): 180.

MacNeice's collection shows the "subtle shifts and
adjustments that have occurred within English
poetic tradition during this century." His mood
changes from his early exuberance to his later
bitterness and melancholy.

"Katherine Mansfield (1940)." 295-97. Titled
"Childhood's False Eden" in SC. 186-88. (Entry
165)

"Edna Millay (1939)." 298-99. Titled "Unofficial
Feminine Laureate" in SC. 154-56. (Entry 158)

"The Minor Shudder: Horace Gregory, Randall
Jarrell, Richard Eberhart, Theodore Roethke
(1952)." 300-2. Titled "The Minor Shudder" in SC.
381-84. (Entry 211)

"Marianne Moore: Nevertheless (1944)." 303-4.
Titled "Marianne Moore 1" in SC. 252-54. (Entry
180)

"Marianne Moore: The Fables of La Fontaine (1954).
304-6. Titled "The Fable and the Song" in SC.
377-80. (Entry 210)

"American to Her Backbone (1947). 306-8. Titled
"Marianne Moore 2" in SC. 254-57. (Entry 181)

272. Edwin Muir (1956). 309-10.
    Review of One Foot in Eden. New Yorker 32
    (6 Oct. 1956): 178-79.

Muir's volume is unusual in that it is spiritual
poetry in an age of Surrealism. Muir's symbols
derive from the Old Testament and Greek mythology.
He is a master of form and of insight. "The
Days," based on the story of creation, is one of
the great lyrics of our time.

"The Secular Hell (1946)." 311-18. Titled "The
Secular Hell" in SC. 305-318. (Entry 194)

273. "The Gods Continue to Arrive (1960)."
     319-25. Review of <u>Larousse Encyclopedia of</u>
     <u>Mythology</u>. <u>New Yorker</u> 35 (6 Feb. 1960):
     131-32, 134-36.

This publication gives Bogan an opportunity to
dwell on the importance of mythology in
contemporary works in music, theater, poetry,
ballet, and literature. She finds the
illustrations in this book the most valuable part.
Many earlier books on myths, derived from Frazer's
<u>Golden Bough</u>, are compared with religious and
psychological studies. Mythology, according to
the introduction by Robert Graves, is the study of
"whatever religious or heroic legends . . . so
foreign to a student's experience that he cannot
believe them to be true." Primitive man used
mythology to put order into his universe and
modern man uses it in the arts. Bogan discusses
Nietzsche's, Freud's, and Jung's theories of myth.
She concludes "the myth transforms the age."

274. "Pablo Neruda (1969)." 326-27.
     Review of <u>Selected Poems</u>. Trans. Ben Belitt.
     <u>New Yorker</u> 38 (17 Nov. 1962): 238, 241-42.

This bilingual edition of Neruda's poems from
1925-1959 focuses on the Surrealist poems in
which, contrasting with other Surrealists, Neruda
"seizes directly upon reality in sharpest detail
and focuses his apprehensions through by means of
conflict and of rhythmic compulsion."

"St. John Perse (1938)." 328-29. Titled Asian
Exoticism" in SC. 81-82. (Entry 144)

"Katherine Anne Porter (1930)." 330-31. Titled
"<u>Flowering Judas</u>" in SC. 33-35. (Entry 129)
"Ezra Pound: <u>Guide to Kulchur</u> (1939)." 332-35.
Titled "Make It New" in SC. 138-41. (Entry 155)

"Ezra Pound: <u>Cantos LII-LXXI</u> (1940)." 335-36.
Titled "Pound's Later Cantos" in SC. 178-80.
(Entry 162)

"Ezra Pound: <u>The Pisan Cantos</u> (1948)." 337-39.

Titled "Pound's Later Cantos 2" in SC. 180-83.
(Entry 163)

275. "Ezra Pound: Section: Rock-Drill 85-95 de Los
     Cantares (1955). 339-41. New Yorker 32
     (1 Sept. 1956) 92-93.

These eleven new cantos are shorter and more
compressed than the earlier ones, and more visual
dimensions have been added. The actual cantos
form "seems slightly fossilized . . . worthy of
note as origin and as process but with no truly
invigorating aspects." The poems show the shadow
of Pound's personality from which "every layer of
self-interest and self-pity has been burned away."

276. "Dorothy Richardson (1967)." 342-48.
     Review of Dorothy Richardson: An Adventure in
     Self-Discovery by Horace Gregory. New York
     Times Book Review (27 Aug.1967): 4-5 (titled
     "Dorothy Richardson and Miriam Henderson").

This new biography helps to set the record
straight on Richardson's first use of the "stream-
of-consciousness" technique before Joyce or
Proust. Her alter ego, Miriam Henderson, is "the
mirror in which all is reflected." Richardson,
writing about feminine reality in the continuous
present in "fresh and alert diction," describes
how it is to be a woman in the early twentieth
century in London.

"Rainer Maria Rilke: In His Age (1937)." 349-55.
Titled "Rilke In His Age" in SC. 70-78. (Entry
142)

"Rainer Maria Rilke: Duino Elegies (1939)." 355-
56. Titled "Rilke In His Age 2" in SC. 78-80.
(Entry 143)

"Rainer Maria Rilke: Wartime Letters (1940)."
356-59. Titled "The Letters of Rainer Maria Rilke
1" in SC. 195-98. (Entry 168)

"Rainer Maria Rilke: Further Letters (1945)."

359-61. Titled "The Letters of Rilke 2" in SC.
199-20. (Entry 169)

"W. R. Rodgers (1942)." 361-64. Titled "War
Poetry" in SC. 216-18. (Entry 216)

277. "Theodore Roethke (1958)." 365.
    Review of Words for the Wind. New Yorker 35
    (24 Oct. 1959): 194-96.

Roethke and Lowell both deal with childhood
memories, but Roethke works "directly with
unconscious images and boldly penetrates
subliminal regions . . . ." Although "terror and
horror come through," in the nonsense verse,
Roethke can laugh without bitterness.

"Carl Sandburg (1936)." 366-67. Titled "The
People Yes and No" in SC. 64-65. (Entry 140)

278. "Karl Shapiro: Poems (1954)." 368-69.
    Review of Poems 1940-1953. New Yorker 30
    (Jun. 1954): 118-19.

Shapiro, spokesman for his generation, has written
"a remarkably full chronicle of a troubled and
tragic era." His war elegies are "distinguished
for their rightness of tone," but his later work
"seems to have become rather embittered."

279. "Karl Shapiro: The Bourgeois Poet (1964)."
    369-370. New Yorker 40 (7 Nov. 1964): 238,
    241-42.

Shapiro "has been carrying on a brisk and bitter
campaign against metre, rhyme, and all stanzaic
patterns." He attacks "all European art before
the Renaissance, . . . all myth, metaphysics and
religion, much general 'culture' and Charles
Baudelaire . . . ." In spite of his desire to
write poetry that is "illimitable, irrational, and
irresponsible," he has written no such poems here.

"Edith Sitwell: Laughter in a Switchback World
(1925)." 372-74. Titled "Laughter in a

Switchback World" in SC. 21-23. (Entry 125)

"Edith Sitwell: A Song of the Cold (1948). 374-76. Titled "2 Satirist to Sybil" in SC. 24-26. (Entry 126)

"Edith Sitwell: Gardeners and Astronomers (1954)." 376-77. Titled "3 Cold Print" in SC. 26-27. (Entry 127)

"Stephen Spender: Trial of A Judge (1938)." 378-79. Titled "Heads Will Roll" in SC. 108. (Entry 148)

"Stephen Spender: Ruins and Visions (1942)." 379-80. Titled "2 Ruins and Visions" in SC. 110-11. (Entry 149)

280. "Stephen Spender Collected Poems (1955)." 380-81. New Yorker 31 (30 Apr. 1955): 116-18.

Spender has become more technically proficient and more open to gradations of thought and feeling. He has revised and improved his early poems, but still retains his "high line of richness and largeness."

"Wallace Stevens: The Auroras of Autumn (1950)." 382-84. Titled "The Auroras of Autumn" in SC. 363-64. (Entry 206)

281. "Wallace Stevens: Collected Poems." 383-85. Review of The Collected Poems of Wallace Stevens and Poems 1923-54 by e. e. cummings. 383-85. New Yorker 30 (11 Dec. 1954): 198, 201-2. Cummings selection reprinted as "The Imaginative Direction of Our Time" in e. e. cummings and the Critics. Ed. Stanley V. Baum. East Lansing: Michigan State University, 1962. pp. 193-94.

Neither of these two large works depart for a moment from "their respective [poet's]

idiosyncratic methods." Cummings "brought into
American post [World War I] poetry a bittersweet
mixture of satire and sentimentality," along with
his typographical experiments and breaking down of
Victorian mores. His verse shows an awareness of
traditional form. Satire is "his main
contribution to the reinvigoration of modern
verse."

Steven's poetry "links the outer world of reality
closely to the ironic world of vision." He was
the first modern poet "to deal with the American
scene in imaginative rather than purely topical or
regional terms. "Subtle discipline" runs
throughout his work.

"Allen Tate (1936)." 386. Titled "The People Yes
and No" in SC. 66. (Entry 40)

282. "Caitlin Thomas (1957)." 387-390.
     Review of Leftover Life to Kill. New Yorker
     33 (12 Oct. 1957): 193-194, 197.

Caitlin Thomas is a "childish woman" who bears the
"terrifying Irish qualities of violence and
rakishness." Her book is a "headlong descriptive
analysis of herself and other people, especially
her late husband, Dylan Thomas . . . ." Her
story is a fairy tale in reverse in which the
expected happy ending turns into a nightmare
world.

"Dylan Thomas (1952)." 391-92. Titled "The Late
Dylan Thomas" in SC. 374-76. (Entry 209)

283. "From the Greek, the Japanese, and the
     Chinese (1956, 1957)." 393-95. Review of
     Greek Lyrics. Trans. Richmond Lattimore.
     New Yorker 31 (4 Feb. 1956): 98, 101-2.
     One Hundred Poems from the Japanese and One
     Hundred Poems from the Chinese. Trans.
     Kenneth Rexroth. New Yorker 33 (4 May 1957):
     167.

Recent translations have improved since Ezra Pound
taught translators to balance formal and
colloquial language and to adhere to the basic

Imagist tenet of natural words in natural order.
Lattimore's translation of Greek poetry has
produced "renderings of great power and beauty,"
while Rexroth has reproduced "both the simplicity
and subtlety of the texts" in his translations of
Japanese haikus and lyrics. The Chinese lyrics
are "simple, direct, and moving with a colloquial
turn of phrase."

284. "Guillaume Apollinaire (1964)."   395.
      Review of Alcools: Poems 1898-1913. Trans.
      William Meredith. New Yorker (40 18 Apr.
      1964): 224.

Meredith's translations of poems by the French
poet who died during the First World War, "bring
[his] subtleties over into English with admirable
effect."

285. "René Char (1956)."   395-96.
      Review of Hypnos Walking. Trans. Jackson
      Matthews. New Yorker 32 (6 Oct. 1956):
      180-81.

This translation into a bilingual edition shows a
poet "whose faith is strongly attached to nature
and to man." His "superb and subtle language . .
. is ultimately untranslatable."

"H. D.'s Euripides (1937)."   396-97. Titled
"Euripides in Modern Dress" in SC.   62-63.
(Entry 139)

286. "Robert Lowell's 'Imitations' (1962)."   397.
      New Yorker 37 (20 Jan. 1962): 118, 120.

"Lowell is primarily concerned with reproducing
the concentrated energy of such poets as Villon,
Heine, Baudelaire, Rimbaud, Rilke, and Pasternak,"
rather then producing "pale replicas" of their
poems.

287. "Ezra Pound's Version of Sophocles' Women of
      Trachis (1959)."   397-98. New Yorker 33
      (2 Nov. 1957): 200.

Pound fails on every point, except perhaps the choruses, in trying to "bring over into a kind of American vernacular the most intimate and touching of Sophocles' plays."

288. "Richard Wilbur's Moliere (1956)." 389. Review of The Misanthrope. Trans. Richard Wilbur. New Yorker 31 (4 Feb. 1956): 101-2.

Wilbur is "a new master of translation's difficult art" in this work in which he "bridges the differences between another time, place, and literary circumstance and today's."

289. "From the Greek and the French: Cavafy, Seferis, St. John Perse, Racine (1961)." 398-402. Review of The Complete Poems of Cavafy, trans. Rae Dalven; Poems by Seferis, trans. Rex Warner; Six poets of Modern Greece, trans. Edmund Keeley and Philip Sherrard; Chronique by St. John Perse, trans. Robert Fitzgerald; and Phedre by Racine, trans. Robert Lowell. New Yorker 37 (7 Oct. 1961): 398-402.

Modern translators have left literalness behind and are true to the emotional tone of the work, as seen in these recent translations of modern Greek and French poems. Cavafy's powerful historical vignettes are a pleasure to read. Seferis "is rich in content and design." The modern Greek poets represented in the Keeley-Sherrard collection have their "roots in Symbolism and Surrealism." Fitzgerald has "brought . . . over into English in full rhetorical splendor," the Chronique of Perse. Robert Lowell's translation of Phedre shows that he understands French "organized rituals of manner, custom, and belief."

"Paul Valery (1939)." 403-6. Titled "Poet in Spite of Himself" in SC. 129-132. (Entry 153)

"Robert Penn Warren (1944)." 407-9. Titled "Young Poets: 1944-154, 4" in SC. 385-88. (Entry 212)

"Eudora Welty (1941)." 410-12. Titled "The
Gothic South" in SC. 207-9. (Entry 172)

"Edith Wharton (1938)." 413-15. Titled "The
Decoration of Novels" in SC. 83-85. (Entry 145)

290. "Walt Whitman (1955)." 416-18.
      Review of The Solitary Singer: A Critical
      Biography of Walt Whitman by Gay Wilson
      Allen; and Leaves of Grass: One Hundred Years
      After, ed. Milton Hindus. New Yorker 31
      (26 Feb. 1955): 98, 100.

These two publications "cut close to the main
facts of Whitman's life and legend and add lustre
to [his] somewhat faded reputation . . . ." The
biography is "a workmanlike piece of
documentation" while the essays in the collection
"subject Whitman to the most searching kind of
criticism." Critical acclaim for Whitman has
vacillated, but his poetry was "the first and last
American poetry with all the swagger left in it."

"Richard Wilbur: The Beautiful Changes (1947)."
419-20. Titled "Young Poets: 1944-54, 4" in SC.
391-92. (Entry 215)

291. "Richard Wilbur: Things of this World
      (1956)." 420. New Yorker 32 (6 Oct. 1956):
      180.

"Wilbur's earlier work announced a lyric talent of
the first order" to which in this collection "he
has added humor and deep discernment."

"Yvor Winters (1944)." 421-23. Titled "Yvor
Winters" in SC. 269-71. (Entry 184)

"Women: The Heart and the Lyre (1947)." 424-29.
 Titled "The Heart and the Lyre" in SC. 334-45.
(Entry 200)

292. "In Balance: Babette Deutsch, Katherine
      Hoskins, Ruth Stone, Barbara Howes, Marianne

Moore (1959)."   429-31.
Review of Coming of Age by Babette Deutsch,
Out in the Open by Katherine Hoskins, In an
Iridescent Time by Ruth Stone, Light and Dark
by Barbara Howes, and Oh to be a Dragon by
Marianne Moore. New Yorker 35
(28 Nov. 1959): 236, 238, 240.

Bogan balances the two extremes of Babette
Deutsche's conventional but dramatically pictorial
poems with the distortion of "baroque" metaphors
in Katherine Hoskins' poetry. In between these
two extremes are Ruth Stone's poems, which can be
extremely artificial, and are the work of a "truly
macabre imagination." Bogan reads with complete
pleasure the books by Howes and Moore.

293. "No Poetesses Maudites: May Swenson, Anne
      Sexton (1963). 431-33.
      Review of To Mix with Time by May Swenson and
      All My Pretty Ones by Anne Sexton. New
      Yorker 39 (27 Apr. 1963): 173-75.

"Women's poetry continues to be unlike men's."
There are still some things a woman cannot do,
including imitating men's rougher conduct and
acting destructively. "There are no poetesses
maudites and . . . no authentic women
Surrealists." May Swenson follows in Marianne
Moore's footsteps with a naturalist's care, but
she can also move through city streets in her
descriptions. Anne Sexton takes risks in "putting
down the primary horrors of life," always at a
"high pitch of emotion," writing from "the center
of feminine experience."

"Virginia Woolf: Three Guineas (1938). 434-36.
Titled "The Ladies and Gentlemen" in SC. 36-39.
(Entry 130)

"Virginia Woolf: The Captain's Death Bed (1950)."
436-37. Titled "The Skirting of Passion in SC.
365-69. (Entry 207)

"The Yale Series of Younger Poets: W. S. Merwin
(1953)." 440-41. Titled "The Young Poets 5" in
SC. 393-94. (Entry 216)

294. "The Yale Series of Younger Poets: John
     Ashbery (1956)."   441-2.
     Review of Some Trees. New Yorker 32 (1 Sept.
     1956): 93-94.

Ashbery's poems "seen a little contrived in both
form and feeling, and are therefore somewhat
boring." He does try "difficult and peculiar
verse forms" in his Surrealistic poems.

295. "The Yale Series of Younger Poets: John
     Hollander (1958)."   442-3.
     Review of A Crackling of Thorns. New Yorker
     34 (6 Dec. 1958): 236-38.

This collection "carries one's attention . . . up
to the verge of interest, only to disappoint it."
Its technical virtuosity makes it "the poetry of
the library and seminar room."

296. "The Yale Series of Younger Poets: George
     Starbuck (1960)."   443.
     Review of Bone Thoughts. New Yorker
     36 (26 Mar. 1960): 157-58.

Starbuck's daring irreverent satire in his poems
is "backed up by an accomplished vocabulary and a
fine ear."

297. "The Yale Series of Younger Poets: Alan Dugan
     (1962)."   443-44.
     Review of Poems. New Yorker 38 (24 Mar.
     1962): 175-76.

"Powerful feeling joined to energetic talent" is
apparent in Dugan's poetry. His satire can be
related to Martial and Swift in the poems'
"balanced language and their unequivocal
utterances of shock and rage."

298. "The Yale Series of Younger Poets: Sandra
     Hochman (1963)." 445.
     Review of Manhattan Pastures. New Yorker 39
     (27 Apr. 1963): 173-75.

"Male Surrealists . . . are made of much sterner
stuff" than Miss Hochman's feminine Surrealism.

"William Butler Yeats: The Greatest Poet Writing
in English Today (1938)." 446-60. Titled "W. B.
Yeats" in SC. 86-104. (Entry 146)

"William Butler Yeats: The Oxford Book of Modern
Verse (1936)." 460-61. Titled "The Oxford Book
of Modern Verse" in SC. 52-54. (Entry 135)

"On the Death of Yeats (1939)." 461-65. Titled
"On the Death of William Butler Yeats" in SC.
133-34. (Entry 154)

"William Butler Yeats: Last Poems and Plays
(1940)." 465-66. Titled "The Later Poetry of
William Butler Yeats" in SC. 202-3. (Entry 170)

"William Butler Yeats: Collected Poems (1951).
466-68. Titled "The Later Poetry of William
Butler Years 2" in SC. 204-6. (Entry 171)

WRITINGS BY LOUISE BOGAN ARRANGED BY OTHERS

Three years after Louise Bogan's death in 1970, a
collection of her letters were published, edited
by the trustee of her estate, Ruth Limmer. Ten
years later, a selection of autobiographical
pieces by Bogan, arranged and edited by Limmer, was
published. These two books are included in this
section.

299. WHAT THE WOMAN LIVED: SELECTED LETTERS OF
     LOUISE BOGAN 1920-1970. Ed. Ruth Limmer.
     New York: Harcourt Brace Jovanovich, Inc.,
     1973.

These edited letters, selected for their literary
importance, illustrate Bogan's intelligence, wit,
and critical perspicacity. They are divided into
five decades, each introduced by a poem
representative of Bogan's life in that period.
The correspondents are literary notables and
friends, including John Hall Wheelock, William
Maxwell, Morton Zabel, Edmund Wilson, Theodore

Roethke, Rolfe Humphries, and May Sarton. Bogan's
letters shed light on her philosophy of writing
poetry and criticism and her disappointment at the
lack of popular acclaim her work received. They
trace her 38-year association with The New Yorker
and her struggles with her increasing inability to
write poetry as she grew older.

300. JOURNEY AROUND MY ROOM: THE AUTOBIOGRAPHY OF
     LOUISE BOGAN, A MOSAIC by Ruth Limmer. New
     York: Viking Press, 1980. Reprinted in
     paperback by Penguin Books, 1981.

The book begins with a 12-page chronology of
Bogan's life and works. This "mosaic" is not an
ordinary autobiography of the events in Bogan's
life, but of her thoughts on the "texture and
meaning of experience." Entries from Bogan's
journals and notebooks, criticism, letters, short
stories, interviews, lectures, and poems are
included. The book is framed by parts of Bogan's
1933 sketch, "Journey Around My Room." Lines from
her poem "Train Tune" provide the chapter titles,
and a photograph from different periods of her
life begins each chapter. Much of the book comes
from Bogan's journals, published in the January
20, 1978, issue of The New Yorker, under the title
"From the Journals of a Poet." Many previously
unpublished poems, such as   "When at Last," "The
Engine," "A Letter," "New Moon," and "Portrait of
the Artist as a Young Woman" are included. A
facsimile of Bogan's handwritten copy of her last
poem, "December Daybreak," closes the book.

        BIBLIOGRAPHY AND ANTHOLOGY COMPILED BY LOUISE
                            BOGAN

301. WORKS IN THE HUMANITIES PUBLISHED IN GREAT
     BRITAIN 1939-1946: A SELECTIVE LIST.
     Washington: U. S. Library of Congress, Oct.
     1950.

The book is a 123-page listing of works published
in Great Britain during the Second World War.
Included are fiction, periodicals, scholarly
studies, poetry, criticism, biography, drama,
anthologies, and annuals. Bogan's brief
introductory notes explain the difficulty of

finding literature from this wartime period. Her
chief aim in compiling this listing from the
resources of the Library of Congress "was to give
the student some explicit information concerning
literary production in a period of crisis and
transition."

302. THE GOLDEN JOURNEY: POEMS FOR YOUNG PEOPLE.
      Compiled by Louise Bogan and William Jay
      Smith. Chicago: Reilly & Lee, 1965.
      London: Evans Bros., 1967.

Collection of poems selected to introduce children
to good poetry. The introduction contains quotes
from Emerson and Frost on the nature of poetry.
Poetry aids in the journey through life. The
compilers state, "We have offered only poems that
we have ourselves enjoyed and read and remembered
with pleasure." Two of Bogan's poems are
included: "M., Singing" and "Musician."

B. NEW YORKER CRITICAL REVIEWS AND ESSAYS

This section lists in chronological order all of Louise Bogan's book reviews and essays in The New Yorker. Her first omnibus critical reviews from 1931-1936 were variously titled. Later reviews were listed under the title "Verse" when they were in a separate section and "Briefly Noted," when they were combined with other short book reviews. Contributors to "Verse" reviews were identified, while the "Briefly Noted" reviews, which may have been longer, were unsigned. An occasional essay focusing on a particular author or subject was identified by a full title. All of these titles are noted in these entries. Reviews collected in Selected Criticism and A Poet's Alphabet are not included here. The following annotations illustrate Louise Bogan's ability to write something new, fresh, and interesting for each of the hundreds of books she reviewed. Each book in the review is listed by author and title, with a brief notation quoted from the review.

1931

303. "Books, Books, Books: The Winter's Verse."
7 (21 Mar. 1931): 80, 82-85.

In her first book review for The New Yorker, Bogan comments on the surprising amount of poetry written and published in spite of the lack of a buyers' market.

W. J. Turner. Miss America. Englishman's satire pricks American social, moral and spiritual myths.

Nathalia Crane. Pocahontas. "One of the most dumbfounding compositions ever written."

Sylvia Townsend Warner. Opus 7. Story of an alcoholic who died dead drunk in a graveyard.

Stephen Vincent Benet. Ballads and Poems: 1915-1930. "Colorful, fast-moving ballads and sensitive lyrics," although not profound.

Conrad Aiken. John Deth and Other Poems. Title

poem sounds "like the work of John Skelton."

E. A. Robinson. The Glory of the Nightingales.
"Perfect example" of Robinson's late style.

Elizabeth Madox Roberts. Under the Tree. No
child should miss this beautiful reprint.

Roy Campbell. Adamaster. Bogan reserves judgment
on this South African poet.

Horace Gregory. Chelsea Rooming House. "Displays
talent and intelligence rare in first books."

Lynn Riggs. The Iron Dish. "Too conscious an
attitude, but not to be lightly passed by."

Thomas Moult, ed. Best Poems of 1930. Choice of
poems "somewhat capricious."

Gerard Manley Hopkins. Poems of Gerard Manley
Hopkins. "The stuff of genius and agony."

304. "Profiles: American Classic." 7 (8 Aug.
     1931): 19-22.

This portrait of Willa Cather celebrates her life
and work on the occasion of her receiving an
honorary doctorate from Princeton University.
Cather is "a writer who can conjure up . . . a
narrative as solid as a house. . . ." And Miss
Cather is as solid as her work. Bogan traces
Cather's literary background from her early
problematic books in which she attempted "to write
beautiful prose about temperamental, ambitious,
enchanting people" to the later popular books,
written about Nebraska, her birthplace, including
O Pioneers. In Bridge of San Luis Rey, Cather has
"made herself complete mistress of her talent."

1932

305. "Plagued by the Nightingales: Books, Books,
     Books." 7 (13 Feb. 1932): 62, 64-65.

Louis Untermeyer, ed. The Book of Living Verse.
From Chaucer to Merrill Moore comprehensively.

Petrarch. The Sonnets of Petrarch. Trans. Joseph
Auslander. Proves poetry is impossible to

translate.

Thomas Moult, ed. Best Poems of 1931. "Why not
the worst" as well as the best poems of 1931?

James Stephens. Strictly Joy. "Not one lyric is
worth" his earlier works.

E. A. Robinson. Matthias at the Door. "Arid days
for his stock characters."

Conrad Aiken. The Coming Forth by Day of Osiris
Jones and Preludes for Memnon. "His world of
melancholy appearances . . . seems to have become
more profound."

e. e. cummings. W (Viva). "Typographical tricks"
with "the saving grace of self-mockery."

John Masefield. Minnie Maylow's Story and Other
Tales and Scenes. Retelling of Tristram story
"lacks poetic life, suffers from neatness."

Peggy Bacon. Animosities. "Wit and sprightly
bitterness."

Selma Robinson. City Child. Same comment as last
review.

Margaret Fishback. I Feel Better Now. Same
comment also.

Phelps Putman. The Five Senses. "Salt enough for
a healthy taste."

George Dillion. The Flowering Stone. "Finest
verse in romantic tradition" produced by a young
man in several years.

T. S. Eliot. Triumphal March. Magnificent
pamphlet published in England.

Robert Bridges. Shorter Poems. No comment.

306. "Books: Half-Pounds and Other Poets."
     8 (30 July 1932): 39-40.

Ezra Pound. Cantos. "Everything is made as
difficult as possible for the reader."

Archibald MacLeish. <u>Conquistador</u>. Cortéz's final
conquest has "every quality necessary to
narrative."

Elinor Wylie. <u>Collected Poems</u>. Beautiful lyrics
are "the final achievements of her life and art."

Hart Crane. <u>The Bridge</u>. "Filled with an
hallucinatory power of communication."

Robinson Jeffers. <u>Thurso's Landing</u>. "Obsessive
talents prevail" as characters cut each other
down.

Padraic Colum. <u>Poems</u>. "A late product of the
Celtic Revival."

Louis Untermeyer. <u>Food and Drink</u>. "So light and
gay," almost in the class of gift books.

Allen Tate. <u>Poems, 1928-31</u>. His "seriousness
shows signs of lifting," and his "talent is sure
to grow."

                        1933

307. "Books: Snarling Under the Sofa and Other
     Attitudes." 9 (18 Feb. 1933): 66-67.

Oliver Wells, ed. <u>An Anthology of the Younger
Poets</u>. Poems ranging from "dull and sententious"
to those written "with the tongues of angels."

Aldous Huxley. <u>Texts and Pretexts: An Anthology
with Commentaries</u>. "Cannot be recommended too
highly for [his] encylopedic interest in poetry."

Frances Frost. <u>These Acres</u>. She "should be
admonished for her unchecked ear."

Wilbert Snow. <u>Down East</u>. Competently written,
"but leaves the reader unsatisfied."

David Morton. <u>Earth's Processional</u>. Same as last
review.

John Masefield. <u>A Tale of Troy</u>. Homeric material
written for the speaking voice may waste his time.

<u>Ballads of the B.E.F.</u>(British Expeditionary
Force). Wartime poems written by fighting men.

Theodore Roosevelt and Grantland Rice, compilers.
Taps: Selected Poems of the Great War. Siegfried
Sasson's poems do much for this.

Edwin Arlington Robinson. Nicodemus. "Great
improvement" on those poems from recent years.

William Rose Benet. Rip Tide. "Excellent novel
in verse . . . [if] novels can be written in
verse."

308. "This Season's Verse." 9 (15 Jul. 1933):
    46-48.

Ezra Pound. A Draft of Thirty Cantos. "Most
irritating poem in English . . . beautifully
written."

D. H. Lawrence. Last Poems. Ed. Kenneth Rexroth.
"Beauty, wisdom, and vision proper to poetry."

Walter de la Mare. The Fleeting. "Nearly bereft
of his early magic."

Harold Lewis Cook. Spell Against Death. Real
talent shows in his "delicate, honest" lyrics.

William Faulkner. A Green Bough. He should go
back to his prose.

1934

309. "Some Months of Poetry." 10 (7 Apr. 1934):
    98.

W. H. Auden is described as an "extremely gifted
disciple of discontinuity." Robinson Jeffers
comes out on the "stupid side of grandiose
tragedies."

Archibald MacLeish. Poems, 1924-1933. Great
poets shadow its pages and his own biases show.

Lizette Woodworth Reese. Pasture. She is still
"mistress of music and emotional vitality."

Winifred Wells. Blossoming Antlers. "Skilled
technician" of "delicate fancy and flawless
style."

Sara Teasdale. <u>Strange Victory</u>. "Posthumous and
most remarkable book."

E. A. Robinson. <u>Talifer</u>. "Mild tragedy for
admirers of Robinson or of foolish feudalism."

Oliver St. John Gogarty. <u>Selected Poems</u>.
"Triumphs of scholarly urbanity, wit, and syntax."

W. B. Yeats. <u>Collected Poems</u>. Poems show his
"sensibility, intellect, conviction, stamina, and
gall."

John Peale Bishop. <u>Now with His Love</u>. "His style
stands up in the crowd of influences."

310. "Briefly Noted." 10 (5 May 1934): 90.

<u>The Poems of Richard Aldington</u>. Formerly an
"influential imagist," now a "tame dilettante."

311. "This Season's Verse." 10 (24 Nov. 1934):
     90.

W. H. Auden and Stephen Spender. <u>Poems</u>. Auden
belongs to Swift's satiric tradition, Spender to
Shelley's romantic tradition. Both are critical
of society and "get lost in their own private
associations."

Edna St. Vincent Millay. <u>Wine from these Grapes</u>.
Poems about the "lonely, imperfect human spirit."

Genevieve Taggard. <u>Not Mine to Finish</u>. She can
be excellent as a romantic, but not as a
revolutionary.

Gerald Bullett, ed. <u>The English Galaxy</u>. "Fine
anthology of English lyrics."

Marya Zaturenska. <u>Threshold and Hearth</u>. This
book "announces a new woman lyricist of
distinction."

E. A. Robinson. <u>Amaranth</u>. "Annual long poem."

Paul Engle. <u>American Song</u>. He shows "evidence of
cultural lag" in his poems of the American
frontier.

<u>Collected Edition of Rudyard Kipling's Verse</u>. The
British Empire's former glories "lie embalmed
here."

T. S. Eliot. <u>The Rock</u>. "A pageant and an act of
piety . . . bursting into poetry comparable to his
best."

Ezra Pound. <u>The Eleven New Cantos</u>. "He advances
unintelligibility . . . into an article of faith."

Edith Sitwell, ed. <u>The Pleasures of Poetry</u>. "She
writes and writes . . . on prosodic texture."

Isidor Schneider. <u>Comrade Mister</u>. His
revolutionary poetry is "worth serious attention."

Elizabeth Drew. <u>Discovering Poetry</u>. A "sensible,
sensitive and scholarly book" for those who care
for poetry.

1935

312. "Briefly Noted." 11 (23 Feb. 1935): 67.

C. Day-Lewis. <u>Collected Poems 1929-1933</u> and <u>A
Hope for Poetry</u>. Expert but monotonous poems and
an intelligent essay.

Stephen Spender. <u>Vienna</u>. An earnest long poem
that "leaves the reader cold."

313. "This Season's Verse." 11 (4 May 1935): 66.

C. Day-Lewis. <u>Collected Poems</u>. Repeat of 23 Feb.
1935 review.

Marianne Moore. <u>Selected Poems</u>. "Close reasoning
and nice description" prefaced by T. S. Eliot's
penetrating sentences on the poetic function.

Lincoln Kirstein. <u>Low Ceiling</u>. "Specimens of
insulated writing."

Archibald MacLeish. <u>Panic</u>. None of the
characters know what they are doing.

W. B. Yeats. <u>Wheels and Butterflies</u>. He explains
his title and his plays are "very beautiful."

Mark Van Doren. <u>A Winter Diary</u>. "Praise of love
and Connecticut in sonnet and narrative form."

Merrill Moore. <u>Six Sides to A Man</u>. "Jottings on
a thousand subjects . . . in wrenched Petrarchian
sonnets."

I. A. Richards. <u>On Imagination</u>. Clarification of
Coleridge's critical theory and its application.

<u>The Sea Sequel to the Week-end Book</u>. A collection
of the finest marine poetry leading up to T. S.
Eliot's poems.

<u>The Bermuda Troubadours</u>. Anthology of Bermuda
verse printed on blue paper.

Kinley Kantor. <u>Turkey in the Straw</u>. Modern
American ballads.

Chaucer. Trans. Frank Ernest Hill. Admirable
translation.

Robert P. Tristram Coffin. <u>Strange Holiness</u>.
"Various unstrange experiences" described.

Horace Gregory. <u>Chorus for Survival</u>. "Well
within the Eliotian shadow, [it] belies earlier
promise."

Thomas McGreevy. <u>Poems</u>. "Perhaps the most
inconsiderable book ever produced by an Irishman."

Leonard Bacon. <u>The Voyage of Autoleon</u>.
"Considerable technical feat."

Lola Ridge. <u>Dance of Fire</u>. "Cries from the
spirit undeniably appear."

Harriet Monroe, ed. <u>Chosen Poems</u>. Recognition by
one with a lifelong dedication to poetic art.

314. "Briefly Noted." 11 (11 May 1935): 84.

e. e. cummings. <u>No Thanks</u>. "When legible, the
words are good and sour on most subjects."

315. "Briefly Noted." 11 (28 Sept. 1935): 72.

T. S. Eliot. <u>Murder in the Cathedral</u>. "Bitter
dissection of martyrdom in general."

316. "Briefly Noted." 11 (12 Oct. 1935): 79.

W. H. Auden with Christopher Isherwood. <u>The Dog
Beneath the Skin</u>. "Fun deflating British antics
and idiocies" with Auden's own poetry and fury.

317. "Briefly Noted." 11 (9 Nov. 1935): 84-87.

<u>The Collected Plays of W. B. Yeats</u>. These "should
be in every English-speaking home."

318. "Briefly Noted." 11 (19 Oct. 1935): 83.

Margaret Fishback. <u>I Take it Back</u>. "Easy and
agreeable."

319. "The Season's Verse." 11 (9 Nov. 1935):
     84-87.

<u>The Selected Poems and Parodies of Louis
Untermeyer</u>. "Light verse skimmed over."

Robinson Jeffers. <u>Solstice</u>. An imitation saga
about infanticide.

T. S. Eliot. <u>Murder in the Cathedral</u>. See 28
Sept. 1935 review. Also, "he splits himself up
into parts and distributes his personality among
the characters."

e. e. cummings. <u>Tom</u>. "Stage directions on the
theme by Harriet Beecher Stowe."

John Gould Fletcher. <u>XXIV Elegies</u>. "Reflective."

Theodore Dreiser. <u>Moods: Philosophic and
Emotional</u>. His "works turn out much as we
expected."

Joseph Auslander. <u>No Traveler Returns</u>. "Less
than natural."

W. H. Davies. <u>Collected Poems</u>. "Simple and fresh
poems" with a "larklike ring."

Winifred Wells. <u>A Spectacle for Scholars</u>. No
comment.

Laurence Whistler. <u>Four Walls</u>. Youth and grace.

Ann Winslow, ed. <u>Trial Balances</u>. Collection of
poets born around 1912.

Arthur Guiterman. <u>Death and General Putnam</u>. Light
verse.

David McCord. <u>Day Window Ballads</u>. Light verse.

Brynner Witter. <u>Guest Book</u>. Light verse.

320. "Briefly Noted." 11 (7 Dec. 1935): 114.

Peggy Bacon. <u>Cat Calls</u>. "Seasoned with delicate
sensibility and mature malice."

1936

321. "The Season's Verse." 12 (22 Feb. 1936):
72-74.

Edwin Rolfe. <u>To My Contemporaries</u>. "Less turgid
and more grounded in action."

Franz Werfel. <u>The Eternal Road</u>. A poetic
biblical mystery play that is rather dull.

William Langland. <u>Piers Plowman</u>. "New scholarly
edition of an early proletariat poem."

<u>A Shakespeare Anthology</u>. Great poetry detached
from the plays "with frequent queer effect."

Siegfried Sassoon. <u>Vigils</u>. "Lyrics of a war poet
turned meditative and resigned."

E. A. Robinson. <u>King Jasper</u>. Posthumous
publication with Frost's "highly readable
preface."

Thomas Moult, ed. <u>The Best Poems of 1935</u>.
"Annual mild Georgian catalog."

Robert Nathan. <u>Selected Poems</u>. Noted in passing.

Peggy Bacon. <u>Cat Calls</u>. See 7 Dec. 1935.

Ruth Pitter. <u>A Mad Lady's Garland</u>. "Witty and
well-made," but also "brittle and indefensibly
minor."

Audrey Wurdemann. <u>The Seven Sins</u>. She does not
show the gifts of her great forebear, Shelley.

Nathalia Crane. <u>Swear by the Night</u>. She "sounds
exactly like a little girl writing verse."

Robert Fitzgerald. <u>Poems</u>. "On the verge of
individual expression."

Kenneth Patchen. <u>Before the Brave</u>. His
"incoherence might fade" if he became more
original.

Muriel Rukeyser. <u>Theory of Flight</u>. She "might
develop a clarion tone, once freed from echoes."

Charles William, ed. <u>The New Book of English
Verse</u>. "A friend of the macabre and an enemy of
cant."

Jean Starr Untermeyer. <u>Winged Flight</u>. She
"profits from maturity" in her latest volume.

322. "Briefly Noted." 12 (28 Mar. 1936): 88.

Archibald MacLeish. <u>Public Speech</u>. He
"admonishes all sides equally" and closes with
words about love.

Paul Engle. <u>Break the Heart's Anger</u>. He "takes
America to task" in poems written in Europe.

C. Day-Lewis. <u>A Time to Dance</u>. "Fluent, but
unconvincing on poetry and the new world."

Robert Penn Warren. <u>Thirty-Six Poems</u>. "The
youngest and . . . most talented Nashville
Fugitive."

John Peale Bishop. <u>Minute Particulars</u>. "A wide
range of effects" from "a poet with a keen eye and
ear."

323. "This Season's Verse." 12 (23 May 1936): 80.

Charlotte Wilder. <u>Phases of the Moon</u>. "Private affirmations used to solve personal problems."

T. S. Eliot. <u>Collected Poems</u>. "Progression from faithless life to balanced calm" in "Burnt Norton."

Baudelaire. <u>Flowers of Evil</u>. Trans. George Dillion and Edna St. Vincent Millay. Translation problems on work by leader of the Symbolists.

Archibald MacLeish. <u>Public Speech</u>. See 28 Mar. 1936.

Paul Engle. <u>Break the Heart's Anger</u>. Same as above.

C. Day-Lewis. <u>A Time to Dance</u>. Same as above.

John Peale Bishop. <u>Minute Particulars</u>. Same as above.

Robert Penn Warren. <u>Thirty-Six Poems</u>. Same as above.

324. "Briefly Noted." 12 (30 May 1936): 67.

Robert Frost. <u>A Farther Range</u>. Sharp satire and beautiful lyrics on the virtues of New England.

325. "Briefly Noted." 12 (6 June 1936): 67-68.

Lionel Wiggam. <u>Landscape with Figures</u>. "He gives evidence of being a born poet" at twenty.

326. "Briefly Noted." 13 (13 June 1936): 75.

Christopher Ward. <u>Sir Galahad and Other Rimes</u>. Twenty-three classics that "tire after the tenth."

Leonard Bacon. <u>The Goose on the Capitol</u>. "He condemns things . . . in a witty and academic way."

327. "Verse." 12 (20 June 1936) 60-62. Stephen Vincent Benet. <u>Burning City</u>. His American audience will appreciate the romance.

John Masefield. <u>A Letter from Pontius</u>. A return
to "humble, endearing characters and
descriptions."

Walter de la Mare. <u>Poems 1919-1934</u>. A modern
poet who can describe the beauties of magic.

Helen Cornelius. <u>In Tract of Time</u>. Metaphysical
poety of "the very first lyric order."

328. "Briefly Noted." 12 (25 July 1936): 64.

<u>Selected Poems of Vachel Lindsay</u>. Best-known
work of poet who expressed "American color and
gusto in rhyme."

329. "Briefly Noted." 12 (15 Aug. 1936): 51-52.

A. T. Quiller-Couch, ed. <u>English Sonnets</u>. New
edition now contains Hopkins and Wilfred Owens.

Arthur Davison Ficke. <u>The Secret and Other Poems</u>.
Makes "no great claims," but "written with a heart
and an ear."

Edgar Lee Masters. <u>Poems of People</u>. "Rousing
celebrations of American historical characters."

Hernández, José. <u>The Gaucho Martín Fierro</u>, trans.
Walter Owen. Argentine national epic of legendary
Gaucho.

330. "Verse." 12 (22 Aug. 1936): 59-62.

Euripides. <u>Alcestis.</u> Trans. Dudley Fitts and
Robert Fitzgerald. "The beauty and dignity of the
play are made clear."

331. "Briefly Noted." 12 (5 Sept. 1936): 67.

A. T. Quiller-Couch, ed. <u>The Oxford Book of
English Verse</u>. "Best all-round and most-read-
aloud" lyrics.

Audrey Wurdemann. <u>Splendor in the Grass</u>. Verse
by youngest Pulitzer winner, but undistinguished.

332. "Briefly Noted." 12 (12 Sept. 1936): 104.
Lizette W. Reese. The Old House in the Country.
Long posthumous poem by one of America's most
"authentic" lyric poets.

333. "Briefly Noted." 12 (19 Sept. 1936): 87.

Corliss Lamont, ed. Man Answers Death: An
Anthology of Poetry. "Mixture of good and bad
poety."

334. "Briefly Noted." 12 (26 Sept. 1936): 76.

Ogden Nash. The Bad Parents' Garden of Verse.
Written "after fatherhood softened up the author."

335. "Review." 12 (3 Oct. 1936): 66.

John Wheelock. Poems, 1911-1936. His awe of the
universe and his forms "sometimes seem outworn."

Frederic Prokosch. The Assassins. Smooth writing
in "good imitation of Perse and MacLeish."

Genevieve Taggard. Calling Western Union. "She
was a better poet before she wrote proletarian
verse."

Virginia Moore. Homer's Golden Chain. "Poems
lifted above the feminine average."

Edgar Lee Masters. The Golden Fleece of
California. "Not particularly dramatic."

336. "Briefly Noted." 12 (17 Oct. 1936): 88.

Collected Poems of Ford Madox Ford. All periods
of his life recorded in verse.

Conrad Aiken. Time in the Rock: Preludes to
Definition. "Collection represents Aiken at his
most vaporous."

Joseph Auslander. More Than Bread. "More banal
romantic poetry."

Edward Doro. Shiloh. "Feebly rhetorical legend

of the Redeemer."
337. "Briefly Noted." 12 (24 Oct. 1936): 67.

Wallace Stevens. Ideas of Order. "Not-to-be
missed item for those who admire Stevens' gifts."

Arthur Guiterman. Gaily the Troubadour. Verses
sound delightful.

Franklin P. Adams. The Melancholy Flute. Wit,
wisdom and "more chipper accomplished rhymes."

338. "Verse." 12 (31 Oct. 1936): 64-65.

A. E. Housman. More Poems. Posthumous collection
shows his despair tempered with joy and virtue.
"He was master of the English lyric."

339. "Briefly Noted." 12 (7 Nov. 1936): 84.

Sara Bard Field. Darkling Plain. "Implicit
Marxist lyrics" written with feminine intensity.

Edward Weismiller. The Deer Come Down. Deft
writing about animals and landscapes.

340. "Briefly Noted." 12 (14 Nov. 1936): 120.

Wallace Stevens. Owl's Clover. Imagination set
against politics in muffled, but beautiful poetry.

Alfred R. Bellinger, ed. Anthology of Verse from
the Yale Literary Magazine 1836-1936.
Undergraduate verse with some antiquarian value.

341. "Briefly Noted." 12 (21 Nov. 1936): 92.

Witter Bynner. Selected Poems. Poems chosen by
Robert Hunt from thirty years' work.

C. A. Millspaugh. In Sight of Mountains. In his
first book "the metaphysics have not entirely
annealed."

Ruth Pitter. A Trophy of Arms. "Her witty,
poised, and graceful talent stands clearly forth."

342. "Briefly Noted." 12 (28 Nov. 1936): 76.

Mark Van Doren, ed. An Anthology of World Poetry.
"Finest anthology of translations extant."

Leonard Bacon. Rhyme and Punishment. "Bitterness
turns out to be snobbery and peevishness."

343. "Poetesses in the Parlor." 12 (5 Dec. 1936):
    42, 45-56, 48, 50, 52.

Bogan explores nineteenth-century feminine poetry
in this essay on Female Poets of America, a 1848
anthology first published by Rufus Wilmot, with
later additions by R. H. Stoddard. Also discussed
is Love Poems of Three Centuries of 1890, edited
by Jessie F. O'Donnell. Bogan describes the early
poets' common attributes: widowed or maiden status
and a wide range of themes in a tone of sturdy and
pious gloom. Later American poetesses incorporate
European travel and a critical view toward
marriage in their poems. Ella Wheeler Wilcox and
others then appear to write aggressive and
possessive love poems.

344. "Briefly Noted." 12 (5 Dec. 1936): 158.

Dorothy Parker. Not So Deep as a Well.
"Collected works in a beautifully designed
edition".

                          1937

345. "Briefly Noted." 12 (2 Jan. 1937): 60.

Shakespeare's Sonnets. Ed. Tucker Brooke.
Sonnets arranged in original order with adult
preface.

346. "Briefly Noted." 12 (16 Jan. 1937): 60.

Frances Frost. Road to America. She appears more
herself "after having served a long apprenticeship
to other poets."

347. "Briefly Noted." 12 (Jan 23. 1937): 68.

<u>Collected Poems and Plays of Rabindranath Tagore</u>.
Great poet twenty years ago, now a minor one.

348. "Verse." 12 (13 Feb. 1937): 63-65.

W. H Auden. <u>On this Island</u> and <u>The Ascent of F6</u>,
a play written with Christopher Isherwood. The
poetry is so well written "it brings tears to the
eyes of the tired reader," but the play, falling
between satire and tragedy, is not so successful.

349. "Briefly Noted." 13 (20 Feb. 1937): 68.

Seldon Rodman. <u>Lawrence: The Last Crusade</u>. "He
does not do Lawrence justice."

350. "Briefly Noted." 13 (27 Feb. 1937): 72.

Lawrence Whistler. <u>The Emperor Heart</u>. Delightful
but "pervaded by English upper-class complacency."

Robert P. Tristram Coffin. <u>Saltwater Farm</u>.
Charming but sentimental descriptions of Maine.

<u>The Poems of Emily Dickinson</u>. Eds. Martha
Dickinson Bianchi and Alfred Leete Hampton.
Preface "contributes no new and illuminates no old
data."

351. "Briefly Noted." 13 (20 Mar. 1937): 88.

John Holmes. <u>Address to the Living</u>. Dexterity
with light verse "carries over into his serious
verse."

352. "Briefly Noted." 13 (27 Mar. 1937): 64.

Winfield Townly Scott. <u>Biography for Traman</u>.
Meditations of a young man who can't take life.

R. P. Blackmur. <u>From Jordan's Delight</u>. His first
book is "more literary than spontaneous, but
shows talent."

353. "Briefly Noted." 13 (3 April 1937): 78-79.

The Agamemnon of Aeschylus. Trans. Louis MacNeice.
"A vigorously written translation."
354. "Briefly Noted." 13 (17 Apr. 1937): 79-80.

Pushkin. Eugene Onegin. Trans. Dorothea Prall
Radin and George Z. Patrick. "Workmanlike
version."

355. "Briefly Noted." 13 (24 Apr. 1937): 76.

Collected Poems of Edwin Arlington Robinson. Poet
"who amplified the finest American literary
tradition."

356. "Verse." 13 (8 May 1937): 70.

Edith Sitwell. Selected Poems. She can become
boring when she attempts to explain her effects.

357. "Briefly Noted." 13 (26 June 1937): 67.

James Still. Hounds on the Mountain. "More
literary style . . . than his material can bear."

358. "Verse." 13 (7 Aug. 1937): 51-53.

Edna St. Vincent Millay. Conversation at Night.
This conversation with herself gets nowhere. The
Liberal, Republican, and Communist characters are
"little more than expert products of taxidermy and
ventriloquism."

359. "Briefly Noted." 13 (14 Aug. 1937): 64.

M. J. Benardete and Rolfe Humphries. eds.
. . . and Spain Sings: Fifty Loyalist Ballads.
Trans. Edna St. Vincent Millay et al. Some
"remarkably effective" English versions.

360. "Briefly Noted." 13 (28 Aug. 1937): 52.

Poems of Jonathan Swift. Ed. Harold Williams.
Definitive ordering throws light on Swift's life.

361. "Briefly Noted." 13 (4 Sept 1937): 68.

Phyllis McGinley. One More Manhattan. She deals
with the problems of life in these hard times.

362. "Briefly Noted." 13 (11 Sept. 1937): 76.

Tom Boggs, ed. 51 Neglected Lyrics. "Illustrates
the wild and delightful things English lyrics
could do."

Ruth Lechliter. Tomorrow's Phoenix. She yields
to theatrical modern feelings and forms.

363. "Verse." 13 (25 Sept. 1937): 72-74.

Federico García Lorca. Lament for the Death of a
Bullfighter. Trans. A. L. Lloyd. Combines "folk-
song directness, Moorish sensibility, gypsy
pathos, and virtuosity of form."

James Joyce. Collected Poems. Poems contain
"seeds of flowing melody which inundates . . .
Ulysses and purls through Anna Livia Plurabelle."

Sara Teasdale. Collected Poems. Early poems
contain too many words, the late poems too few.

Marya Zaturenska. Cold Morning Sky. Her lyrics
have a "cool liquid quality," but lack "real
solidarity."

Ten Principal Upanishads. Trans. Shree Purohit
Swami and W. B. Yeats. Rendered with "touching
devotion and humor."

Mark Van Doren. The Last Look and Other Poems.
"Oblique but realistic" new style.

364. "Briefly Noted." 13 (2 Oct. 1937): 68.

Allen Tate. Selected Poems. His poems show
"continual enlightened poetic growth and
revision."

Robinson Jeffers. Such Counsels You Gave to Me,
and Other Poems. He explores "the last possible
incest combination" and states he is not a

prophet.

365. "Briefly Noted." 13 (9 Oct. 1937): 76.

Wallace Stevens. The Man with the Blue Guitar.
He "strikes odd and lovely notes from the
imagination."

366. "Briefly Noted." 13 (16 Oct, 1937): 80.

Edgar Lee Masters. The New World. This "sweep
through American history . . . offers good
anecdotes."

367. "Briefly Noted." 13 (23 Oct. 1937): 72.

Margaret Haley. The Gardener Mind. She has a
"wider-than-usual range of language and emotion."

Jake Falstaff. The Bulls of Spain. "Lusty and
tender ballads" by a "legend in his own time."

Margaret Fishback. One to a Customer. "An
omnibus of cheerful verse."

368. "Briefly Noted." 13 (13 Nov. 1937): 84.

The Book of Songs. Trans. Arthur Waley.
"Traditional Chinese poems in a simple and
scholarly translation."

369. "Briefly Noted." 13 (27 Nov. 1937): 80.

Three Greek Plays: Prometheus Bound, Agamemnon,
The Trojan War. Trans. Edith Hamilton.
"Remarkably successful" in "simplicity and
naturalness."

Russell Lord, ed. Voices from the Fields: A Book
of Country Songs by Farming People. Poetry that is
unprofessional, but sincere and of real beauty.

370. "Review." 13 (18 Dec. 1937): 93-94. ·

Louis MacNeice. Poems. His talent is to
"set the telling image into the simple line."

Ezra Pound. Fifth Decad of Cantos. "Extremely
tiresome hymn" against usury, but the Italian
weather is good.
Recognition of Robert Frost. The result of this
tribute is somewhat confusing, but Americans'
gratitude is clear.

371. "Verse." 13 (25 Dec. 1937): 50-52.

Alice R. Longworth and Theodore Roosevelt,
compilers. The Desk Drawer Anthology. The poems
sent in by the public are "feeble, insipid, and
vacuous beyond belief."

                         1938

372. "Briefly Noted." 13 (Jan. 1938): 64.

Rex Warner. Poems. "A seizure of Gerard Manley
Hopkins unfortunately attacks him at times."

Carl Sandburg. Smoke and Steel, and the Stab of
the Sunburnt West. "Two characteristic early
volumes combined."

373. "Briefly Noted." 13 (5 Feb. 1938): 60.

Muriel Rukeyser. U.S. 1. "Her manner still tends
to obscure her matter" and her cure for current
problems is revolution.

374. "Briefly Noted." 14 (26 Feb. 1938): 64.

Collected Poems of E. E. Cummings. Beneath his
typography he is "tough, tender, snobbish, [and]
funny."

W. Henderson, ed. Victorian Street Ballads. How
people got "shocks and sentiment before tabloids."

375. "Briefly Noted." 14 (5 Mar. 1938): 64.

Raymond Holden. Natural History. His poems "bear
the mark of the craftsman" with fine phrasing.

Dudley Fitts, ed. One Hundred Poems from the
Palatine Anthology. "Rendered with many bleak

Palatine Anthology. "Rendered with many bleak spots in the Poundian manner."

Louis MacNeice. Out of the Picture. "Silly and disjointed puppet show" with some good language.

376. "Verse." 14 (2 Apr. 1938): 61-62.

Archibald MacLeish. Land of the Free. A poem in "the form of a soundtrack inspired by photographs of poor and homeless Americans in the scarred landscape, debris . . . of a money-grabbing society."

377. "Briefly Noted." 14 (9 Apr. 1938): 79.

Eileen Hall. The Fountain and the Bough. Truly distinguished lyrics with their own accent.

T. F. Highman and C. M. Bowra, eds. Oxford Book of Greek Verse in Translation. Translations by experts and hacks from Homer through the Alexandrians.

Robert N. Neeser, ed. American Naval Songs and Ballads. Songs of navy of sailing ships with reproduced broadsides.

378. "Verse." 14 (16 Apr. 1938): 61-62.

W. B. Yeats. The Herme's Egg. Yeats' three mystery plays are "reduced to the barest elements of music, movement and speech." The poetry is magnificent, but the subjects are obscure legends.

379. "Verse." 14 (23 Apr. 1938). 64-65.

Laurence Housman. My Brother A. E. Housman. He humanizes his brother "often at his own expense." "The poems add nothing of interest to the canon."

380. "Briefly Noted." 14 (30 Apr. 1938): 64.

Lindley Hubbell. Winter-Burning. "Closely written with real vigor and epithet and sincere feeling."

John Milton. <u>The Mask of Comus</u>. Ed. E. H.
Visiak. Superb folio edition reprinted from the
original.

381. "Briefly Noted." 14 (7 May 1938): 96.

John Masefield. <u>Selected Poems</u>. Early volume
reissued with new poems.

382. "Briefly Noted." 14 (4 June 1938): 64.

John Gould Fletcher. <u>Selected Poems</u>. The early
poems have some worth as examples of American
Imagism.

383. "Briefly Noted." 14 (11 June 1938): 60.

Ogden Nash. <u>I'm a Stranger Here Myself</u>. Poems by
"the man who put the muses on roller skates."

384. "Briefly Noted." 14 (23 July 1938): 58-59.

Seldon Rodman, ed. <u>New Anthology of Modern
Poetry</u>. He errs at times in matters of taste.

385. "Briefly Noted." 14 (30 July, 1938): 44.

<u>Verona Press Rhyme Sheet 1-6</u>. Review of verses
from the Greek and Chinese decorated in color.

386. "Briefly Noted." 14 (20 Aug. 1938): 51.

Abbie H. Evans. <u>The Bright North</u>. This New
Englander writes deeply contemplative poems.

387. "Briefly Noted." 14 (24 Aug. 1938): 60.

John A. and Alan Lomax, compilers. <u>Cowboy Songs
and Other Frontier Ballads</u>. "Sentimental lonely
songs of the range."

Sean O'Faolain, ed. <u>The Silver Branch, An
Anthology of Old Irish Poetry</u>. "Fresh and lovely."

388. "Briefly Noted." 14 (17 Sept. 1938): 76.

Walter de la Mare. Memory and Other Poems. "Not the completely memorable de la Mare." Marjorie Allen Seiffert. The Name of Life. "Mature feminine emotion and self analysis."

389. "Briefly Noted." 14 (15 Oct. 1938): 72.

Ben Belitt. The Five-Fold Mesh. "A packed close lyric style with a bright intellectual edge."

E. B. White. The Fox of Peapack and Other Poems. "One of the best light versifiers" writing on many things.

390. Verse." 14 (22 Oct. 1938): 95-96.

Charles Henri Ford. The Garden of Disorder. He "writes as though he were describing a series of [poor] surrealistic pictures."

Kay Boyle. A Glad Day. She lacks discipline and overworks mannerisms, but has wonderful emotion.

Hudson Strode, ed. Immortal Lyrics. "A serious attempt to arouse interest for beautiful lyrics."

Frederic Prokosch. The Carnival. Poems frought with emotion sound lovely to anyone.

391. "Briefly Noted." 14 (5 Nov. 1938): 72.

The Collected Poems of Genevieve Taggard. "The total effect of this collection is a blur."

392. "Briefly Noted." 14 (19 Nov. 1938): 92.

The Selected Poetry of Robinson Jeffers. His "formative principle" is not to tell lies in verse.

The Complete Collected Poems of William Carlos Williams. "Clinical candor" comes through clearly.

James Stephens. Kings and the Moon. Nothing

memorable, but much "happy and peaceful
mysticism."

393. "Verse." 14 (24 Dec. 1938): 50-52.

Translation from the Poetry of Rainer Maria Rilke.
Trans. M. D. Herter Norton. First comprehensive
collection in America. A suggestion of his purity
and strength comes through.

Laura Riding. Collected Poems. "Intelligent and
purposeful seeming," her poetry hardly exists.

1939

394. "Briefly Noted." 14 (7 Jan. 1939): 47.

Merrill Moore. M: One Thousand Autobiographical
Sonnets. "Marginalia and random thoughts."

Kenneth Fearing. Dead Reckoning. "Crisp
merciless shafts at the American setup."

395. "Briefly Noted." 14 (11 Feb. 1939): 75-76.

Mark Van Doren. Collected Poems. Late poems
display a distinctly mystical American idiom.

396. "Briefly Noted." 15 (18 Feb. 1939): 72.

The Antigone of Sophocles. Trans. Dudley Fitts
and Robert Fitzgerald. A slightly edited version,
"cleanly and ably put into English."

397. "Briefly Noted." (11 Mar. 1939): 80.

Josephine Miles. Lines at Intersection. Her
first book's poems "combine intellect and emotion
evenly."

398. "Briefly Noted." 15 (18 Mar. 1939): 88.

W. H. Auden and Christopher Isherwood. On the
Frontier: A Melodrama in Three Acts. A decided
letdown from their first collaboration. "A well-
worn dilute Leftist stereotype of indoctrination."

399. "Briefly Noted." 15 (22 Apr. 1939): 72.

Robert Graves. Collected Poems. "A real and
original poet with influence on younger poets."

John Holmes, ed. The Poet's Work. "The sound
quotations are very good indeed."

Collected Poems of Robert P. Tristram Coffin.
Poetic appreciation of Maine can be sentimental.

In America: The Collected Works of John V. A
Weaver. "His dialects now seem a bit dated."

400. "Briefly Noted." 15 (27 May 1939): 84.

V. Sackville-West. Solitude: A Poem. A simple
and complicated examination of faith.

The Fountain of Magic. Trans. Frank O'Connor.
Irish heroic songs of bards and folk poetry.

401. "Briefly Noted." 15 (5 Aug. 1939): 68.

Louise Townsend Nicoll. Water and Light. "Filled
with genuine mysticism, quietly done."

402. "Briefly Noted." 15 (19 Aug. 1939): 59.

Louise MacNeill. Gauley Mountain. "Good hearty
verse about West Virginia mountains and people."

403. "Briefly Noted." 15 (2 Sept. 1939): 62.

Charlotte Wilder. Mortal Sequence. Shelley award
winner writes tight metaphysical verse.

Poems of Federico García Lorca. Trans. Stephen
Spender and J. L. Gili. "Rather spiffy" literal
translations which "tone down the original's
brilliance and harden its poignant simplicity."

404. "Briefly Noted." 15 (7 Oct. 1939): 79-80.

Sarah Henderson Hay. This My Letter.
"Technically competent" and "warmhearted" poems.

405. "Briefly Noted."   15 (4 Nov. 1939): 72.

John Holmes. Fair Warning. "Medium-light poems
about weather, food, bores, etc."

406. "Briefly Noted."   15 (18 Nov. 1939): 91-92.

Edith Wharton and Robert Norton, compilers.
Eternal Passion in English Poetry. "Solid
conventional anthology of English love poems."

T. S. Eliot. Old Possum's Book of Practical Cats.
Delightful verse on very English cat characters.

Kenneth Patchen. First Will and Testament.
"Hymns the pure revolution in standard gloomy
fashion."

A Greek Garland: Selection from the Palantine
Anthology. Trans. F. L Lucas. "Pleasant
renderings by a Cambridge scholar."

Nathalia Crane and Leonard Feeney. The Ark and
the Alphabet. "Charming and queer" zoological
verses which are over children's heads.

407. "Briefly Noted."   15 (30 Dec. 1939): 52.

Revel Denny. The Connecticut River and Other
Poems. He is "best when he allows himself to be
lyrical."

Babette Deutsch. One Part Love. "Poems on
contemporary subjects, especially lack of peace."

John Masefield. Some Verses to the Germans. "A
tired but touching peace-loving poem."

James Laughlin, ed. Poems from the Greenberg
Manuscripts. Some poems have a "psychopathic
brilliance."

Federico García Lorca. Blood Wedding. Trans.
Gilbert Neiman. Some of the flashing quality of
the original Spanish comes through.

1940

408. "Verse."   15 (27 Jan. 1940): 52-54.

Rimbaud. *Une Saison en Enfer*. Trans. Delmore
Schwartz. Rimbaud reacted against his society in
"an absolutely mature and ruthless fashion." The
"truth in his work is absolute and inexhaustible."

John Ciardi. *Homeward to America*. His book,
influenced by Rimbaud, contains social criticism.

Dylan Thomas. *The World I Breathe*. Also
influenced by Rimbaud, Thomas writes pure but
"perfectly hollow poetry with a surrealistic
coloring."

Louis MacNeice. *Autumn Diary*. An ironic
examination of London and Ireland in autumn, 1938.

409. "Verse." 16 (24 Feb. 1940): 68-69.

W. H. Auden. *Another Time*. Rewrite of "Spain
1937," his worst poem. His style is more varied,
serious and objective. The love poems are the
weakest.

410. "Briefly Noted." 16 (16 Mar. 1940): 96.

A. T. Quiller-Couch, ed. *The Oxford Book of
English Verse*. "Interesting additions in medieval
section, metaphysicals given their due."

The Collected Poems of H. E. Housman. A
beautifully and finely planned volume.

411. "Briefly Noted." 16 (23 Mar. 1940): 76.

Kimball Flaccus. *The White Stranger*. Mexican
Indian poetry "relies too much on traditional
form."

Mary B. Duryce. *No Special Pleading*. "Very
light, very feminine lyrics and sonnets."

412. "Verse." 16 (20 Apr. 1940): 75-76.

Oscar Williams. *The Man Coming Toward You*.
"Thoroughly synthetic poet" who "has rehashed
poetry from the last thirty years" in these
"repulsive poems."

Ruth Pitter. The Spirit Watches. She lacks
ardor, but has "a fine ear and sensitive insight."

413. "Briefly Noted." 16 (4 May 1940): 76.

Elizabeth Madox Roberts. Song in the Meadow.
Ballads in the Kentucky folk tradition.

414. "Briefly Noted." 16 (24 Aug. 1940): 59-60.

Edna St. Vincent Millay. There Are No Islands,
Any More. Lines written by a former pacifist "in
deep concern for England, France, and her
country."

Stephen Vincent Benet. Nightmare at Noon. He
fears enemy planes will soon fly over America.

F. R. Higgins. The Gap of Brightness. Irish
poet's "writing is humorous, dramatic, and tough."

415. "Briefly Noted." 16 (31 Aug. 1940): 48.

M. E. Speare, ed. Great English and American
Poems. "Worth its popular purpose and price."

Robert Hillyer. Pattern of a Day. "Skillful
though sometimes conventional verse."

416. "Briefly Noted." 16 (21 Sept. 1940): 68.

David Cecil, ed. The Oxford Book of Christian
Verse. All varieties of English devotional verse.

Elder Olsen. The Cock of Heaven. His
commentaries are "rather blownup and derivative,"
but he writes good lyrics.

417. "Briefly Noted." 16 (12 Oct. 1940): 88.

Phyllis McGinley. A Pocketful of Wry. "Light
verse which is helpful to many these days."

Raymond Holden. The Arrow at the Heel. "Limited
diction, but a sound, conservative technique."

418. "Verse." 16 (19 Oct. 1940): 87-89.

Letters on Poetry from W. B. Yeats to Dorothy
Wellesley. Yeat's last five years of
correspondence deals with his return to the
popular idiom, influenced by Dorothy Wellesley.
The letters show the poetic process at work.

420. "Verse." 16 (9 Nov. 1940): 78.

Kenneth Fearing. Collected Poems. "Poetry of
social consciousness" with a sense of timing.

421. "Briefly Noted." 16 (16 Nov. 1940): 87.

Margaret Fishback. Time for a Quick One. Minor
matters considered by a sound versifier.

The Face is Familiar: The Selected Verse of Ogden
Nash. The "dizziest rhythms and rhymes of the
day."

421. "Verse." 16 (28 Dec. 1940): 62-63.

Conrad Aiken. And In the Human Heart. He loses
his own accent and method in this book.

Edna St. Vincent Millay. Make Bright the Arrows.
Her expressions of horror are "sincere but
sentimental in their noble tone." She urges the
reader to sharpen his tools to make a better
world.

Frederic Prokosch. Death at Sea. His yearly book
of Auden adaptations in his melodious style.

Thomas Hardy. Selected Poems. Tough poems with
unmistakable vigor from the end of an era.

1941

422. "Briefly Noted. 16 (18 Jan. 1941): 80.

Rudyard Kipling's Verse: Definitive Edition.
"Large badly arranged but inclusive volume."

Five Young American Poets. First of annual
anthology including unpublished poets under

thirty. In this edition Mary Barnard, John
Berryman, Randall Farrell, W. R. Moses and George
Marion O'Donnell write serious, formal,
nonderivative poetry.

423. "Briefly Noted." 17 (22 Feb. 1941): 72.

Jan Struther. The Glass Blower and Other Poems.
"Not wholly light and not wholly serious."

Edmund Blunden. Poems 1930-1940. Georgian's work
has "style, emotion, and meditative substance."

424. "Verse." 17 (1 Mar. 1941): 55-57.

Donne's religio-erotic poetry influenced Pound and
Eliot and others right through the thirties.
Current poets have turned against his death-
obsessed poetry, especially the following:

Louis MacNeice. Poems 1925-1940. He has "broken
out of the rhetorical cage of the academy."

John Peale Bishop. Selected Poems. His tone
never varies, "but his taste is unimpeachable."

e. e. cummings. 50 Poems. "Irrevocably stuck in
the past," with the usual "toughness and
tenderness."

425. "Briefly Noted." 17 (15 Mar. 1941): 76.

Gerald Bullet, ed. The English Galaxy of Shorter
Poems. "One of the best modern lyric
anthologies."

426. "Briefly Noted." 17 (29 Mar. 1941): 64.

Arthur Waley, ed. Translations from the Chinese.
Poetry from third century B.C. to seventeenth A.D.

Walter de la Mare. Collected Poems. Six early
books in one, excluding Peacock Pie.

Theodore Roethke. Open House. His first book
with a "real sense of lyric style, a fine bitter
wit."

David McCord. And What's More. "More odd and
droll rhymes and rhythms."

427. "Briefly Noted." 17 (5 Apr. 1941): 76.

Siegfred Sassoon. Rhymed Ruminations. "Rather
startlingly gentle sentimental verse."

428. "Verse." 17 (12 Apr. 1941): 85.

Horace Gregory. Poems 1930-1940. "Apogee of
modern style and dead end of poetry."

429. "Briefly Noted." 17 (26 Apr. 1941): 76.

The Poems of Alice Meynell. "An Englishwoman of
true lyric and intellectual endowment."

The Ages of Man: The Standard Shakespeare
Anthology, ed. George Rylands. "Critical insight
and faultless taste in arrangement of passages."

430. "Briefly Noted." 17 (3 May 1941): 88.

Marya Zaturenska. The Listening Landscape. Use
of myth to explore her own sense of time.

431. "Verse." 17 (17 May 1941): 91-94.

James Laughlin, ed. Poet of the Month. Latest
pamphlet End of a Decade, by Harry Brown. He
should drop classic influences and become ironic
about himself.

Yvor Winters. Poems. He writes with "informed
reticence" in this privately printed book of
poems.

432. "Briefly Noted." 17 (30 Aug. 1941): 56.

Hilaire Bellou. Cautionary Verses. "A grand
omnibus" by "an old master."

433. "Verse." 17 (6 Sept. 1941): 75-76.

Ridgely Terrance. <u>Poems</u>. "His poem, "The Son,"
is one of most beautiful lyrics ever written."

John Wheelwright. <u>Selected Poems</u>. He is a mystic
whose posthumous collection shows native vigor.

Josephine Miles. <u>Poems on Several Occasions</u>. A
satirist without "a malicious ingredient in her."

E. M. Butler. <u>Rainer Maria Rilke</u>. Makes Rilke
appear "a nincompoop and rather a knave."

434. "Briefly Noted." 17 (20 Sept. 1941): 111.

Marjorie Barrows, compiler. <u>Pulitzer Prize Poems</u>.
Collection clearly shows wavering committee taste.

<u>Sophocles: Oedipus at Colonus</u>. Trans. Robert
Fitzgerald. Accurate, not particularly moving.

435. "Verse." 17 (18 Oct. 1941): 94.

Richard Aldington, ed. <u>Viking Book of Poetry of
the English-Speaking World</u>. "Remarkably complete
anthology" up to the twentieth century.

Hugh MacDiarmid, compiler. <u>The Golden Treasury of
Scottish Poetry</u>. "Special pleading" for the
Scottish unappreciated literary treasure shows in
these enchanting poems.

436. "Verse." 17 (1 Nov. 1941): 87-88.

Marianne Moore. <u>What are Years</u>. Her objects
become symbols in the deepest sense. She could be
published only in an advanced civilization.

Harry Brown. <u>The Poem of Bunker Hill</u>. "Full of
the look and sound of ordinary life."

George Zabriskie. <u>The Mind's Geography</u>. He can
describe anything in poetry without condescension.

437. "Verse." 17 (29 Nov. 1941): 104-5.

Mark Van Doren. The Mayfield Deer. His "most
subtle, oblique, and lofty treatment" of a
backwood field does not work.

Delmore Schwartz. Shenandoah. Play in prose with
verse comment is "sophomoric to a degree."

438. "Briefly Noted." 17 (6 Dec. 1941): 136.
Collected Sonnets of Edna St. Vincent Millay. One
hundred-sixty-one sonnets with a foreword by the
author.

Robinson Jeffers. Be Angry at the Sun and Other
Poems. He "sticks to his usual gloomy view of
man's fate."

Dilys Benet Laing. Another England. "A first
book of sensitive and incisive verse."

Phyllis McGinley. Husbands are Difficult or the
Book of Oliver Ames. Thirty-two witty variations
on the theme of matrimony.

439. "Verse." 17 (14 Feb. 1941): 68-69.

F. T. Prince. Poems. The new poem "The
Babiaantje" is a "lovely lyric."

Malcolm Cowley. Dry Season. He "tries
everything, but not often wisely or well."

Rilke. Poems from the Book of Hours. Trans.
Babette Deutsch. She has wisely kept the tone of
the originals in these early Rilke poems.

More Poems from the Palatine. Trans. Dudley
Fitts. "Great store of Greek epigrams and elegy."

John Masefield. Gautama the Enlightened. "A
touching purity of soul" is in this old poet.

Complete Poems of Emily Jane Brontë. Ed. O. W.
Hatfield. A basis for all future studies of the
writer.

440. "Verse." 18 (7 Mar. 1941): 54-55.

Five Young American Poets: Second Series 1941.

These poets can comment on their scene without
depression. Shapiro is "the prize of the lot,"
which also includes Paul Goodman, David Schubert,
and Jeanne McGahey.

Rolfe Humphries. Out of the Jewel. (Dedicated to
Louise Bogan.) Traces slowly developing spiritual
history.

1942

441. "Briefly Noted." 18 (9 May 1942): 63-64.

Robert Frost. A Witness Tree. "Gnomic epigrams
and arch philosophizing" of his later period.

Arthur Davison Ficke. Tumultuous Shores.
Conservative and sensitive sonnets and lyrics.

Robert Penn Warren. Eleven Poems on the Same
Theme. Poems "remarkable for their variety and
effects" by one of America's most expert
craftsmen.

442. "Briefly Noted." 18 (30 May 1942): 56.

Morris Bishop. Spilt Milk. "Verses of a light
order . . . by this versatile professor."

443. "Briefly Noted." 18 (27 June 1942.): 56.

John Masefield. Natalie Maisie and Pavilastukay:
Two Tales in Verse. Old-time Masefield touches in
romance of Russia's past and England's future.

Walter de la Mare. Bells and Grass. "Continuing
the Peacock Pie tradition with some of its charm."

444. "Verse." 18 (10 Oct. 1942): 73-74.

Wallace Stevens. Parts of a World. He "now seems
obsessed by his defense of the imagination against
the world of fact." American scholarship should
decide his place in American poetry.

445. "Briefly Noted." 18 (17 Oct. 1942): 91.

Rainer Maria Rilke. Sonnets to Orpheus. Trans.
M. D. Herter. Literal verse "well above trot
class."

Randall Jarrell. Blood for a Stranger. Real
power and originality under "heavy Auden
wrappings."

Louis Untermeyer, ed. A Treasury of Great Poems,
English and American. "A Cook's tour of verses."

446. "Verse." (31 Oct. 1942): 80

Patricia Ledward and Colin Strang, ed. Poems of
this War by Younger Poets. Joy set against a
background of fiery shadow. John Hall has talent.

Muriel Rukeyser. Wake Island. Her technique is
filled with "rhetorical hollowness."

José García Villa. Have Come, Am Here. He is
given to "religious mysticism and surrealism."

447. "Briefly Noted." 18 (21 Nov. 1942): 100.

Ogden Nash. Good Intentions. Matters "submitted
to the acid test of Mr. Nash's wit and rhyme."

1943

448. "Verse." 18 (9 Jan. 1943): 49-51.

Karl Shapiro. Person, Place, and Thing. This
fine young poet's satire can be compared with
Heine's.

Edmund Wilson. Notebooks of Night. "A sensitive,
sensual preception" of reality's color and shape.

449. "Briefly Noted. 18 (30 Jan. 1943): 63.

Dudley Fitts, ed. An Anthology of Contemporary
Latin-American Poetry. "The translations
emphasize meaning rather than music" in this
"interesting job."

Goethe's Faust: A New American Translation.
Trans. Carlyle F. MacIntyre. "Part One is

translated into English more easy than stylish."
Edith Sitwell. Street Songs. "Much less shrill
than her earlier work," with "real pathos and
charm."

450. "Briefly Noted." 19 (20 Mar. 1943): 63.

Charles Henri Ford, ed. The Mirror of Baudelaire.
Three poems with "odd-in-spots" translations.

Last Poems of Elinor Wylie. "A collection of new
and fugitive poems by the late gifted lyricist."

Walter Benton. This Is My Beloved. "Rather
freshly done" sensuous love poetry in free verse.

Hortense Flexner. North Window. "Intelligent
notes on life."

451. "Verse." 19 (12 June 1943): 67-68.

John Masefield. A Generation Risen. "Shrewd
pungent comments" on England's young defenders.

Delmore Schwartz. Genesis, Book One. "An
experiment which makes hard reading."

Rainer Maria Rilke. Poems. Trans. Jessie Lemont.
Miss Lemont's versions are "somewhat softening."

452. "Verse." 19 (7 Aug. 1943): 62-64.

The Poets of the Year Series now includes these
two long-dead, almost ignored poets:

John Wilmot. A Satire Against Mankind and Other
Poems. Ed. Harry Levin. This work by the Earl
of Rochester contains his "most witty, bitter, and
uninhibited views about his contemporaries."

Some Poems of Frederich Holderin. Trans. Frederic
Prokosch. Prokosch has difficulty translating the
classic forms and atmosphere of eighteenth-century
Germany.

453. "Briefly Noted." 19 (25 Sept. 1943): 75.

Oscar Williams, ed.   Book of New Poems. Wordy
recent poems from modern English and Americans.

A. J. M. Smith, ed.   The Book of Canadian Poetry.
Comprehensive critical and historical anthology.

Kenneth Fearing.   Afternoon of a Pawnbroker and
Other Poems. In spite of a light tone, the poems
"arouse a nameless dread."

454. "Verse." 19 (2 Oct. 1943): 76-78.

A Choice of Kipling's Verse Made by T. S. Eliot.
Although Kipling had skill in writing ballads, he
never developed into a human's poet, preferring
machines over men. In spite of Eliot's special
pleading, Kipling's sentimentality is hopeless.

455. "Briefly Noted." 19 (9 Oct. 1943): 84.

Arthur Guiterman.   Brave Laughter. The last
collection of this "skillful versifier" contains
his best work.

456. "Verse." 19 (13 Nov. 1943): 98-104.

Horace Gregory, ed.   The Triumph of Life: Poems of
Consolation for the English-Speaking World.
Gregory's choices resemble Victorian periodical
literature, but he does include the great elegies.

457. "Briefly Noted." 19 (20 Nov. 1943): .96.

George Herbert Clarke, ed.   The New Treasury of
War Poetry: Poems of the Second World War. More
sentimental than World War I poetry.

The Violent: New Poems by Harry Brown. "Well-made
verse . . . reminiscent of Auden's early work."

458. "Briefly Noted." 19 (27 Nov. 1943): 110.

John Holmes.   Map of My Country. He tries to
"delineate his place" in a dislocated world.

1944

459. "Briefly Noted." 19 (15 Jan. 1944): 72.

Paul Claudel. Coronal. Trans. Sister Mary David.
"A serious, but not always successful
translation."

John Masefield. Wonderings (Between One and Six
Years). This long poem mixes "realistic
humanitarianism with charming memories of
childhood."

Weldon Kees. The Last Man. "A literate talent
with a satiric edge."

460. "Verse." 20 (26 Feb. 1944): 82, 84, 86.

Kenneth Patchen. Cloth of the Tempest. Childish
verse with strange titles.

George Barker. Sacred and Secular Elegies. An
Auden imitator with emotion and a musical ear.

Dunstan Thompson. Poems. A former Harvard editor
who knows all the trends and writes every sort of
verse "like a virtuoso," but has no ear.

Rimbaud. Les Illuminations. Trans. Helen
Rootham. She shows what "eloquence and
hallucinatory beauty" came from this schoolboy.

461. "Briefly Noted." 20 (25 Mar. 1944): 91.

e. e. cummings. 1 x 1 (One Times One). His
satire and delight are best without the tricks.

Mark Van Doren. The Seven Sleepers. "A kind of
somnabulist style . . . mood, and point of view."

Ralph Gristafson, ed. The Little Anthology of
Canadian Poets. "The writing and general
observation are far from provincial."

462. "Verse." 20 (22 July 1944): 58.

John Pudney. Flight Above Clouds. Sometimes his
war poetry breaks away from propaganda.

William Justema. _Private Papers_. He describes
his war experiences without affectations.

463. "Briefly Noted. 20 (30 Sept. 1944): 71-72.

William Rose Benet. _Day of Deliverance_. "Verse
written hot on the steps of war."

No Road Back: Poems by Walter Mehring. Trans. S.
A. De Witt. "Hard hitting in the original German,
but rather limply translated."

Poems from the Desert by Members of the British
Eighth Army. Interesting and human poems written
during the fighting in the Western African desert.

Karl Shapiro. _V-Letter_. "The most complex
reaction to the war yet heard by his generation."

464. "Briefly Noted." 20 (7 Oct. 1944): 75-76.

Jess Stuart. _Album of Destiny_. He has "tamed
folk material to magazine-verse standards."

Oliver St. John Gogarty. _Perennial_. "Witty and
well-made verse . . . too malicious to be large."

465. "Briefly Noted." 20 (14 Oct. 1944): 87-88.

_The Iliad of Homer: A line-for-Line Translation in
Dactylic Hexameters_. Trans. William Benjamin
Smith and Walter Miller. Professor Smith's
feeling for and skill with the hexameter line is
its interest.

Christopher Morley. _The Middle Kingdom: Poems
1929-1944)_. "A master of light occasional verse."

Rolfe Humphries. _The Summer Landscape_. He "moves
back and forth between the real and dream world."

466. "Verse." 20 (21 Oct. 1944): 91-92.
Muriel Rukeyser. _Beast in View_. This current
work is "almost lushly romantic and brightly
hopeful."

Marya Zaturenska. _The Golden Mirror_. Her best

work resembles "a bibelot collection arrangement."
Babette Deutsch. <u>Take Them, Stranger</u>. "At times
[her poetry] shows the brief touch of gentility."

Dilys Bennett Laing. <u>Birth Is Farewell</u>. "Her
talent is small but genuine."

Margaret Young. <u>Moderate Fable</u>. "Metaphysical
concepts and semi-surrealistic technique."
H. D. <u>The Walls Do Not Fall</u>. Her writing has
increased in scope in this book on bombed London.

467. "Briefly Noted." 20 (18 Nov. 1944): 95-96.

W. H. Auden. <u>A Selection from the Works of Alfred
Lord Tennyson</u>. Auden successfully shows
Tennyson's musical ear and limited intellect.

<u>Herman Melville: Selected Poems</u>. Ed. F. O.
Matthiessen. Melville's poetic insights and
emotions [appear] in "compressed and compelling
form."

Russell Davenport. <u>My Country: A Poem of America</u>.
An "old-fashioned sentimental tract" written to
put over verse on the public.

<u>The Way of Life According to Lao Tzu: An American
Version by Witter Bynner</u>. "Lucid, flexible,
witty."

468. "Briefly Noted." 10 (30 Dec. 1944): 54, 56.

Conrad Aiken. <u>The Soldier: A Poem</u>. A civilian
onlooker cheers himself by writing about Mars.

Thomas Merton. <u>Thirty Poems</u>. His poems "unite
semi-surrealistic technique with religious
feeling."

Robert Lowell. <u>Land of Unlikeliness</u>.
"Combination of a fine sense of form" with
"brutal emotion."

Kenneth Rexroth. <u>The Phoenix and the Turtle</u>. He
translates the classics and examines his
conscience.

1945

469. "Verse."   20 (13 Jan. 1945): 74, 76-78.

Oscar Williams, ed. New Poems: 1944. Usual
sounding selections from American and British
poets.   "The war poems have a definite humanity."

Young American Poets. This latest crop "seems
rather overcharged in the baroque sense."
Included are Eve Merriam, Jean Garrigue, John
Frederick Nims, Tennessee Williams, and Alejandro
Corrion.

470. "Briefly Noted."   21 (24 Feb. 1945): 70.

Richard Eberhart. Poems, New and Selected. He
now has more control and sometimes a Blakean
vision.

Rafael Alberti. Selected Poems. These
translations lack the wit and brilliance necessary
for surrealism.

Three Russian Poets. Trans. Vladimir Nabokov.
Selections from Pushkin in which "the epigrammatic
tenseness survives;" and Lermontov and Tyutchev,
who are rendered into "soggy, romantic English."

471. "Verse."   21 (7 Apr. 1945): 86.

Allen Tate. The Winter Sea. His most memorable
poems are written in high tradition and are
satirical.

472. "Verse."   21 (16 June 1945): 58, 61-62.

William Rose Benet. The Dust that Is God.
Republication of 1941 Pulitzer-prize winning novel
in verse is now found to be a "technical failure."

Robert P. Tristram Coffin. Poems for a Son with
Wings. His productions "elude formal critical
attention," so Bogan quotes publisher's blurbs.

George Zabriskie. Like the Root. "Rather quiet
and unself-regarding" with insight and gentle
control over self and material.

Hubert Read. <u>A World Within a War</u>. Same as
above.

Charles Edward Butler. <u>Art is the Branch</u>. Same
as above.

473. "Briefly Noted." 21 (23 June 1945): 71-72.

Jeremy Ingalls. <u>Tahl</u>. "Pure romantic
phantasmagoria . . . almost stifles the reader."

Edward Fenton. <u>Soldiers and Strangers</u>. His
tougher poems on wartime are better than his
tender ones.

Oscar Williams. <u>That's All That Matters</u>. "Sharp
pictures of a nightmare world."

William Rose Benet and Norman Cousins, eds. <u>The
Poetry of Freedom</u>. Some dull verse, but the scope
of the anthology makes it interesting.

474. "Briefly Noted." 21 (7 July 1945): 67-68.

John Crowe Ransom. <u>Selected Poems</u>. His
"mannerisms are perfectly suited to his subject
matter."

Charles Henri Ford. <u>Poems for Painters</u>. His
poems are strongly influenced by Paul Eluard.

475. "Briefly Noted." 21 (28 Jul. 1945): 63-64.

Oscar Williams, ed. <u>The War Poets: An Anthology
of the War Poetry of the Twentieth Century</u>.
Excellent poems "surrounded by . . . dull
observation and double talk."

C. Day-Lewis. <u>Short Is the Time: Poems 1936-1943</u>.
Lewis is "still capable of a lovely song."

476. "Briefly Noted." 21 (22 Sept. 1945): 79-80.

Gwendolyn Brooks. <u>A Street in Bronzeville</u>. She
"successfully crosses the vigorous folk poetry of
her people with traditional forms."

477. "Briefly Noted." 21 (29 Sept. 1945): 87.

Frances Meynell. Seventeen Poems. Civilized
charm and insight in light and serious verse.

478. "Briefly Noted." 21 (6 Oct. 1945): 91.

Paul Engle. American Child. Rhetorical portrait
in sixty sonnets of the poet's child.

Thomas Wolfe. A Stone, a Leaf, a Door. Ed. John
S. Barnes. Wolfe's prose in verse forms is
"enervating and fiberless."

Ogden Nash. Many Long Years Ago. Culling earlier
collections results in this book.

479. "Briefly Noted." 21 (Oct. 1945): 99.

Alum Lewis. Ha! Ha! Among the Trumpets. This
posthumously published poem has "a rough vigor and
a tragic tone."

480. "Briefly Noted." 21 (3 Nov. 1945): 93.

Edmund Blunden. Shells by a Stream. "His later
poetry seems battered, mossy, and blurred."

Louis MacNeice. Springboard: Poems 1941-1944. A
completely new side "without his mocking mask."

Norman Nicholson. Five Rivers. This English
regionalist is "a technician of the highest
order."

Alex Comfort. The Song of Lazarus. His poems
deal with the borderline between emotion and
dreams.

481. "Briefly Noted." 21 (1 Dec. 1945): 136, 138.

David McCord, ed. What Cheer. "On the whole a
successful anthology of American and British
humorous and witty verse."

482. "Briefly Noted." 21 (29 Dec. 1945): 68.

Karl Shapiro. <u>Essay on Rime</u>. Long, too-serious poem with "transitional pontifications."

Wallace Stevens. <u>Esthétique du Mal: A Poem</u>. "A good example of his later style in which ideas and language shift from . . . transparency to opacity."

H. D. <u>Tribute to the Angels</u>. Reaffirmation of "her faith in a future rising from the ruins."

Marsden Hartley. <u>Selected Poems</u>. "The Maine poems by this painter are particularly vivid."

Walter de la Mare. <u>The Burning Glass and Other Poems</u>. These later lyrics "exhibit his wit and exquisite lyrical gift."

1946

483. "Verse." 21 (9 Feb. 1946)" 95.

Richard Eberhart and Selden Rodman, eds. <u>War and the Poet: An Anthology Expressing Man's Attitudes Toward War from Ancient Times to the Present</u>. War poetry has gradually changed from the action level to the psychological level and has become anti-war poetry.

Randall Jarrell. <u>Little Friend, Little Friend</u>. "Subconscious springs of action" in war poetry.

Louis Aragon. <u>Aragon: Poet of the French Resistance</u>. Ed. Malcolm Cowley and Hannah Josephson. "Artful pastiches" which have a "painfully hollow sound," but make a profound impression.

484. "Briefly Noted." 22 (23 Feb. 1946): 91.

Richard Aldington. <u>A Wreath for San Gemignano</u>. Translation of profane bard's delightful <u>I Sonnetti</u>.

Ruth Pitter. <u>The Bridge: Poems 1939-1944</u>. Her artificiality has given way to modern effects.

Rainer Maria Rilke. <u>Sonnets to Orpheus: Duino Elegies</u>. Trans. Jessie Lemont. She successfully gets around some of the poems' difficulties.

Laurence Housman, ed. <u>A Wordsworth Anthology</u>. He "freshens up the rather faded Laureate."

William Rose Benet and Conrad Aiken. <u>An Anthology of Famous English and American Poetry</u>. The publisher excised Pound from this anthology.

485. "Briefly Noted." 22 (4 May 1946): 112.

Powys Mathers, trans. <u>Love Songs of Asia</u>. "Charming translations of Asiatic poetry."

486. "Briefly Noted." 22 (20 July 1946): 75-76.

Oscar Williams, ed. <u>A Little Treasury of Modern Verse</u>. Good job giving neglected poets their due.

Henry Treece. <u>Collected Poems</u>. The "father of the New Apocalypse movement" shows his "glib talent."

Denis Devlin. <u>Lough Derg and Other Poems</u>. "Celtic intellect, boldness and uncommon sense."

Josephine Miles. <u>Local Measures</u>. She is more interested in language than in describing reality.

487. "Briefly Noted." 22 (7 Sept. 1946): 102-3.

Jorge Carrera Andrade. <u>Secret Country: Poems</u>. Trans. Muna Lee. Sympathetic translation shows his innovative, lyrical work.

488. "Verse." 22 (5 Oct. 1946): 122.

Thomas Merton. <u>A Man in the Divided Sea</u>. He is moving toward a synthesis between his religious and poetic gifts.

John Manifold. <u>Selected Verse</u>. An occasional bright song makes this a pleasant volume.

489. Briefly Noted." 22 (26 Oct. 1946): 119-120.

William Carlos Williams. <u>Paterson: Book 1</u>. His Imagism continues in this poem which has "moments of success . . . and exasperating failure."

Petrarch Sonnets and Songs. Trans. Anna Maria
Armi. Able translation of a "seemingly faded"
poet.

V. Sackville-West. _The Garden_. "Old-fashioned
sentimentality and well-observed details."

Robert P. Tristram Coffin. _People Behave Like
Ballads_. He "varnishes New England people,
objects, and weather in his gay fashion."

490. "Verse." 22 (9 Nov. 1946): 121-23.

Rimbaud. _Illuminations_. Trans. Louise Varese.
Rimbaud's adolescent poety now appears "vital and
mature." He allows his subconscious to take
control.

André Breton. _Young Cherry Trees Secured Against
Hares_. Trans. Edouard Roditi. Breton's poetry
written at fifty preserves childishness. He
attempts to manipulate his subconscious.

491. "Verse." 22 (30 Nov. 1946): 140.

Janet Lewis. _Earth-Bound_. Special 300-copy
edition with the beautiful poem "In the Egyptian
Museum."

492. "Briefly Noted." 22 (14 Dec. 1946): 147.

Mark Van Doren. _The Country Year: Poems_. Little
of his "master Frost's" wit or music are found.

H. D. _The Flowering of the Rod_. "Thin shrill
mysticism" in works with a biblical background.

Helen Devington. _Doctor Johnson's Waterfall and
Other Poems_. She is able to blend wit, literary
criticism, and observation.

The Collected Poems of Hart Crane. Ed. Waldo
Frank. Reprint of the 1933 edition.

493. "Briefly Noted." 22 (21 Dec. 1946): 99.

The Selected Writings of Dylan Thomas. His
"wilder Surrealist tendencies" are less in
evidence.

Pablo Neruda. Residence on Earth and Other Poems.
Trans. Angel Flores. He combines a Surrealistic
technique with emotional drive.

1947

494. "Briefly Noted." 22 (11 Jan. 1947)) 87.

e. e. cummings. Santa Claus: A Morality. "The
theme of love vs. death, hate, science, and the
mob . . . [is] simplified to the point of parody."

Anne Finch. Essay on Marriage. A "refreshingly
crisp and adult survey" of modern love.

Edith Sitwell. Green Song and Other Poems. Her
work has become "excessively romantic."

Reed Whittemore. Heroes and Heroines. His best
verses make the worst sound artificial.

495. "Briefly Noted." 22 (8 Feb. 1947): 99.

Kenneth Yasuda (Shoson). A Pepper-pod: Classic
Japanese Poems Together with Original Haiku. His
translations and own haiku are "rhymed and thus
sweetened over the originals."

Hubert Creekmore. The Long Reprieve. His
interest in prosody as such impedes his poetry.

Seldon Rodman, ed. The New Anthology of Modern
Poetry. Thoroughly up-to-date revision.

496. "Briefly Noted." 23 (15 Mar. 1947): 119.

Speaking for Scotland: Selected Poems of Hugh
MacDiarmid. He functions better in Scots dialect
than in plain English.

Kathleen Hoagland, ed. 1000 Years of Irish
Poetry: The Gaelic and Anglo-Irish Poets from
Pagan Time to the Present. Her attempts to link
Irish history and poetry seem superficial.

497. "Verse." 23 (5 Apr. 1947): 102-104.
John Frederick Nims. The Iron Pastoral. His
poems seem complex but boil down to universal
truths. He lacks seriousness of purpose.

Stephen Spender. Poems of Dedication. Although
he has dropped romanticism, his sincerity is still
apparent in this "uneven collection."

498. "Verse." 23 (3 May 1947): 116.

Wallace Stevens. Transport to Summer. His later
elaborate style almost destroys sustained emotion
and ideas.

Frederic Prokosch. Chosen Poems. His "verbal
sweetness [is] so thick that everything floats in
it like preserved fruit in syrup."

499. "Briefly Noted." 23 (17 May 1947): 118.

The Portable Dante. Ed. Paolo Milano, trans.
Laurence Binyon. A valuable collection.

Oscar Williams, ed. A Little Treasury of Great
Poetry, English and American, from Chaucer to the
Present. "Some fine things turn up with the old
indispensable war horses."

Stephen Spender, ed. A Choice of English Romantic
Poetry. His "attitude toward the Romantics is
curiously ambivalent."

Claire and Ivan Goll. Love Poems. "A sad and
tender charm pervades these verses."

500. "Briefly Noted." 23 (7 June 1947): 128.

Robert Frost. Steeple Bush. "Effective words
fall delightfully into effective order."

501. "Briefly Noted." 23 (14 June 1947): 99.

Poems by Samuel Greenberg. Ed. Harold Holden and
Jack McManis. Poems of simple intensity by a man
who died young and "somewhat influenced Hart
Crane."

The Collected Poems of Sidney Keyes. Ed. Michael
Meyer. Although he was dead before he was twenty-
one, he influenced his generation.

502. "Briefly Noted." 23 (21 June 1947): 79-80.

The Georgics of Virgil. Trans. C. Day-Lewis.
"Charm and rural wisdom come through."

Baudelaire. One Hundred Poems from Les Fleurs du
Mal. Trans. C. F. MacIntyre. "A good modern
version . . . keeping Baudelaire's form reasonably
intact."

503. "Briefly Noted." 23 (19 July 1947): 72.

Joan Murray. Poems. Posthumous volume showing
"unmistakably poetic" original point of view.

504. "Verse." 23 (13 Sept. 1947): 118-19.

Jean Garrigue. The Ego and the Centaur. Smooth
poems interrupted by obscure phrases.

Louis Cox. The Sea Faring. Like Garrigue, he
searches for the "tortuous, overelaborate phrase."

505. "Briefly Noted." 23 (20 Sept. 1947): 106-7.

The Sonnets of Louise Labe. Trans. Frederic
Prokosch. The French Renaissance sonnets sound
like "products of Romanticism."

Laurie Lee. The Sun My Monument. "Sparkling gay
impressionism" which is unlike contemporaries'
gloom.

Ezra Pound. Personnae: The Collected Poems of
Ezra Pound. The best poems written before his
"mental illness."

506. "Briefly Noted." 23 (4 Oct. 1947): 111.

Conrad Aiken. The Kid. A synthesis of the
untamable American genius into a romantic figure.

Seldon Rodman. <u>The Amazing Year: A Diary in
Verse</u>. The personal verse is more interesting.

507. "Briefly Noted." 23 (18 Oct. 1947): 128.

Samuel Hoffenstein. <u>Pencil in the Air</u>. A
fitting obituary showing his technical mastery.

Tristan Corbière. <u>Poems</u>. Trans. Walter McElroy.
"Complex and primitive, sincere and harsh," he
influenced T. S. Eliot and others.

508. "Briefly Noted." 23 (1 Nov. 1947): 115.
     Robert Frost. <u>A Masque of Mercy</u>. "Lightly
satirical discussion of divine motives."

509. "Verse." 23 (15 Nov. 1947): 133-34.

Howard Nemerov. <u>The Image and the Law</u>. His anti-
Romantic poems are abstractions which progress
from one concept to another.

William Jay Smith. <u>Poems</u>. He writes "a true
lyric often edged with effective satire."

John Ciardi. <u>Other Skies</u>. He covers his war
experiences and his postwar letdown.

Karl Shapiro. <u>Trial of a Poet</u>. Successful
dramatic verse defends poet who is "confronted by
modern materialistic society and religion."

510. "Briefly Noted." 23 (22 Nov. 1947): 140.

Henry Reed. <u>A Map of Verona and Other Poems</u>. It
contains the memorable war verse "Naming the
Parts."

Rolfe Humphries. <u>Forbid Thy Ravens</u>. His latest
collection.

511. "Briefly Noted." 23 (29 Nov. 1947): 143.

<u>Poems from Giacomo Leopardi</u>. Trans. John Heath-
Stubbs. Successful translation of Leopardi's
"anti-romantic view of man."

512. "Briefly Noted." 23 (20 Dec. 1947): 98, 100.

Selected Poems of Bertolt Brecht. Trans. H. R.
Hays. His early vigor and brilliance are "later
replaced by dullness and rigidity."

Wallace Stevens. Three Academic Pieces. Two new
poems and a prose address at Harvard.

Selected Poems of Federico García Lorca, trans.
Stephen Spender and J. L. Gili. New poems are
added and old poems are "rendered more poetic,
less literal."

R. P. Blackmur. The Good European. Fine limited
edition with "cryptic and slow-paced verse."

1948

513. "Verse." 23 (21 Jan. 1948): 64-66.

Poets at Work. Sponsored by University of
Buffalo. A volume with two essays by poets W. H.
Auden and Karl Shapiro; and two essays by
professors Donald Stauffer and Rudolph Arnheim.
It includes poets' worksheets and Auden's
discussion of the poetic vocation.

514. "Briefly Noted." 24 (6 Mar. 1948): 100.

Allen Tate. Poems 1922-1947. This collection
shows Tate's development from "purely Southern
idealism" to broad humanity.

Bernard Spencer. Aegean Islands and Other Poems.
These war poems illustrate his "sense of history."

515. "Briefly Noted." 24 (13 Mar. 1945): 127-28.

Stephen Spender. Returning to Vienna 1947.
Elegiac poems to the author's humanitarianism.

516. "Briefly Noted." 24 (24 Apr. 1948): 110.

Padriac Colum, ed. An Anthology of Irish Verse.
An addition to the 1922 collection with both
Gaelic and Anglo-Irish poets.

Dante. The Divine Comedy. Trans. Laurence Grant
White. "Rather pedestrian" blank verse.

Thomas Merton. Figures for an Apocalypse. His
dislike of wealth often reaches a prophetic tone.

517. "Briefly Noted." 8 (May 1948): 115.

Muriel Rukeyser. The Green Wave. "Her writing is
increasingly complicated and heavy-handed."

Mark Van Doren. New Poems. He is "never out of a
subject and never firmly in possession of one."

Selden Rodman, ed. 100 American Poems:
Masterpieces of Lyric, Epic, and Ballad from
Colonial Times to the Present. The editor has
"eliminated driftwood" and brought his material up
to date.

Four Poems by Rimbaud. Trans. Ben Belitt. He
succeeds in getting the tension and brilliance.

518. "Verse." 24 (15 May 1948): 117-21.

Randall Jarrell. Losses. His wartime poetry
contains simple, direct, and moving emotional
responses. His other work is "superficially
modern" when he uses tricks from the academy.

Theodore Roethke. The Lost Son. "He relives his
deep subconscious fears" and writes about his
childhood with complete control.

519. "Briefly Noted." 24 (12 June 1948): 99-100.

Robert Horan. A Beginning. "Although the baroque
style is too evident," he is gifted.

Collected Poems of Robert P. Tristram Coffin. "He
is as irrepressible as ever."

520. "Briefly Noted." 24 (4 Sept. 1948): 83-84.

Robinson Jeffers. The Double Axe and Other Poems.
"His antihumanism shows up in his ghoulish and
incestuous plots."

William Carlos Williams. Paterson - Book Two.
"The overall plan sacrifices [his] sense of form."

Vernon Watkins. Selected Poems. The late Yeats
is implied in his lyricism and imagery.

Oscar Williams, ed. The Little Treasury of
American Poetry: the Chief Poets from Colonial
Times to the Present. The editor's point of view
is "pedestrian," even though he misses nothing.

Louis Untermeyer, ed. An Anthology of the New
England Poets from Colonial Time to the Present
Day. His selections outside the mainstream are
more interesting.

521. "Briefly Noted." 24 (2 Oct. 1948): 106-7.

The Collected Poems of John Peale Bishop. His
later poems show mature strength.

John Arlott, ed. First Time in America: A
Selection of Poems Never Before Published in the
U. S. A. The "dead hand of the Georgians" shows.

Poems of Gerard Manley Hopkins. Ed. W. H.
Gardner. The "third definitive edition will
establish a basis for his legitimate and lasting
fame."

John Berryman. The Dispossessed. His
experimental verse frightens the reader with its
language.

522. "Briefly Noted." 24 (13 Nov. 1948): 151-52.

Archibald MacLeish. Act Five and Others. His
"humanitarian sadness" is bearable in small forms.

Winfield Townley Scott. Mr. Whittier and Other
Poems. At times these poems continue the
satirical New England tradition of Frost and
Robinson.

Lilian Bowes Lyon. Collected Poems. "Uneven
poems with a sense of language and sincerity."

523. "Verse." 24 (25 Dec. 1948): 56-57.

A Celebration for Edith Sitwell, by seventeen
contributors. A touching tribute for her war
verse when she became the voice of the English
people.

T. S. Eliot. Recordings available from Harvard
Vocarium, H. M. V., and Library of Congress.

1949

524. Briefly Noted." 24 (22 Jan. 1949): 86.

Devin A. Garrity, ed. New Irish Poets. They are
too lyrical, although they do show some Irish
bitterness.

C. Day-Lewis. Poems 1943-1947. The poems "seem
brilliant singly," but inconsequential together.

Peter Viereck. Terror and Decorum. "He fails to
reconcile the emotion in the title."

525. "Briefly Noted." 24 (29 Jan. 1949): 71-72.

Lanston Hughes and Arna Bontemps, eds. The Poetry
of the Negro 1746-1949. The amount of good poetry
is the same as in "any longterm racial cross-
section."

Langston Hughes. One Way Ticket. He has trouble
"reproducing authentic Negro folk poetry."

Siegfred Sassoon. Collected Poems. His war
poetry "contrasts with his later mildly satirical
verse."

William Carlos Williams. The Clouds, Aigeltinger,
Russis, etc. "Beautifully bound limited edition
of his latest lyrics."

526. "Briefly Noted." 24 (12 Feb. 1949): 95.

Sacheverell Sitwell. Selected Poems. This "does
not demonstrate a large or strong poetic talent."

527. "Briefly Noted." 24 (12 Feb. 1949): 95.

Ogden Nash. Versus. A good part of the

collection was previously published in <u>The New Yorker</u>.

528. "Briefly Noted." 24 (12 Mar. 1949): 108.

C.M. Bowra. ed. <u>A Second Book of Russian Verse</u>.
"Much of the material makes a poignant impression."

Elizabeth Daryush. <u>Selected Poems</u>. Her poetry is "ordinary in epithet and idea, [and] flat in sound."

529. "Verse." 25 (26 Mar. 1949): 110-11.

Louis MacNeice. <u>Holes in the Sky</u>. This has moments of wit and charm, "but the long poem is diluted Eliot."

John Heath-Stubbs. <u>The Charity of the Stars</u>. "Liquid and sweet."

530. "Briefly Noted." 25 (7 May 1949): 114-15.

Cecily Mackworth, ed. <u>A Mirror for French Poetry</u>. "A good many poems are rather warped."

<u>Collected Poems of William Empson</u>. His striving for ambiguity succeeds in "brilliant obscurity."

531. "Briefly Noted." 25 (21 May 1949): 119-20.

John Neihardt. <u>A Cycle of the West</u>. Old-fashioned poetic technique in action stories.

<u>Selected Poems of William Carlos Williams</u>. Randall Jarrell, intro.; and <u>The Pink Church</u>, a pamphlet. The introduction puts Williams' work in proper perspective for his solid achievement. The pamphlet is "full of his charm and unexpectedness."

St. John Perse. <u>Exile and Other Poems</u>. Trans. Denis Devlin. Powerful feelings expressed in difficult, but not arbitrary language.

532. Briefly Noted." 25 (28 May 1949): 104.

Norman Ault, ed. Elizabethan Lyrics. Classic
anthology with selections arranged in order they
became known to the public.

Richard Eberhart. Brotherhood of Man. Moving
poem of a captured soldier in Anglo-Saxon rhythms.

533. "Briefly Noted." 25 (11 June 1949): 103.

Avrahm Yarmolinsky, ed. A Treasury of Russian
Verse. Trans. Babette Deutsch. The variety of
Russian poetry comes through.

Mediaeval Latin Lyrics. Trans. Helen Waddell. Gay
and human monkish Latin.

The Edge of Being: Poems by Stephen Spender. The
more "simplicity and actuality" Spender achieves,
the better.

Some Poems of Thomas Wyatt. Ed. Alan Swallow.
"His variety, intensity, and directness delight."

534. "Briefly Noted." 25 (15 Oct.1949): 139.

Complete Poems of Robert Frost: 1949. The "lyric
runs pure," but "middle-class thought emerges."

Ivor Winters, ed. Poets of the Pacific: Second
Series. Twelve students of Winters show his
influence in well-written but monotonous poetry.

Robert Tristram Coffin. One-Horse Farm. He has
theatricalized his verse, himself, and Maine.

535. "Verse." 25 (26 Nov. 1949): 126, 129-30.

A discussion of experimental verse.

Harry Brown. The Beast in His Hunger. Compared
with the other volumes in this review, Brown
regresses into old-fashioned rhetoric.

José García Villa. Volume Two. He uses commas to
set apart every word, which does not work.

Rosalie Moore. The Grasshopper's Man. Her
Imagist manner is hampered by rhetorical demands.

Herbert Cahoon. Thanatopsis. Compared to the
others, his poems are "simple, cool and pellucid."

536. "Briefly Noted." 25 (17 Dec. 1949): 130.

Skylight One: Fifteen Poems by Conrad Aiken. His
improvisations are neither very profound nor very
shallow."

Gwendolyn Brooks. Annie Allen. Her sense of form
is remarkable, but not all of her experimentation
comes off.

Demetrios Capetanakis. The Shores of Darkness.
"Posthumous publication of touching poetry."

Francis R. D. Godolphin, ed. The Latin Poets.
Dry translations in this exploration of Latin
poetry's effect on later English literature.

Theodore Spencer. An Acre in the Seed. His five-
line stanza shows his wit and perception.

Herbert Read and Bonamy Dobree, eds. The London
Book of English Verse. The arrangement runs from
"the most simple to the most complex."

1950

537. "Briefly Noted." 26 (11 Mar. 1950): 105-6.

Thomas Merton. The Tears of the Blind Lions. His
sincerity underlies his "rhetorical intensity."

Edith Sitwell. The Canticle of the Rose: Poems
1917-1949. A drastic editing of her earlier work.

Osbert Sitwell. England Reclaimed and Other
Poems. His satire tends towards sentimentality.

Charles Henri Ford. Sleep in a Nest of Flames.
He resembles Eluard, but he has a sense of humor.

St. John Perse. Anabasis. Trans. T. S. Eliot.
Eliot has corrected his translations.

André Gide, compiler. Anthologie de la Poésie

Française.   French anthology which was years in
the works.

V. Sackville West and Harold Nicholson, compilers.
Another World Than This.   They chose the poems in
this anthology from the books with underlined
passages of verse in their library.

538. "Verse."   26 (18 Mar. 1950): 116-17.

Seldon Rodman, ed.   _100 Modern Poems_.   He makes
his work an act of criticism, unlike most American
anthologies, which resemble college readers.

539. "Briefly Noted."   26 (22 April 1950): 127.

Edmund Blunden.   _After the Bombing_.   Although a
Georgian, "his poetry is fresh and appealing."

Wilfred Owen.   _Poems_.   Corrected version of the
1931 edition.   He influenced Spender and Auden.

Ezra Pound.   _Selected Poems_.   Fragments from the
Cantos and other representational poems.

_The Goliard Poets: Medieval Latin Songs and
Satires_.   Trans. George F. Whicher.   "Gay and
reprobate literature by outcast scholars."

540. "Verse."   26 (20 May 1950): 112-14, 117.

A reflection upon the differences between
nineteenth- and twentieth-century poetry, which is
"vigorous, mature, flexible, varied and open."

Robert Nathan.   _The Green Leaf_.   He has adhered to
a "Parnassian formality."   His principal emotions
are sadness and nostalgia.

e. e. cummings.   _Chaire: Seventy-one Poems_.
Addicted to the sonnet like Nathan, he has
experimented in technique and subject matter.   "He
gives up mankind as a bad job."

Alfred Hayes.   _Welcome to the Castle_.   "Stubborn
gloom and self-pity" are found in his poetry.

Peter Viereck.   _Strike Through the Mask_.   He works

from a basis of ideas without monotony.

Muriel Rukeyser. Orpheus and Elegies. She
attempts a "spiritual journey from chaos to
order."

Kenneth Rexroth. The Signature of All Things.
This is a "continuation of deeply felt variations"
on his themes.

Emma Swan. The Lion and the Lady. There is a
"sense of inevitability in everything she writes."

541. "Briefly Noted." 26 (1 July 1950): 72.

Helen Bevington. 19 Million Elephants. Her
lighthearted verse is best dealing with bygone
literary figures.

542. "Briefly Noted." 26 (22 July 1950): 74-75.

John Masefield. On the Hill. He can "wring an
eerie and primitive charm" from the simplest
ballad.

The Collected Poems of Isaac Rosenberg. Poems and
fragments by soldier killed in France in 1918.

Charles Péguy. The Mystery of Joan of Arc.
Trans. Julian Green. Also killed in the First
World War, he combines reasoning with mysticism.

William Carlos Williams. Paterson: Books 1 and 2
and Paterson Book 3. "The third volume is the
most poignant yet produced by the poet-physician."

543. "Briefly Noted." 26 (9 Sept. 1950): 124.

Christopher Smart. Poems. Ed. Robert Brittain
reprints Smart's poetry and examines his life.

Paul Valéry: Selected Writings. Republication of
his miscellanea with seventeen new works.

544. "Verse." 26 (28 Oct. 1950): 126, 129-130.

Selected Writings of Guillaume Apollinaire.

Trans. Roger Shattuck. Although he pushed
frankness to absurdity, the translations are dull.
William Van O'Connor. The Shaping Spirit: A Study
of Wallace Stevens. The first long scholarly
analysis of Steven's work to appear.

545. "Verse." 26 (4 Nov. 1950): 157-58, 161.

Marcel Raymond. From Baudelaire to Surrealism.
Most important history of French poetic thought in
America in 75 years traces its "sustained
opposition to materialism and positivism."

Lloyd Frankenberg. Pleasure Dome: On Reading
Modern Poetry. Companion volume to recordings of
modern poets "vacillates in fact and theory."

John Ciardi, ed. Mid-Century American Poets.
Subjects his poets to a thoroughly positivist
questionnaire "guaranteed to chill" wit and fancy.

546. "Briefly Noted." 26 (25 Nov. 1950): 159-160.

F. O. Matthiessen, ed. The Oxford Book of
American Verse. A large sample of "pure American
poetic gold" from Colonial times to the present.

547. "Briefly Noted." 26 (9 Dec. 1950): 172.

Ogden Nash. Family Reunion. Poems collected from
previous books about a heartwarming family.

Carl Sandburg. Complete Poems. "Pure moonshine"
in this poetic record of thirty years.

Peter Quennell, ed. The Pleasures of Pope.
Enjoyment even for heroic couplet haters.

Series devoted to poets with a particular appeal
for our day includes:

The Muses Library: Collected Poems of Sir Thomas
Wyatt. Ed. Kenneth Muir.

Collected Poems of Christopher Smart. Ed. Norman
Callan.

Selected Poems of William Barnes. Ed. Geoffrey

Grigon.

Plays and Poems of Thomas Lovell Beddoes.   Ed. H.
W. Donner.
                           1951

548. "Briefly Noted." 27 (10 Mar. 1951): 123-24.

Hugh MacDonald, ed. _England's Helicon._ Reprint
of 1600 edition as part of new series of poets
"scholarly appreciation has caught up with."

549. "Verse." 27 (9 June 1951): 109-110, 113.

Delmore Schwartz. _Vaudeville for a Princess._
There is a lack of emotion in his "extreme
burlesque methods."

James Merrill. _First Poems._ This graduate
student's poetry is "impeccably written," but it
is "frigid and dry."

Robert Lowell. _The Mills of the Kavanaughs._ His
relation to his subjects is direct and dramatic;
his writing is "compressed and morbid."

W. H. Auden. _Nones._ In this work is "a mature
simplicity of style and a new openness toward
experience."

Richard Wilbur. _Ceremony and Other Poems._ His
second volume proves "the authencity of this
remarkable lyric talent."

William Jay Smith. _Celebration of Dark._ He
"shows moments of color, simplicity, and charm."

550. "Briefly Noted." 27 (7 Jul. 1951): 67-68.

The Aeneid of Virgil: A Verse Translation by Rolfe
Humphries. The English version "brings out its
power without losing . . . its variety of mood and
tone."

Mark Van Doren. _Introduction to Poetry._ Close
analysis of theme and technique of thirty poems.

551. "Briefly Noted." 27 (20 Oct. 1951): 152.

Alan Swallow, ed. <u>Key Poets</u> <u>1-10</u>. Charmingly
designed chapbooks including <u>Poor Man's Music</u> by
Edith Sitwell, <u>True Confessions</u> by George Barker,
<u>The God in the Cave</u> by Randall Swingler, and
<u>Forgive Me, Sire</u> by Norman Cameron.

<u>Selected Poems of John Clare</u>. Ed. Geoffrey
Grigson. (repeat of Muses Library selection of
Dec. 9, 1950).

552. "Verse." 27 (3 Nov. 1951): 150-51.

Adrienne Rich. <u>A Change of World</u>. Her first book
is commended for "honesty, shape, tone, and
modesty."

Muriel Rukeyser. <u>Selected Poems</u>. She has moved
from "materialistic fields to spiritual ones."

Janet Lewis. <u>Poems 1924-1944</u>. Although her
audience is small, her work shows "rare lyric
fire."
                         1952

553. "Briefly Noted." 28 (8 Mar. 1952): 127.

Edith Sitwell, compiler. <u>A Book of the Winter</u>. A
"garland of verse and prose" from her wide
reading.

Oscar Williams, ed. <u>A Little Treasury of British
Poetry</u>. He cuts out the "underbrush," presenting
British poetry as a culmination of British
tradition.

<u>Selected Writings of Paul Eluard</u>. Trans. Lloyd
Alexander. Eluard's talent was inflated by the
Surrealistic methods he developed.

<u>Iliad of Homer</u>. Trans. Richard Lattimore.
"Strikingly modern" translation which conveys the
"speed and tone" of the Greek.

<u>The Agamemnon of Aeschylus</u>. Trans. Louis
MacNeice. The 1936 translation is "accurate and
vivid."

554. "Briefly Noted." 28 (12 Apr. 1952): 138-40.

Arthur Waley. The Poetry and Career of Li Po.
China's greatest outcast poet's life and poetry.

Walter de la Mare. Winged Chariot and Other New
Poems. The old master's craft brings to light that
"fabulous world-beyond-appearance."

Mallarmé. Poems. Trans. Roger Fry. This is the
best English introduction to the great French
symbolist.

Paul Engle. The Word of Love. "A mature and
rewarding collection" unpredicted by earlier work.

The Poems of St. John of the Cross. Trans. Roy
Campbell. A sometimes successful translation of
"ecstatic 16th century lyrics."

555. "Verse." 28 (2 Aug. 1952) 65-66.

Marianne Moore. Collected Poems. This collection
finally has gained her the official laurels she
long deserved. Her "poems are always beautifully
about something."

556. "Verse." 28 (8 Nov. 1952): 165-66, 169.

Babette Deutsch. Poetry in Our Time. Her
criticism stresses "how poetry grows out of life."
She organizes poets by their unifying qualities.

Elizabeth Sewell. The Structure of Poetry. A
study of Rimbaud, Mallarmé, and basic linguistics.

1953

557. "Verse." 28 (31 Jan. 1953): 75-75.

T. S. Eliot. The Complete Poems and Plays. The
poet who has been "modern from the beginning"
shows his sense of humor as well.

558. "Briefly Noted." 29 (7 Mar. 1953): 111-12.

The Aeneid of Virgil. Trans. C. Day-Lewis. The
radio translation loses much music and pathos.

Chaucer. The Canterbury Tales. Trans. Nevill

Coghill. He successfully transposes "Chaucer's 14
century picture into a modern framework."

Goethe's Faust, Parts I and II. Trans. Louis
MacNeice. His abridged version removes much
obscurity and he dazzles in the lyric passages.

559. "Verse." 29 (9 May 1953): 133-34, 137.

This American and this French poet share a large
vision, an eloquence and an inexhaustible
curiosity.

Kenneth Rexroth. The Dragon and the Unicorn. A
vivid long poem of a modern grand tour.

St. John Perse. Winds. Trans. Hugh Chisholm.
Long poem of the rise and fall of civilizations,
"oracular and exalted."

560. "Briefly Noted." 29 (12 Sept. 1953): 147-48.

Gerard Manley Hopkins. The Hopkins Reader. Ed.
John Pick. "An admirable and useful selection."

Archibald MacLeish. Collected Poems. Over time a
gain in theme and dramatic tension occur.

The Collected Plays of W. B. Yeats. 48 years of
widening interests and growing dramatic power.

561. "Verse." 29 (19 Sept. 1953): 113-14.

Botteghe Oscure: An International Review of
Literature. Ed. Marguerite Caetini. Magazine of
poetry and prose in three languages carries on the
standards of the little magazines of the 1920's.

Edward Bogardus. Jangling Keys. This poet in the
fifth volume of the Yale Series of Younger Poets
can "construct a poetic line."

562. "Briefly Noted." 29 (10 Oct. 1953): 159-60.

The Collected Poems of Edwin Muir: 1921-1952. He
keeps a "deceptively simple and colorless style."

The Collected Poems of Dylan Thomas. "From a
roaring boy to a master of exuberant effects."

George Williamson. A Reader's Guide to T. S.
Eliot: A Poem-by-Poem Analysis. He deals with
Eliot's "large purposes and principal methods."

563. "Verse." 29 (24 Oct. 1953): 157-58.

Robert Penn Warren. Brother to Dragons. A long
poem on frontier violence in folk speech.

Theodore Roethke. The Waking. His poems describe
his childhood by delving into his subconscious.

                          1954

564. "Verse." 30 (27 Feb. 1954): 115.

May Sarton. The Land of Silence. She "begins to
show an insight into the life of things."

565. "Briefly Noted." 30 (6 Mar. 1954): 119-120.

Gertrude Stein. Bee Time Vine and Other Pieces,
Ed. Virgil Thomson. In spite of her ability with
words, much is "trivial and tiresome."

Dylan Thomas. The Doctor and the Devils. His
last work is a film scenario of body-snatching
murders.

Rolfe Humphries, ed. New Poems by American Poets.
An anthology "with an air of freshness and
vitality" with poems the poets chose from their
own work.

566. "Briefly Noted." 30 (20 Mar. 1954): 118.

Tilbury Town: Selected Poems of Edwin Arlington
Robinson. The short New England poems "lie at the
heart of his work and show his full range."

Louis MacNeice. Ten Burnt Offerings. "Sober and
meditative poems" written in Greece.

567. "Briefly Noted." 30 (20 Mar. 1954): 119-20.

Conrad Aiken. <u>Collected Poems</u>. His "French-style
romanticism" shows over the years.
Christopher La Farge. <u>Beauty for Ashes</u>. This
novel in verse cancels out the literary effects of
both.

<u>Poems of Michael Drayton</u>. Ed. John Buxton.
A professional poet and Shakespeare's
contemporary.

Randall Jarrell. <u>Poetry and the Age</u>. Critical
essays on the importance of the poet's work.

568. "Briefly Noted." 30 (1 May 1954): 123-24.

John Masefield. <u>Poems</u>. His diction and meter are
still as "fresh and undated" as when he began.

<u>The Gypsy Ballads of García Lorca</u>. Trans. Rolfe
Humphries. The reader is aware of the power and
color of the original because of the translation.

<u>The Translations of Ezra Pound</u>. Ed. Hugh Kenner.
These translations "permanently extended the
bounds of English verse."

569. "Briefly Noted." 30 (8 May 1954): 147-48.

Osbert Sitwell. <u>Wrack at Tidesend: A Book of
Balnearies</u>. "Charmingly obsolete and unorthodox."

<u>The Collected Poems of Padriac Colum</u>. His fresh
and meaningful lyrics have not diminished.

Robinson Jeffers. <u>Hungerfield and Other Poems</u>.
He remains "unchangeably misanthropic" and
violent.

Note: The Noonday Press has published LB's
<u>Collected Poems</u>.

570. "Briefly Noted." 30 (29 May 1954): 104.

Edna St. Vincent Millay. <u>Mine the Harvest</u>. This
posthumous book's tone is "melancholy and
nostalgic."

Dylan Thomas. <u>Under Milk Wood</u>. His radio play

shows his gaiety and his skill with folk ways.

571. "Briefly Noted." 30 (12 June 1954): 120.

Babette Deutsch. _Animal, Vegetable, Mineral_.
Balanced, varied, and mature occasional poems.

572. "Briefly Noted." 30 (10 July 1954): 76.

Selected Poems of Winthrop Mackworth Praed. Praed
(1802-1839) "recorded the worldy life and manners
disdained by the Romantics."

William Carlos Williams. _The Desert Music and
Other Poems_. He "continues his meditations with a
serious, but never melancholy detachment."

573. "Briefly Noted." 30 (14 Aug. 1954): 84.

C. Day Lewis. _An Italian Visit_. His parody is
"rather hollow" in this description of an air
journey to Rome.

574. "Briefly Noted." 30 (9 Oct. 1954): 171-172.

Oliver St. John Gogarty. _Collected Poems_. The
lyrics and satires are "delightful and memorable."

Christopher Smart. _Jubilate Agno_. "Remarkable
fragmentary work" written in an insane asylum.

Tristan Corbière. _Selections from Les Amours
Jaunes_. Trans. C. F. MacIntyre. "Modern taste
has come to relish his originality."

James Stevens. _Collected Poems_. He "broke
through Georgian dullness with his wit and
lyricism."

575. "Verse." 30 (16 Oct. 1954): 158, 161.

Poets of Today. Three poets who are dissimilar in
subject, technique, and aim. Included are _Poems
and Translations_ by Harry Duncan; _Samurai and
Serpent Poems_ by Murray Noss; and _Another Animal:
Poems_ by May Swenson.

Vernon Watkins. <u>The Death Bell: Poems and Ballads</u>. He is musical in a rather traditional way with a "monotonously grand tone."

576. "Briefly Noted." 30 (6 Nov. 1954): 195-96.

<u>The Classic Anthology Defined by Confucius</u>. Trans. Ezra Pound. These fragments show Pound's translating abilities and universal folk themes.

<u>Collected Poems of Charlotte Mew</u>. This legendary Georgian produced "freshly poignant lyrics."

Marya Zaturenska. <u>Selected Poems</u>. A delicate dreamworld with a "monotonous emotional climate."

1955

577. "Briefly Noted." 30 (15 Jan. 1955): 106-7.

Rolfe Humphries. <u>Poems Collected and New</u>. "A fine lyricist" who searches for new breadth.

Archibald MacLeisch. <u>Songs for Eve</u>. "His view of modern civilization is still full of doom."

Mark Van Doren. <u>Selected Poems</u>. "Representatives of his free-floating poems."

578. "Briefly Noted." 31 (5 Mar. 1955): 120.

<u>The Collected Poems of Edith Sitwell</u>. "Much undeliberate emotion and imagination" are involved in these poems.

Millicent Todd Bingham. <u>Emily Dickinson: A Revelation</u>. Her letters written to older men outline her "extravagant attachment" to a father figure.

579. "Verse." 31 (30 Apr. 1955): 118.

Howard Nemerov. <u>The Salt Garden</u>. He has a "concise and orderly" way of putting experience into form.

Elder Olsen. <u>The Scarecrow Christ</u>. He has "moments of terror and horror" in his formal lyrics.

Ben Belitt. <u>Wilderness Stair: Poems 1938-1954</u>.
These Impressionist poems make demands on the
reader.

580. "Briefly Noted." 31 (14 May 1955): 180.

Randall Jarrell. <u>Selected Poems</u>. His war poems
"continue to have more impact than his other
work."

Roy Campbell. <u>Selected Poems</u>. His "tendency to
tirade" obscures his ability to produce lyrics.

581. "Verse." 31 (30 July 1955): 63-64.

Marianne Moore. <u>Predilections</u>. Her prose
collection shows her talent for miscellany.

Ovid. <u>Metamorphoses</u>. Trans. Rolfe Humphries.
Humphries uses the "natural phrase and telling
idiom" in this translation of the world of Ovid.

Robert Graves. <u>Collected Poems</u>. He has "pruned
his total poetic output" to these timeless poems.

Ruthven Todd. <u>A Masterpiece of Shells</u>. Natural
forms observed with a naturalist's eye.

Constance Carrier. <u>The Middle Voice</u>. She has
observed her countryside precisely.

582. "Verse." 31 (8 Oct. 1955): 179.

Elizabeth Bishop. <u>Poems</u>. "Her powers of
description are astonishing."

Adrienne Rich. <u>The Diamond Cutters</u>. Her poems
are "most compressed, demanding, and subtle."

583. "Briefly Noted." 31 (15 Oct. 1955): 196.

Baudelaire. <u>The Flowers of Evil</u>. Ed. Marthiel
and Jackson Mathews. A "remarkable
reconstitution" of one of the greatest poetic
works with various translators.

584. "Briefly Noted." 31 (14 Jan. 1956): 112.

The Selected Poems of Federico García Lorca. Ed.
Donald M. Allen and Francisco García Lorca. The
English versions bring out the contrast and color.
Federico García Lorca. Poet in New York. Trans.
Ben Belitt. These poems show his break from
allegiance to Flamenco tradition and surrealism.

1956

585. "Briefly Noted." 32 (31 Mar. 1956): 111-12.

Thomas H. Johnson. Emily Dickinson: An
Interpretive Biography. "A good many enigmas
[about Dickinson] disappear" in this book..

C. M. Bowra. Inspiration and Poetry. These
studies "illustrate workings of the creative
imagination."

The Complete Poetical Works of Amy Lowell. She
had an "indomitable will, amazing energy," and "a
talent that never exceeded the bounds of the
mediocre."

586. "Briefly Noted." 32 (14 Apr. 1936): 176.

Rolfe Humphries. Green Armor on Green Ground:
Poems in the Twenty-four Official Welsh Meters and
Some in Free Meters, on Welsh Themes. Musical,
subtle, varied intricacies of ancient bardic form.

587. "Briefly Noted." 32 (9 June 1956): 143-44.

Walter de la Mare. Lovely England and Other
Poems. His "old evocative themes of sleep, death,
and the eerie regions" remain "touched with
sorcery."

588. "Briefly Noted." 32 (9 June 1956): 144.

Witter Brynner. Book of Lyrics. Many poems are
"untouched by the passage of time."

589. "Briefly Noted." 32 (17 Nov. 1956): 243-44.
Anne Marrow Lindbergh. The Unicorn and Other

Poems. Brief, simple, and sincere lyrics.

John Hall Wheelock. Poems Old and New. "A steady
progress towards a kind of tragic severity."

Albert B. Friedman, ed. The Viking Book of Folk
Ballads of the English-Speaking World. A
compilation starting where Child's left off.

1957

590. "Verse." 33 (2 Mar. 1957): 111-12.

Little presses discussion. The multiplication of
little presses shows twentieth-century poetry is
not static.

John Berryman. Homage to Mistress Bradstreet.
His language and rhythms are sometimes close to
Hopkins, and sometimes original in this portrait
of a Colonial poetess.

Marianne Moore. Like a Bulwark. Variations on
theme of courage linked to excellence in nature.

W. S. Merwin. Green with Beasts. He is starting
to work in "larger, freer, dramatic forms."

Peter Viereck. The Persimmon Tree. He "bears
down hard on metre and rhyme in his lyrics."

591. "Briefly Noted." 33 (4 May 1957): 167-68.

Selected Writings of Jules Laforgue. Trans.
William Jay Smith. Smith maintains the "speed and
freshness of the original."

502. "Briefly Noted." 33 (8 June 1957): 144.

Aristophanes: The Birds. Trans. Dudley Fitts. He
has kept the lyrics smooth, the comedy rough.

593. "Verse." 33 (14 Sept. 1957): 170, 173-75.

A discussion of the new lyric poets who are
avoiding intellectual and flattened out poems.

New World Writing. A group of lyric poems showing

a great range of subjects and style.

James Wright. <u>The Green Wall</u>. The most recent
volume in Yale Series of Younger Poets draws on
contemporary ideas in thought and action.

Philip Booth. <u>Letter from a Distant Land</u>. His
natural scenes are "untouched by machines or
cities."

<u>Poets of Today, Vol. IV</u>. Three books in one
volume including George Garrett's <u>The Reverend
Ghost</u>, Robert Wallace's <u>The Various World</u>, and
Theodore Holmes' long line of poetry.

594. "Briefly Noted." 33 (2 Nov. 1957): 199-200.

Vivian de Sola Pinto and Allan Edwin Ordway, eds.
<u>The Common Muse: An Anthology of Popular British
Ballad Poetry, 15th-20th Centuries</u>. A scholarly
collection of songs and broadsides.

1958

595. "Briefly Noted." 34 (22 Mar. 1958): 156.

May Sarton. <u>In Time Like Air</u>. She does not
subject her poetry to the "usual crucial
tensions."

John Updike. <u>The Carpentered Hen</u>. Note only that
book has been published by Harper.

596. "Briefly Noted." 34 (16 Apr. 1958): 96.

Ted Hughes. <u>The Hawk in the Rain</u>. He is given to
"terror and anguish that sometimes get out of
hand."

597. "Briefly Noted." 34 (16 Aug. 1958): 96.

Archibald MacLeish. <u>J.B. A Play in Verse</u>. Modern
version of Job story.

598. "Verse." 34 (6 Dec. 1958): 238.

Mary Phelps. <u>A Bed of Strawberries</u>. First book

announces an original feminist lyricist.

599. "Briefly Noted." 34 (20 Dec. 1958): 120.

e. e. cummings. 95 Poems. His "sentiment flows
more broadly" in typographically puzzling poems.

William Carlos Williams. Paterson: Book Five.
"He has not lost his knack of observing objects."

600. "Briefly Noted." 34 (7 Feb. 1959): 144.

Nikos Kazantzakis. The Odyssey: A Modern Sequel.
Trans. Kimon Friar. These "scenes have more
relation to Jules Verne than to Homer."

601. "Briefly Noted." 35 (21 Mar. 1959): 178-80.

Donagh MacDonagh and Lennox Robinson, eds. The
Oxford Book of Irish Verse, 17th-20th Centuries.
They present the Irish voice in its many
"inflections."

Edith Sitwell, ed. The Atlantic Book of British
and American Poetry. She selects poems that give
her pleasure and she ignores structure.

St. John Perse. Seamarks. Trans. Wallace Fowlie.
This is a celebration of the sea in a long prose
poem that cannot be reproduced in English.

Ezra Pound. Pavannes and Divagations. A
"gathering of Pound's lighter writings."

602. "Briefly Noted." 35 (27 June 1959): 96.

T. S. Eliot. The Elder Statesman: A Play. Ed.
John Hayward. The play "depends on simple
structure and speech," revealing human qualities.

603. "Briefly Noted." 35 (119 Sept. 1958): 196.

Kings, Lords, and Commons. Trans. Frank O'Connor.
"Fine and moving translations" of Gaelic poems.

604. "Verse." 36 (8 Oct. 1960): 197.

George W. Nitchie. <u>Human Values in the Poetry of
Robert Frost</u>. He "emphasizes the more neglected
aspects . . . of this exceedingly complex artist."

Elizabeth Shepley Sergeant. <u>Robert Frost: The
Trial by Existence</u>. A sympathetic biography of
"affectionate impressionism" with darker aspects.

605. "Briefly Noted." 36 (29 Oct. 1960): 187-88

<u>The Poems of Edward Taylor</u>. Ed. Donald E.
Stanford. Contains details of Taylor's life and
shows his use of elaborate forms in his poems.

Ezra Pound. <u>96-109 De Los Cantares</u>. "His chief
concern continues to be money's use and misuse."

606. "Briefly Noted." 36 (14 Jan. 1961): 120.

Rainer Maria Rilke. <u>Selected Works, Vol. II</u>.
Trans. J. B. Leishman. "His difficult German
verse is translated into comprehensible graceful
English."

607. "Briefly Noted." 37 (25 Feb. 1961): 135-36.

A. J. M. Smith, ed. <u>Oxford Book of Canadian
Verse</u>. The first anthology with French and
English poems side by side with modern poetic
idiom in both.

<u>Swinburne: A Selection</u>. Compiler, Edith Sitwell.
"Swinburne's poetry remains fixed in its time."

608. "Briefly Noted." 37 (20 May 1961): 168.

<u>Homer: The Odyssey</u>. Trans. Robert Fitzgerald.
"The semi-incantatory quality" is restored.

                          1962

609. "Verse." 38 (24 Mar. 1962): 175-76.

X. J. Kennedy. <u>Nude Descending a Staircase</u>. His
first book shows he can "hit important targets."

Peter Viereck. <u>The Tree Witch</u>. His poem and play
are "examples of failed satire."

610. "Briefly Noted." 38 (14 Apr. 1962): 188.

John Hall Wheelock. <u>The Gardener and Other Poems</u>.
The 50th anniversary volume shows he has not
deviated in his approach to life and art.

611. "Verse." 38 (17 Nov. 1962): 242, 244.

Robert Frost. <u>In the Clearing</u>. Published on
Frost's 88 birthday, the collection is very
direct, formal, nice, and "is written in
American."

                        1963

612. "Briefly Noted." 38 (26 Jan. 1963): 124.

<u>Love Poems of Ancient Egypt</u>. Trans. Ezra Pound
and Noel Stock. "A delightful picture of
youthfully disorganized emotion" in ancient times.

613. "Briefly Noted." 38 (9 Feb. 1963): 148.

<u>Yevtushenko: Selected Poems</u>. Trans. Robin Milner-
Guilland and Peter Levi. This translation allows
vigorous emotions to come through.

614. "Briefly Noted." 39 (6 July 1963): 76.

Paul Engle and Joseph Langland, eds. <u>Poet's
Choice</u>. 103 poets choose their own poems for
anthology, making delightful reading. (Entry 696)

615. "Briefly Noted." 39 (23 Nov. 1963): 248.

William Cole, ed. <u>Erotic Poetry: The Lyrics,
Ballads, Idyls and Epics of Love: Classical to
Contemporary</u>. Most of the poems have literary
merit.

616. "Briefly Noted." 39 (121 Dec. 1963): 96.

Monroe Spears. <u>The Poetry of W. H. Auden: The
Disenchanted Island</u>. Spears attempts to describe
the diverse elements of the "most complex and
audacious poet" writing in English today.

1964

617. "Verse."   40 (11 Apr. 1964): 180-81.

Vernon Watkins. <u>Affinities</u>. "He never deviates
from a tone of high seriousness."

Edith Sitwell. <u>Music and Ceremonies</u>. The book
concentrates on her "phantasmagoric symbols."

618. "Briefly Noted." 40 (25 Apr. 1964): 208

John Malcolm Brinnin and Bill Reid. <u>The Modern
Poets: An American-British Anthology</u>. Poems,
pictures of, and notes by 82 modern poets.

619. "Briefly Noted." 40 (23 May 1964): 188.

<u>The Collected Poems of Wilfred Owen</u>. Ed. C. Day-
Lewis. "Greatest war poems in our literature."

620. "Briefly Noted." 40 (3 Oct. 1964): 227-28.

John Hayward, ed. <u>Oxford Book of Nineteenth
Century English Verse</u>. "Great Romantics and
Victorians are properly side by side."

621. "Verse."   40 (7 Nov. 1964):   243.

Theodore Roethke. <u>The Far Field</u>. "A final moving
contribution to the high metaphysical tradition."

William Meredith. <u>The Wreck of the Thresher</u>. "He
deals imaginatively with reality" and has style.

J. V. Cunningham. <u>To What Strangers, What
Welcome</u>. Account of a transcontinental journey.

Ben Belitt. <u>The Enemy Joy</u>. "This should be read
slowly to savor its crowded, authentic detail."

Robert Seward. <u>Kissing the Dancer</u>. "A complete lack of current cliche."

622. "Briefly Noted." 41 (13 Mar. 1965): 204.

<u>The Complete Poems of D. H. Lawrence</u>. Ed. Vivian de Sola Pinto and F. Warren Roberts. All of Lawrence's poetic successes and failures are included.

623. "Briefly Noted." 41 (4 Sept. 1965): 108.

W. H. Auden. <u>About the House</u>. "There is nothing quite like [this book] in English verse annals."

624. "Briefly Noted." 42 (5 Mar. 1966): 159.

Ezra Pound. <u>A Lume Spento and Other Early Poems</u>. These derivative efforts were disowned by Pound.

625. "Briefly Noted." 42 (12 Mar. 1966): 179-80.

John Clare. <u>The Shepherd's Calender</u>. Eds. Eric Robinson and Geoffrey Summerfield. The restored original text may be the "truest poem of country life."

626. "Briefly Noted." 42 (2 Apr. 1966): 176.

W. H. Auden, ed. <u>Nineteenth Century British Minor Poets</u>. A "remarkably readable anthology."

627. "Briefly Noted." 42 (24 Sept. 1966): 239-40.

<u>The Collected Poems of Theodore Roethke</u>. This "traces [the] poet's progress in technique and spiritual illumination."

Andrei Voznesensky. <u>Antiworlds</u>. Eds. Patricia Blake and Max Hayward. A reproduction of Russian poems by America's most brilliant lyric talents.

628. "Briefly Noted." 42 (3 Dec. 1966): 248.

Avrahm Yarmolinsky, ed. Two Centuries of Russian
Verse: An Anthology from Lomonosovto to
Voznesensky. Trans. Babette Deutsch. The
translations bring out "Russian nostalgia and
sweetness."

1967

629. "Verse." 43 (4 Mar. 1967): 161-62.

Rolfe Humphries. Collected Poems. He has
received little critical notice for his work.

Barbara Howes. Looking Up at Leaves. She still
"writes occasional poetry affirmatively."

George Starbuck. White Paper. He brings the
"underside of . . . life to brilliant
illumination.

The William Carlos Williams Reader. Ed. M. L
Rosenthal. A balanced sampling of prose and verse
by one who has "a perfect ear" and "is alert."

William Jay Smith. The Tin Can and Other Poems.
He recognizes tough reality and laughs at
machines.

Lawrence Thompson. Robert Frost: The Early Years.
Frost's unhappy childhood and youth.

Holly Stevens, ed. Letters of Wallace Stevens.
His idiosyncrasies and curious nature are shown.

630. "Briefly Noted." 43 (20 May 1967): 180.

James Dickey. Poems 1957-67. "A number of
[these] poems appeared originally in The New
Yorker."

631. "Briefly Noted." 43 (29 Jul. 1967): 84.

John MacQueen and Tom Scott, eds. The Oxford Book
of Scottish Verse. A full and neat compilation in
spite of language problems.

632. "Briefly Noted." 43 (2 Sept. 1967): 87-88.

John Betjeman. <u>High and Low</u>. "Many of his
pieties seem rather baffling to Americans."

T. S. Eliot. <u>Poems Written in Early Youth</u>. A
"handful of juvenilia [which] adds little
interest."

1968

633. "Verse." 44 (30 Mar. 1968): 133-38.

<u>Sixty Poems of Martial</u>. Trans. Dudley Fitts.
"Short biting epigrams" in free translation.

Hugh MacDiarmid. <u>The Company I Keep</u>. "Evidences
of a life lived almost entirely as an
exhibitionist."

Elizabeth Salter. <u>The Last Years of A Rebel: A
Memoir of Edith Sitwell</u>. A sad and terrifying
account of Dame Edith's "obsessive
preoccupations."

Michael Reck. <u>Ezra Pound: A Close-up</u>. An account
of Pound's incarceration and return to Italy.

Forrest Read, ed. <u>Pound/Joyce: The Letters of
Ezra Pound to James Joyce, with Pound's Essays on
Joyce</u>. Two men make up the "mutual magic" that
"changed English for good."

Noel Stock. <u>Reading the Cantos: The Study of
Meaning in Ezra Pound</u>. Stock takes a
"straightforward and irreverent approach" to
Pound.

Richard Ellman. <u>Eminent Domain: Yeats Among
Wilde, Joyce, Pound, Eliot, and Auden</u>. Ellman
assigns Yeats' influence among his contemporaries.

<u>The Odyssey of Homer</u>. Trans. Richmond Lattimore.
"The most accurate verse translations" written in
English with intelligent comments.

Nelly Sachs. <u>O the Chimney</u>. "Mercy and goodness
remain" in the symbol of heaven's presence.

Christian Morgenstern. <u>Gallows Songs</u>. Trans. W.
D. Snodgrass and Lore Segal. They have faced up
well to an almost "impossible task of
translation."

William Cole, ed. <u>Eight Lines and Under: An Anthology of Short, Short Poems</u>. "Charmingly arranged and faultlessly selected."

<u>The Complete Poems of Marianne Moore</u>. The poems are arranged in rough chronological order with a "few retouches."

W. H. Auden. <u>Shorter Collected Poems 1927-1957</u>. Like Marianne Moore, Auden is a "conscious and diligent maker of poetry."

Ted Hughes. <u>Wodwo</u>. He "advances farther into the regions of the monstrous."

Alan Dugan. <u>Poems 3</u>. "Centrally black poems lit up now and then with a glimmer of myth."

John Berryman. <u>Short Poems</u> and <u>Berryman's Sonnets</u>. His Petrarchan sonnets show the "irritating virtuosity" of his later work.

Anthony Hecht. <u>The Hard Hours</u>. Baroque characteristics express "color and profusion."

Jean Garrigue. <u>New and Selected Poems</u>. Baroque characteristics "call up joy and release."

634. "Verse." 44 (28 Dec. 1968): 62-63.

Robert Gittings. <u>John Keats</u>. With Keats' death the ode went out of English poetry.

W. D. Snodgrass. <u>After Experience</u>. He returns to form with natural and unnatural horrors.

W. S. Merwin. <u>The Lice</u>. "His adherence to the nonlogical now makes even his titles opaque."

Galway Kinnell. <u>Body Rags</u>. Journeys back through time are described in "shattered statements."

Ralph Pomeroy. <u>In the Financial District</u>. "It is a pleasure to recognize" his lyrics' components.

Ned O'Gorman. <u>The Harvester's Vase</u>. His ground of religious belief is "rich and elaborate."

Thomas Kinsella. <u>Nightwalker and Other Poems</u>. A distinctive Irish poet with "all-round skill."

C. CRITICAL REVIEWS NOT IN THE NEW YORKER

This section lists in chronological order book, movie, and play reviews from sources other than The New Yorker that were not published in Selected Criticism nor A Poet's Alphabet. Information on later reprintings is also included.

1924

635. "Water Running Up Hill." Measure 46 (Dec. 1924): 17-18. Review of The Sleeping Beauty by Edith Sitwell.

Sitwell's fairy-tale, unlike the children's story, is "encased from the world's accidents and consequences very rigidly." Her characters are poppets in a painted landscape of "clowns, carrousel animals and clever clockwork birds" where the princess sleeps on forever. For a moment a human voice cries for lost innocence, but at the end everything is forgotten. She has "protected us for a little from reality."

1925

636. "Viola Meynell." Saturday Review of Literature 1 (25 Apr, 1925): 703. Review of Young Mrs. Cruise by Viola Meynell. Revised and reprinted in Literary Opinion in America, ed. Morton Zabel. New York: Harper, 1937, pp. 1390-96

The stories in this collection show Miss Meynell's ability to get below the surface of peoples' lives and to present reality. She observes her characters closely and describes their passions "with complete simplicity."

637. "The Espalier." New Republic 47 (18 Aug. 1926): 371. Review of The Espalier by Sylvia Townsend Warner.

In spite of their echoes of Hardy and de la Mare,
Warner's poems surpass those of other English
women poets. Her ballads are the most beautiful.
"That note of hale unselfish bawdy of the old
wives' tradition sounds whereat . . . women should
more often excel."

1927

638. "True to the Medium." New Republic 52 (26
     Oct. 1927): 263-64. Review of movies
     Sunrise, directed by Murnau; Underworld,
     directed by Joseph von Sternberg; and The Cat
     and the Canary, directed by Paul Leni.

Each director uses his camera technique well.
Murnau places the action in his film against other
movement, making "motion-beside-within motion" in
the story of a young peasant who plans to murder
his wife to join the woman from the city. Von
Sternberg devises four flashes of action to
signify a jewelry story robbery. "Grim lighting
and sinister composition" comprise Leni's
invention in this tale of horror.

639. "Louise Imogen Guiney." New Republic 53 (14
     Dec. 1927): 113. Review of The Letters of
     Louise Imogen Guiney and Happy Ending: The
     Collected Poems of Louise Imogen Guiney.

Worn-out New England genteel traditions and Old
Oxford, England, gave Guiney her inspiration. Her
poetic temperament came from the memory of her
father killed in the United States Civil War, and
her Roman Catholic religion. Her poems are "made
up of seemly abstinences," but "for a poet,
negative choosing is not enough."

1928

640. "Artists and Models: Through the
     Stereoscope." New Republic 54 (11 Apr.
     1928): 246-47. Play Review by Louise Bogan
     and Rolfe Humphries.

In adjacent columns the reviewers satirize two
different types of threater reviews of the musical
comedy, Artists and Models. Bogan ridicules
reviews which emphasize sensuous qualities in her
half of the stereoscope, "Left Eye: The Senses."

Humphries makes fun of learned reviewers in his
half, "Right Eye: The Intellect." Bogan describes
the semi-naked "satin girls," the raucous
comedienne, and the "so-called clockwork
creature: twenty girls in line . . . engagingly
mechanical flesh and blood."

641. "Viola Meynell." New Republic 55 (27 June
     1928): 151. Review of A Girl Adoring by
     Viola Meynell. Revised and reprinted in
     Literary Opinion in America. Ed. Morton
     Zabel. New York: Harper, 1937. pp. 390-96.

Her novels and stories revolve around heroines who
are childlike women struck by passion. The main
characters who are involved in various stages of
love affairs are set apart as seemingly real
people. Her prose style is quiet and natural. She
tells the simplest story with "explicitness and
tragedy."

642. "Wrong Reasons." New Republic 55 (8 Aug.
     1928): 311. Review of Armed with Madness by
     Mary Butts.

This book concerns the unbelievable doings of a
group of youths, of "indeterminate sex, adept at
torturing themselves and others" (including the
reader). The style "leans hard on a modern
metonymy" and the book is "off-key in every
possible way."

                        1929

643. "Mary Webb." New Republic 59 (14 Apr. 1929):
     348. Review of The House in Dormer Forest,
     Seven for a Secret, and Poems and the Spring
     of Joy.

Her novels, with traditional rural English
characters and scenes, succeed in their narrative
style and fail in their approach to nature. This
defect is not so apparent in her poetry.

644. "Hildegard Flanner." New Republic 60
     (18 Sept. 1929): 130. Review of Times
     Profile by Hildegard Flanner.

"Miss Flanner's maturity as a craftsman [is] far
from complete in this her second book of poetry."

645. "Lizette Woodworth Reese." New Republic 60
     (6 Nov. 1929): 327. Review of A Victorian
     Village by Lizette Woodworth Reese.

The culture of the Victorian village outside of
Baltimore, now extinct, where Miss Reese grew up,
influenced the "delicate firmness, the fragility
and fragrance of her poetry."

646. "New England and Virginian Ladies." New
     Republic 61 (4 Dec. 1929): 50-51.   Review of
     They Stooped to Folly by Ellen Glasgow and
     Short as Any Dream by Elizabeth Shepley
     Sergeant.

Miss Glasgow's superficial novel about unfortunate
Southern love affairs fails because the ladies in
the book remain figurines. "Miss Sergeant's fault
is to distort her scene with sentiment when she
discusses the New England past."

647. "Virginia Woolf on Women." New Republic 61
     (18 Dec. 1929): 105. Review of A Room of
     One's Own by Virginia Woolf.

In respect to Woolf's argument for women taking
their destiny in their own hands, Bogan suggests
women should stop envying and disliking their
female counterparts, stop imitating their male
counterparts, and make use of their "androgynous"
minds. "Such minds do not lean too hard upon arid
intellectual processes, but have the leaven of
feminine wit and (invidious term!) intuition
within them."

                         1930

648. "Fantasy and Obsession." New Republic 62
     (26 Feb. 1930): 52-53. Review of Harriet
     Hume by Rebecca West and A Night Among the
     Horses by Djuna Barnes.

The two chief characters, Harriet Hume and Arnold
Condorex, in Miss West's fantasy are "automatons
produced by joinery of a high order." Her chief

excellence . . . lies in her style of writing."
The stories in Miss Barnes' book deal with the
same obsessive characters and themes, and her
style has the "precision of good French prose."

649. "Ann Hutchinson." New Republic 62
     (9 April 1930): 223. Review of Unafraid: A
     Life of Anne Hutchinson by Winifred King Rugg
     and An American Jezebel by Helen Augur.

A biography of Hutchinson takes up most of the
review. Bogan states "Miss Augur and Miss Rugg
have not attempted a psychological interpretation
. . . . They have set her in her time and given
her sympathy. Miss Rugg has written
comprehensively of Hutchinson's English life and
Miss Augur of her American years."

650. "Tolstoy's Wife." New Republic 63
     (2 July 1930): 187. Review of The Diary of
     Tolstoy's Wife, 1860-61 and The Countess
     Tolstoy's Later Diary 1891-97, both
     translated by Alexander Werth.

These diaries relate thirty-five years of marriage
to a genuis and fanatic. They are a "record of
pathetic human inadequacy before the demands of
the ideal." In the early years of their marriage,
the bourgeois Sofie Angreyevna managed the family
and her amanuensis tasks, but Tolstoy's religious
conversion turned her into a woman who cared
little for life.

1931

651. "Tilbury Town and Beyond." Poetry 37, No 4
     (Jan 1931): 216-21. Review of Collected
     Poems of Edwin Arlington Robinson and The
     Glory of the Nightingales by Robinson.

Robinson's background as a New England Yankee
explains his poetry which describes small town
"failures, dreamers and do-nothings" with wit.
His early volumes collected in the first book
present the conflict between townspeople and these
pariahs. Even the lovers are touched with an
"emotional paralysis." In the later work he sees
the same themes in New York City, which "casts out
its thinkers in much the same way as had the small

. . . town." His Arthurian poems and the non-
legendary narratives of his later period are "a
distinct lapse in power."

1932

652. "Allen Tate's New Poems." New Republic 70
     (30 March 1932): 186-87. Review of Poems:
     1928-1931.

His new poems are sometimes unsuccessful, because
of his "long and determined attack on his own
poetic equipment." His early membership in the
Fugitive group fostered in him a confusion of
poetic processes and logical processes. The new
successful poems in contrast "have a solidarity
. . . and even in some cases, a kind of
magnificence."

653. "Viola Meynell." Poetry 40, No. 4 (July
     1932): 226-29. Review of The Frozen Ocean by
     Viola Meynell. Revised and reprinted in
     Literary Opinion in America, ed. Morton
     Zabel. New York: Harper, 1937. pp. 390-96.

Her poetry, like her novels, is limited in scope
to the contemplative, "the most neglected field
wherein women have exercised their emotional and
intellectual capacities." Her love poems,
especially "The Maid in the Rice-fields" quoted in
full, are "elaborate in conceit, frugal in form,
and candid as thoughtful speech."

1933

654. "The Shadow of the Laureateship." Poetry 41
     No. 6 (Mar. 1933): 332-35. Review of A Tale
     of Troy by John Masefield.

Masefield did not need "time-honored theme and
traditional heroic figures" in his early poetry.
His strengths lie in storytelling and ballads.
This book on legendary material seems to have been
influenced by Masefield's laureateship and by the
contests in verse speaking he initiated at Oxford.
He should return to his earlier world.

655. "Sara Teasdale's Last Poems." New Republic
     77 (15 Nov. 1933): 25. Review of Strange

<u>Victory</u> by Sara Teasdale.

This review of Teasdale's last twenty-two
published poems gives Bogan an opportunity to
define lyric poetry and lament the lack of a
contemporary audience for it. These poems are
"the final expression of a purely lyrical talent
and of a poetic career remarkable for its
integrity throughout."

1934

656. "True Flight." <u>Poetry</u> 44 (June 1934):
      159-62. Review of <u>Blossoming Antlers</u> by
      Winifred Welles.

Her fancy, "the delicate incandescence of aspect,"
places her poems alongside those of John Clare.
Her poem, "Immaculate Task," is quoted in full as
an example of Welles' "certain and pure talent."

1935

657. "Conversion into Self." <u>Poetry</u> 45, No. 5
      (Feb. 1935): 277-79. Review of <u>Wine from
      These Grapes</u> by Edna St. Vincent Millay.

"Edna Millay at last gives evidence that she
recognizes and is prepared to meet the task of
becoming a mature and self-suffering woman and
artist." Many of her previous poems were "based
on the immature impulse to experience beyond
limits of experience," but the poems in this book
show her ability to express herself within her own
frame of reference without becoming embroiled in
the turmoils of new political or social orders.

658. "For Garrets and Cellars." <u>Poetry</u> 46, No. 2
      (May 1935): 100-4. Review of <u>Wheels and
      Butterflies</u> by William Butler Yeats.

Yeats' signs for wisdom are the butterfly and his
wheel of Time and Destiny. The four plays include
<u>The Words Upon the Window-pane</u>, a prose play in a
Dublin lodging house in which a seance brings
together Swift and Vanessa; <u>Fighting the Waves</u>,
<u>Resurrection</u>, and <u>The Cat and the Moon</u>, which are
poetic plays "written with the utmost severity and
restraint."

659. "Lyric Prophet." New Republic 83 (10 July
     1935): 258. Review of Dance of Fire by Lola
     Ridge.

Her poetry has retained its original "zeal for
social justice," while it has increased in
technical power. Her "endowment is of the sort to
celebrate the noblest and the bravest, and to cast
on them some reflection from her inner symbolic
fire."

660. "Action and Charity." The New Republic 85
     (27 Nov. 1935): 79. Review of The Dog
     Beneath the Skin or, Where Is Francis? a play
     by W. H. Auden and Christopher Isherwood.

Auden's satire on the English upper class succeeds
in its aim to "give humanity in general a hard and
unprejudiced stare." The hero and his dog
progress through the symptomatic institutions of a
debased and lunatic society in search of Sir
Francis Crewe. Auden's "poetic endowment . . . is
gaining in power and scope."

                        1936

661. "The Poet Dickinson." Poetry 48, No. 3
     (June 1936): 162-66. Review of Unpublished
     Poems by Emily Dickinson. Ed. Martha
     Dickinson Bianchi and Alfred Lute Hampson.

"We lack histories . . . of [Dickinson's] form,
language and spiritual development" as well as an
understanding of the great upheavals in her life,
all of which influenced her work. It is
impossible to know from this collection which
poems, including the "imaginative-intellectual
flights that reach as far as lyric poetry has ever
reached," and "the poems with the sentiment and
archness of a child" were written at which periods
in her life.

                        1937

662. "Dead Sea." New Republic 91 (14 June 1937):
     285-86. Review of The Wheel Turns by Gian
     Davli.

Davli's novel, set in Italy at the beginning of
the twentieth century, describes "the

interrelationship of a violent people and the
constriction put upon them by pre-war petty
bourgeois society." Its hero, Giovannino,
deteriorates throughout the novel, becoming a
beggar in the end, illustrating "the impact of an
imperfect society on the imperfect human beings
who inhabit it."

663. "Imitate Him If You Dare." Nation 145
      (28 Aug. 1937): 223-24. Review of Jonathan
      Swift by Bertram Newman.

This professional biography deals sympathetically
with Swift's life, especially his political and
religious careers and his final illness. Newman
"brings out . . . both the native qualitites of
Swift's mind and the coloring it took from his
age." He describes Swift's neurotic dependency on
Stella, his hatred and obsessions, as well as his
humor and generosity, all in superb prose.

664. "Miss Pedder's Governess." Nation 145
      (25 Sept. 1937): 324-25. Review of Miss
      Weeton: Journal of a Governess.

Miss Weeton's journals record a peculiar
transitional period in English life. At this time
"an inarticulate and grisly section of English
society, the Northern lower middle class and the
argriculture [society were] just beginning to pass
over into the industrial." She describes their
"penury, violence, avarice, spleen, class-
consciousness . . . provincial alcoholism,
boredom, and lust."

                         1938

665. "Revolution in Wonderland." Nation 146
      (29 Jan. 1938): 129-30. Review of The Wild
      Goose Chase and Poems by Rex Warner.

Compared to Swift and Kafka, Warner's allegory of
Marxist revolution in The Wild Goose Chase fails
utterly. His Poems is better than his prose.

666. "Padded Shelves." Nation 146 (18 June 1938):
      703-4. Review of House of All Nations by
      Christina Stead.

"She has given the freest possible rein to her thoroughly self-believed-in-gifts" in this long unbelievable book of international finance.

667. "Life of St. Patrick." Nation 147
     (24 Sept. 1938): 303. Review of I Follow
     Saint Patrick by Oliver St. John Gogarty.

His life of St. Patrick emphasizes the influence of Roman Christianity's spiritual values on the character and manners of the Irish.

668. "Brave Immortal Dan." Nation 147
     (12 Nov. 1938): 512-513. Review of King of
     the Beggars: Daniel O'Connell and the Rise of
     Irish Democracy by Sean O'Faolain.

This fine modern biography presents O'Connell as a complete man, showing his corrupt political side as well as his heroic side. It gives the actual shocking facts instead of the false romance of Irish history.

1939

669. "Rilke Literally." New Republic 98
     (22 Feb. 1939): 78, 80. Review of
     Translations from the Poetry of Rainer Maria
     Rilke. Trans. M. D. Herder Norton.

This is a literal translation of the poems without any regard for their forms. The German original is printed opposite the translation. Many poems are missing, particularly the late lyrics. Bogan discusses Rilke's "condition of being entirely alone, his early romanticism and later repudiation of idealistic romanticism." She berates scholarly attempts to elucidate and systematize the ideas in Rilke's work because "the poetic quality is the only true worth."

670. "Memoir of D. H. Lawrence." Nation 149
     (5 Aug. 1939): 153-54. Review of A Poet and
     Two Painters: A Memoir of D. H. Lawrence by
     Knud Merrild.

The Danish author, who is a painter, tells the story of a winter on the Del Monte Farm with the

Lawrences. "Lawrence emerges from the pages a tortured man, a genuine and warm friend, and an almost completely self-deceived, dependent, childishly neurotic human being."

671. "Professor Versus Poet." Nation 149 (7 Oct. 1939): 392-93. Review of D. H. Lawrence and Susan His Cow by William York Tindall.

The author, who is a professor, has treated Lawrence only as a novelist and prophet, omitting his poetry and damning his private religion, the female element symbolized by the cow. Tindall's scholarly book leaves out anything that would contradict his points and his tone is mocking. He also ignores Lawrence's complexity.

1940

672. "The Defense of Belles-Lettres." Nation 150 (13 Apr. 1940): 480-81. Review of the new publication Horizon edited by Stephen Spender and Cyril Connolly.

"Can a review dedicated to disinterested comment upon literature and life . . . survive or are the guilt-fear-hatred holders of the last decade still too unresolved to allow its survival?" Publication of this review and Cyril Connolly's Enemies of Promise may herald the return of the artist as a "brave fighter, sensitive thinker and good workman . . . ."

673. "Guidebook to World Literature." Nation 150 (18 May 1940): 631-32. Review of Preface to World Literature by Albert Guerard.

This middle-class textbook is an introduction to the "best which has been thought and said" in the world. It breaks no fresh ground, but is "served forth with good sense and good nature."

674. "A Note on Jean Sans Terre." Partisan Review 7, No. 4 (July/Aug. 1940): 294-95. Review of Jean Sans Terre by Ivan Goll.

"An actual Romantic spirit and feeling reappears" after the terrors of the Gothic and Surrealistic

periods in this poetry. Nature and emotion
return. Man is free. Jean Sans Terre is the new
romantic hero who has modern adventures in the
modern city in this modern epic.

675. "Exile and Cunning." <u>Partisan Review</u> 7,
      No. 4 (July/Aug. 1940): 318-320. Review of
      <u>James Joyce: His First Forty Years</u>, by
      Herbert S. Gorman.

This biography explores undiscovered sides of
Joyce, even though Gorman's naivete does not allow
him to draw conclusions from his findings.
Joyce's battles with British and Irish publishers,
as well as English and American censors, are the
most valuable parts of the book. Bogan compares
Joyce and Yeats in their contempt for town-
Irishmen. Unlike Yeats, Joyce never succeeded
cutting his ties with Dublin, even in exile. In
his <u>Ulysses</u>, Dublin becomes the Mediterranean, the
known world of the ancients. In <u>Finnegan's Wake</u>
"Dublin is the point from which the circumference
springs and to which it returns."

                        1941

676. "The Abstract Bicycle." <u>Nation</u> 153
      (12 Jul. 1941): 37. Review of <u>The New</u>
      <u>Criticism</u> by John Crowe Ransom.

Ransom's preferences "are continually congealing
into prejudice" in this very tense book of
academic criticism which leaves out any reference
to image and finally dissolves into a confused
blur. I. A. Richards says more about emotions
than Ransom in these "structural and technical
feats," of "ontological criticism."

677. "The Brontë Fantasies." <u>New Republic</u> 105
      (1 Sept. 1941): 285-86. Review of <u>The</u>
      <u>Brontës' Web of Childhood</u> by Fannie E.
      Ratchford.

Miss Ratchford's twenty-year collection and
integration of the Brontë juvenilia is "a true
feat of scholarly research;" however, she "has no
clear idea of the profound worth of her
discoveries." She does not see the differences
between the mythical countries of Emily, Branwell,

and Charlotte. In Emily's Gondol poems "we are
offered the complete key to Emily's mature
genius."

678. "Theory and Practice." Nation 153
     (25 Oct. 1941): 406-6. Review of Look at All
     Those Roses by Elizabeth Bowen.

In contrast to her usual writing, these short
stories are grim and formulaic, except for those
in which she returns to a psychological situation
as a basis for the story.

679. "The Gothic South." Nation 153 (6 Dec.
     1941): 572. Review of A Curtain of Green by
     Eudora Welty.

Bogan compares Welty's short stories to Gogol's in
that they both deal with the same sort of subjects
in a kind of oblique humor. Welty "opens the door
and describes the setting, almost inch by inch."
Her method is suitable only for Southern
characters and does not work with Nothern stories.
In her writing "the slenderest unifying device"
produces a fine novel.

1942

680. "Gaelic Captain: Fuedal Earl." New Republic
     107 (16 Nov. 1942): 645-46. Review of The
     Great O'Neill by Sean O'Faolain.

The book describes the great Gaelic earl, Hugh
O'Neill of Ulster, and his leadership of the Irish
clans in their continuing warfare against Queen
Elizabeth's takeover of Northern Ireland.
O'Faolain's work gives the reader "a view of the
true nature of Irish history and culture."

1943

681. "Yeats and His Ireland." Partisan Review
     10 (Mar.-Apr. 1943): 198-201. Review of W.
     B. Yeats 1865-1939 by Joseph Hone.

Hone, Yeats' official biographer, has recorded the
poet's life fully. This book fills in the gaps in
early years of Yeats' Autobiography, showing his
heroic defense of Synge during the Playboy riots
and Synge's influence on Yeats' own poetry.

Events in Ireland, including the Easter Rising of
1916 and the Civil War after 1919 "directed
[Yeats] to more ruthless and intense work." Yeats
took upon himself the role of shaman, as well as
the artistic consciousness of Ireland. His
"cabalistic jargon," A Vision, is the least
attractive of his writings. Yeats "remained
inexorably . . . pitted against that genteel and
semi-genteel section of the public . . . from
which rise . . . the savage and hollow ideas of
our day."

1945

682. "Words and Pictures." Nation 160
     (21 Apr. 1945): 454, 456. Review of The
     Romance of English Literature.

Lavish pictures in color and black and white of
familiar English writers and their works are
combined with seven critical essays on English
Letters by such authors as Graham Greene and
Elizabeth Bowen. "A wonderful spirited . . .
book."

683. "The Mystic Experience." Nation 161
     (7 July 1945): 15. Review of The Soul Afire:
     Revelation of the Mystics. Ed. H. A.
     Reinhold.

This collection of writings on mysticism sheds
light on the development of Christian mystics who
are neither spiritualists nor theosophists. But
the selections are stiff and resemble each other
because the writings of mystic poets such as
Blake, Rimbaud, Baudelaire, Rilke, and T. S. Eliot
are not included.

1947

684. "The Citizen and the Ideal." Nation 164
     (8 Feb. 1947): 159-60. Review of The Blue
     Flower: Best Stories of the Romantics. Ed.
     Hermann Kesten.

These forty-five stories gathered from thirteen
countries emphasize romantic idealism and downplay
romantic horror, particularly in the English
section. The new bourgeois audiences of the
period read and enjoyed these simple tales before

industry and power "became the moral ideal of the
bourgeois age."

685. "Experiment and Post-Experiment." American
     Scholar 16 (Spring 1947): 237-38, 240, 242,
     244, 246, 248, 250, 252. Review of
     Apollinaire's Choix des Poésies, Lord Weary's
     Castle by Robert Lowell and Esthétique du Mal
     by Wallace Stevens, The Collected Poems of W.
     H. Auden, The Selected Writings of Dylan
     Thomas, and Selected Writings of Gertrude
     Stein. Also included are bilingual editions
     of A Season in Hell and Prose Poems from
     Illuminations by Rimbaud, as well as Young
     Cherry Trees Secured Against Hares by Andre
     Breton, and New Direction 9, edited by James
     Laughlin.

Current post-experimental literature derives
principally from poetry of Rimbaud and Baudelaire
rather than the English Romantics. French avant-
garde poetry generated the Symbolist revolution
which degenerated into the Dadaists and
Surrealists, whose work is the exhausted end of
experimental poetry. Apollinaire's work "marks a
point where pure experientation intersects the
humane poetic line of all times and all
countries." In contrast, André Breton's work is
"singularly empty." Gertrude Stein's experiments
"detached words from hampering connotative
accretions." Wallace Steven's "poetic talent is
rich and varied, although marked by a tendency
toward affectation." Dylan Thomas' early
surrealistic technique later became more lyrical.
T. S. Eliot's joy and religious emotion in the
Four Quartets also appears in Auden's Collected
Poems. Religious fervor appears in Lowell's Lord
Weary's Castle. These last three poets have found
a sane way to live in this anarchic world.

1956

686. "MacNeice." Poetry London-New York 1, No. 1
     (Mar-Apr. 1956): 40-42. Review of Autumn
     Sequel: A Rhetorical Poem in XXVI Cantos by
     Louis MacNeice.

Rhetoric is not enough in this long undeveloped
sequel to his 1939 occasional poem, Autumn
Journal. It is a "perfectly well-sounding rhymed

discourse, suitable for broadcasting;" however the
form, terza rima, is not suitable for the poem.

D. CRITICAL ESSAYS NOT IN THE NEW YORKER

These articles and essays were published in various journals and as chapters of books. They are listed in chronological order of date of publication. Information on later reprints is also given.

1923

687. "The Springs of Poetry." New Republic 37 (5 Dec. 1923): 9.

"The poem is always the last resort." Even though the poet would choose to do anything else rather than write down his emotions, those who let the moment pass and write about the emotion at second hand become second-rate poets. Yeats, in his later years, wrote poetry directly from his emotions "as though his mind had a tongue."

1925

688. "The Darkness of the Contemporaries." Measure 48 (Feb. 1925): 14.

Bogan warns young poets against imitation and posturing. She sees nothing wrong with them serving an apprenticeship by biting "old bones [which] are good for young teeth. But when the teeth are cut, they should bite into their own food."

1935

689. "Stitched on Bone." In Trial Balances, ed. Ann Winslow. New York: Macmillan Co., 1935. pp. 135-39.

This chapter contains the text of seven poems by Roethke including "Epidermal Macabre," "Silence," "Genius," "Death-piece," "Fugitive," "Essay," and "Prayer," along with comments by Bogan. She states that Roethke has been working toward

himself "as opposed to any echo or premature
silence." These poems show "the strength of his
determination to yield in no way to the poorer
tricks of style" even though he has not "yet
mastered the difficult art of writing lyric
poetry."

1938

690. "Poetry." <u>An Inquiry into Civilization in
     the United States by Thirty-six Americans</u>.
     Ed. Harold E. Stearns. New York: Charles
     Scribner's Sons, 1938. pp. 48-61.

This chapter discusses Pound's and Eliot's
influences on the barren American literary scene.
<u>The Waste Land</u> proved to be "the triumph of the
American Poetic Renaissance" after the long sleep
since the nineteenth century. The popular poetry
movement began with Harriet Monroe's founding of
<u>Poetry</u> in Chicago in 1912, while Amy Lowell
advanced the Imagist group. T. S. Eliot wrote the
critical bible of the younger generation of
American poets, <u>The Sacred Wood</u>. Edna St. Vincent
Millay and Elinor Wylie ushered in a short-lived
lyric revival.

Little magazines, especially <u>The Dial</u>, provided
vehicles for literary experimentation in American.
The literary intelligentsia fled to Europe during
the twenties and their work was published in
<u>Transition</u>. Hart Crane led the field of
unconventional form. Regional phenomena included
the Fugitive Group of Nashville, Robinson Jeffers
on the West Coast, and Archibald MacLeish's poem
<u>Conquistador</u>, which attained popular success.
Leftist poets wrote "political verse infused with
gloom." W. H. Auden, C. Day Lewis, and Stephen
Spender came from England to "espouse the cause of
the proletariat." The great poets Rilke and Yeats
ignored political ideologies. At the present
"signs of spiritual health in American poetry are
few, but the current . . . may again be ready to
discharge its spirit."

1939

691. "The Situation in American Writing, 1939."
     <u>Partisan Review</u> 6, No. 5 (Fall 1939): 105-8.
     Reprinted in <u>The Partisan Reader 1934-44: An
     Anthology</u>. Eds. William Philips and Philip

Rahv. New York: The Dial Press, 1946.
pp. 601-4. Also reprinted in Critical
Essays on Louise Bogan. Ed. Martha Collins.
Boston: G. K. Hall & Co., 1984. pp. 49-53.

In this Partisan Review symposium several American
writers answer questions on their influences from
the past, audiences for their work, the value of
criticism, the possibility of making a living by
writing, allegiance to any group, the political
tendency of American writing, and their attitude
towards the next war.

Bogan replies that the influences on her work were
mainly the classics, as well as Arthur Symon's
Symbolist movement, French poets, English
metaphysics, Yeats, Poe, Thoreau, Emily Dickinson,
and Henry James. Poetry has a small static
audience with inborn literary appreciation.
Although Bogan has never had any pressure on her
own criticism, she finds "corruption [by
advertising] of literary supplements is nearly
complete." She has never been able to make a
living by writing poetry. She has been influenced
by the Catholic liturgy, Celtic language, racial
and religious prejudice, and her own development
as an individual. The spiritual malaise in
American writing is due to the intellectuals
throwing off their freedoms and taking refuge in
closed political systems. She plans to oppose war
with Japan with "every means in my power."

                          1953

692. "Reading Contemporary Poetry." English
     Journal 42 (Feb. 1953): 57-62.

"The function of art is to express feeling and
transmit understanding." Modern poetry readers
should not demand Romantic frenzy and pathos nor
Victorian moralistic exhortations. W. B. Yeats is
an example of the transformation of a "Romantic
poet in his youth into the modern poet of his
later years." Modern poetic style includes
adaptation of masks, use of irony, and
compression. "Sheer incoherence and sheer
formlessness" have given way to straightforward
syntax and the poetic line, as well as rhyme and
assonance. Not all modern poets work in the same
way, however.

Bogan suggests that readers should not read
anthologies, but "go directly to a poet's work as
a whole and read it chronologically." Marianne
Moore's poem "The Steeple-Jack" is used by Bogan
to show how the reader can draw general inferences
from observed facts. Its theme is "safety versus
danger." Modern poetry is less popular but more
profound than Victorian.

1954

693. "Poetic Background: A Period of
     Consolidation." <u>Times Literary Supplement</u>
     (17 Sept. 1954): ii. Unsigned essay in
     special section "American Writing Today."
     Reprinted in <u>American Writing Today</u>. Ed.
     Allan Angoff. Washington Square: New York
     University Press, 1957. pp. 11-18.

Bogan gives background for the growing
appreciation of poetry in the United States. It
has become a respectable study for academicians,
poets, and critics. Conflicts arise because of
the new criticism and "graduate school poetry,"
which is well written but without spirit.

Fellowships, awards, and grants grow in amount and
numbers. The Marxist ideology of the 30s and the
populist poets, such as Carl Sandburg, have
declined as quickly as they ascended. The
<u>Partisan Review</u> has withdrawn from its extreme
left-wing position. <u>New Directions</u> still prints
avant-garde poetry.

Translations and critical appraisals of European
writers have appeared, filling the gap in new
American poetry. No great new American originals
such as Whitman or Dickinson are evident. Even
though much American poetry is standardized,
Roethke and others have "attempted to express the
vulgarity and violence usual in modern life."
Perhaps the future will bring American poets
freedom from the old alienation and the new
university allegiance.

1960

694. "Homo Additos Naturae." <u>Literary Review</u> 3
     (Spring 1960): 412-13. Also in Polish
     language weekly <u>Wiadomosci</u>, published in
     London. Contribution to article "Karimierz

Wierzynski: a Symposium," a discussion of the
translation of <u>Selected Poems</u> by Wierzynski.

"Largeness and breadth characteristic of Romantic
poetry at its most vital show up in Wierzynski's
choice as well as in his treatment of the
subject." Poetry can be translated by other poets
with "a close approximation to form and rhythm"
and turn out to be "not only a true rendering of
the original, but a fine poem in its own right."
His poetry deals with man added to nature, man
pressing forward to extreme limits of prowess and
endurance. His humor is charming, his form is
traditional and his pathos comes from the memory
of his homeland, Poland.

1962

695.   <u>Poet's Choice</u>.   Ed. Paul Engle and Joseph
       Langland.   New York: The Dial Press, 1962.
       pp. 33-34.

In this book, over one hundred living artists
chose a favorite or crucial poem from their own
work and commented on it.   Bogan chose "Zone."
She commented, "'Zone' was written in the late
30's in a transitional period of my outer
circumstances and my central beliefs . . . a time
of emotional crisis." The poem's imagery expresses
"some reflection of those relentless universal
laws under which we live, which we must not only
accept, but in some manner forgive . . . ."
(Entries 98 and 614)

1964

696.   "On Richard Eberhart's 'Am I My Neighbor's
       Keeper?'" in <u>The Contemporary Poet as Author
       and Critic</u>.   Ed. Anthony J. Ostroff.   Boston:
       Little, Brown, 1964.   pp. 143-46.

The format of this book is a symposia in which
three distinguished poets write three independent
critiques of a recent poem by a contemporary, who
then writes a response.   Bogan traces the history
and development of the sonnet and tries to analyze
Eberhart's poem which "feels itself a sonnet"
according to these established conventions.   She
finds that his first four lines are mostly wasted.
However, the anecdote of the farmer's killing and
the universal implication of this tragedy somewhat

succeed in the end of the poem.

1967

697. "Tribute to Wystan Hugh Auden on His Sixtieth
     Birthday." <u>Shenandoah</u> 18 (Winter 1967):
     45-46. Also poem "To Wystan Auden On His
     Birthday" with alternating lines by Bogan and
     Edmund Wilson. (Entry 787)

"Auden has never failed the active idealism of his
early years." He looks toward the future in his
new literary ventures. He searches for "all that
is lively in the modern mind and imagination." He
continues to seek out "fresh diction, central
emotion, sound assumptions."

E. SHORT STORIES AND JOURNALS

This section lists Louise Bogan's short stories, journals, and sketches. Many excerpts from these works were later incorporated into <u>Journey Around My Room</u> by Ruth Limmer. Information on other reprints is given.

1927

698. "Keramik." <u>The American Caravan for 1927</u>.
     Eds. Van Wyck Brooks, Alfred Kreymborg,
     Lewis Mumford, Paul Rosenfeld. New York:
     J. J Little and Ives Co., 1927.
     pp. 673-678.

This is a story of an older man and his young mistress, Else, whom he has just stood up. It takes place in autumn in a nameless European city. The two go their separate ways, he to his quiet apartment to contemplete his many affairs, she to a young man she has just met.

1928

699. "Soliloquy." <u>The Second American Caravan</u>.
     Eds. Alfred Kreymborg, Lewis Mumford, Paul
     Rosenfeld. New York: The MacCaulay Company,
     1928. pp. 216-18.

An odd, self-pitying reminiscence of unhappy home scenes and depressing maturity is presented in uncharacteristic surrealistic metaphors such as: "This is a well-bred rock garden. It has been to the best schools. It received a cane with a diamond ferrule of the occasion of its engagement."

700. "Winter Morning." <u>The New Republic</u>
     54 (14 Mar. 1928): 125.

In this sketch Bogan lists the sights in an unpopulated New York street scene on a winter

morning with an artist's sensibility and a poet's
eye. She sees "carefully arranged rhomboids and
stars of the nut-shop windows" and "empty
theaters, the ceilings bent like rococo foreheads
in sleep." She animates her landscape with an
earth-eating steam shovel.

701. "Art Embroidery." The New Republic
     54 (21 Mar. 1928): 156.

Ordinary housewives go to a department store to
learn how to embroider their babies' clothing and
make home decorations to kill the time they have
on their hands. While these women crowd the fifth
floor, "tons of machinery, enough to crack them
all to bits, rock behind the walls, over the
ceiling, under the floors."

                        1931

702. "Hydrotherapy." New Yorker 7 (27 June 1931):
     18-19.

In this brief possibly autobiographical vignette,
Bogan describes a woman patient suffering from a
broken heart who stops suffering momentarily after
sitting in a heat cabinet and getting a cold hose
treatment from a Swedish nurse.

703. "Sabbatical Summer." New Yorker 7
     (11 July 1931): 18-21.

The insipid hero, a poor young English teacher,
Duncan MacNeil, comes to New York City for a
summer to "observe life, make interesting
contacts, and to study music." He gets more than
he bargained for when he falls in love with
Sigrid, a beautiful cosmopolitan blond who works
in a small, exclusive bookstore. All goes well
with the romance until the day Duncan takes Sigrid
to the museum to propose and accidentally meets a
friend of his sister. Duncan suddenly sees Sigrid
through the friend's bourgeois eyes and is
repulsed by her "slightly soiled" odd fruit and
vegetable dress.

704. "A Speakeasy Life." New Yorker 7
     (29 Aug. 1931): 14-16.

Mrs. Scarcey, a dumb young New York City matron,
suggests that her bored husband "really needs a
speakeasy life." Instead, when her old friend
Kay, who is full of "zip" comes into Mrs.
Scarcey's life, bringing her lawyer friend Fred,
Mrs. Scarcey joins them in a speakeasy in
Greenwich village for late lunches several times a
week. She finally learns who really needs the
speakeasy life.

705. "Zest." New Yorker 7 (24 Oct. 1931): 16-19.

An unnamed neurotic New Yorker sets out to find
happiness in the city after she reads a modern
philospher's advice to "Love someone or something,
take interest in things outside yourself and
cultivate zest." In her quest for zest she
contemplates the News Building, takes a street car
ride, and goes to a restaurant for a late lunch.
She finally finds zest when she telephones a
friend to gossip about her former boyfriend.

706. "Sunday at Five." New Yorker 7
     (12 Dec. 1931): 19.

Between drinks, the narrator, trapped at a Sunday
afternoon cocktail party, rages internally at the
artificiality, smugness, and pretentiousness of
the guests and the hostess. The bland
conversation drives her into a rage. She wonders
why the glaze that coats the others doesn't crack
and she waits for another drink.

                          1933

707. "Journey Around My Room." New Yorker 8
     (14 Jan. 1933): 16-18. Reprinted in The
     Poet's Story. Ed. Harold Moss. New York:
     Macmillan Publishing Co., Inc. 1973.
     pp. 17-20. Title and organizing device for
     the book Journey Around My Room: The
     Autobiography of Louise Bogan.

The "adventurous traveler" lying in her bed,
describes the four walls, the furniture, and the
decorations of her room and wonders how she got to
this point in her journey though life. She began
her childhood journey in March 1909 on a train to
Boston from Ballardvale.

708. "The Short Life of Emily." New Yorker 9
     (6 May 1933) 17-18.

The heroine has a brief epiphany on the way to her
lawyer's office to hear the provisions of her
aunt's will. She suddenly realizes that she and
all the other people on the Manhattan street are
alive, "an unprecedented experience for Emily
Hough" who has lived in New York City for five
years, yet still thinks that "all avenues down
which elevated trains run are one and the same
avenue."

709. "The Last Tear." New Yorker 9
     (22 Jul. 1933): 21-22.

The vaguely alcholic Mrs. Read, who spent her life
"arduously earning a living," brought up her
daughter Claire to have one talent, "making nice
friends." Both of them were leaving Rome where
they had spent the winter, as usual. They were
going to Florence, a city Mrs. Read hated but
which was cheaper than Rome. Claire was traveling
to Salzburg to be with friends, leaving her mother
alone. However, Mrs. Read had already shed her
last tear two years earlier when Claire first left
her to be with "one of [her] groups of nice
people."

710. "Conversation Piece." New Yorker 9
     (12 Aug. 1933): 13-14. Reprinted in Short
     Stories from The New Yorker. New York: Simon
     and Schuster, 1945. pp. 141-44.

Mr. and Mrs. Tracy visit Mr. and Mrs. Williams in
their cool, dark, highly-decorated apartment on a
hot August afternoon in New York City. In the
process of drinking five cocktails and listening
to Mr. Williams pontificate about art, the couples
find they have many common acquaintances, whom
they gossip about unmercifully. Mrs. Tracy
expects that Mr. Williams will gossip about her to
his next guests.

711. "Coming Out." New Yorker 9 (14 Oct. 1933):
     22-23.

In this brief sketch with a second person point of

view, Bogan describes mental illness as feeling
that the entire world, except for the sick
individual, is happy and follows well-ordered
patterns. "The entire habitable globe, to your
distraught imagination, is peopled by human
beings," as well as animals, fish, and insects,
who "go their way rejoicing." Recovery from the
black pit of the nervous system depends upon
making choices to love or hate and to no longer
feel as if you are "the world's lost child
. . . ." The normal person realizes that everyone
else is odd too.

712. "Dove and Serpent." New Yorker 9
     (18 Nov. 1933): 24-26.

Ballardvale's strong influence on Bogan shows in
this reminiscence of Jack Leonard, a frightening
old neighbor who visited her mother in the late
winter afternoons for a cup of tea and someone to
talk to. Bogan as a young girl was terribly
afraid of him, especially when he screamed at the
children returning from school while beating his
porch railing with a stick. She could not
understand why her mother let Leonard into the
house, nor his comment to her, "We must be as wise
as the serpent and as gentle as the dove."

                    1934

713. "Letdown." New Yorker 10 (20 Oct. 1934):
     18-19.

In this coming-of-age story from Bogan's
adolescence, she tells of the art lessons she took
from the artistic, proper Bostonian Miss Cooper,
whose studio was in the Oxford Hotel in Boston.
The hotel, Miss Cooper, and nearby Copley Square,
surrounded by the Boston Public Library's
"imitation Italian Renaissance," and Trinity
Church's "imitation false Gothic revival," gave
her "that sensation in the pit of the stomach
which heralds both love and an intense aesthetic
experience." But she became disillusioned with
Miss Cooper and her studio when during one lesson
Miss Cooper appeared with a "greasy paper bag in
one hand and a half-eaten doughnut in the other."

                    1935

714. "To Take Leave." The New Yorker 10
     (26 Jan. 1935): 26-27.

The speaker bids farewell to her constant
companions, Sorrow and Romantic Attachment, who
have dogged her footsteps for many years through
her travels and her daily life. "This is a short
speech to take leave. So goodbye, grief.
Goodbye, love."

1977

715. "From the Notebooks of Louise Bogan
     (1935-36)." Ed. Ruth Limmer. Antaeus 27
     (1977): 120-29.

These musings from Bogan's notebook for 1935-36
show her talent "for the short cry or the cahier."
The entries range from an overheard conversation
on a bus, to reflection of James' colloquial style
and Turgenev's analysis of the mystical
revolutionary. Sometimes she follows Thoreau's
suggestion "In a journal it is important to
describe the weather." One thread that runs
through these entries is Bogan's disparaging
treatment of women, "the frightful collection [of]
old female wrecks in the uptown streets."
Discussing her own writing, she finds she could
never be happy writing fiction "because fiction is
always a put up job on reality. Poetry gives
reality freedom and meaning."

1978

716. "From the Journals of a Poet." New Yorker 53
     (30 Jan. 1978): 39-70.

Bogan muses about her difficult childhood and
unhappy marriages, her daily life, the weather and
the seasons of the year, and famous literary
figures such as Virginia Woolf in this
posthumously published journal. Her
reminiscences, written with the "most careful
detail and feeling for truth," center on her
unhappy relationship with her mother. She
contrasts her mother's untidy housekeeping with
Mrs. Gardner's orderly home in Ballardvale, where
the Bogan family had boarded when she was a child.
Mrs. Gardner's house, the symbol of "blessed
order, blessed thrift" impressed Bogan for the
rest of her life. She states the "final antidote"

in dealing with people from the past is to "love
and forgive them," especially her parents, in
spite of their domestic violence and her mother's
obvious infidelities. Bogan's efforts to "get at
the quotidian essence" in this journal result in
the brief sad entries at the end, when she
describes her daily struggle with dependency on
tranquilizers and her thoughts about her
approaching death.

F. TRANSLATIONS

This section contains translations of individual
poems and complete books. Several of these
translations were done with others. Reprints are
noted.

1939

717. "The Poetry of Paul Eluard." Partisan Review
6 (Fall 1939): 86-89.

Two poems from Cours Naturel, 1939, translated by
Louise Bogan: an untitled poem and "Painted Words
to Pablo Picasso" with the originals. These
translations are not included in the reprints of
the original article in SC and APA.

1940

718. "Kapuzinerberg (Salzburg)." New Republic 103
(18 Nov. 1940): 699.

Translation of work by Pierre-Jean Jouvre
describing the view out of a window of the plain
of Bavaria and the schloss above the town which
reminds the speaker of Goethe and how his work
inspired all Germany.

1958

719. Goll, Ivan. Jean Sans Terre. New York:
Thomas Yoseloff, 1940. Critical notes
pp. 13-16.

Bogan's translations include: "Jean Sans Terre
Sacrifices Himself to the Sun," p. 93; "Jean Sans
Terre the Prodigal Son," p. 116; "John the Fire,"
p. 135; "Jean Sans Terre's Race," p. 145; "Jean
Sans Terre Sings an Ode to France in May 1940," p.
158; "Jean Sans Terre on the Bowery," p. 168; Jean
Sans Terre in Cuba " (trans. with Paul Goodman),
p. 172; and "Jean Sans Terre's Rights of
Inheritance," p. 187.

1959

720. "Translations from Valéry." <u>Hudson Review</u> 12
     (Spring 1959): 92-93.

Translations by May Sarton and Louise Bogan of
four poems by Paul Valéry: "Birth of Venus,"
"Bather," "In Sleeping Beauty's Wood," and
"Caesar."   The French originals are not
included.

721. "Paul Valéry."   <u>Poetry</u> 194 (Apr. 1959): 1-7.

Translations by May Sarton and Louise Bogan of
three poems by Valéry: "Canticle of the Columns,"
"Spinner," and "To the Plane Trees."   The French
originals are not included.

1960

722. Ernst Junger. <u>The Glass Bees</u>. Trans. Louise
     Bogan and Elizabeth Mayer. New York: Noonday
     Press, 1960.

Captain Richard, a German officer, narrates this
story of the mechanization of war and life
symbolized by Zapparoni's robots.

1962

723. Ivan Goll. <u>Four Poems of the Occult</u>. Ed.
     Frances Carmody. Kentfield, California: The
     Allen Press, 1962. 130 copies published,
     unbound folios, no page numbers.

Book 3. <u>Elegy of Ipetonga</u>. Translated by Babette
Deutsch, Louise Bogan, and Claire Goll. Themes of
New York City as a busy rich mass of stone,
destined to become a dead city. The title comes
from the Canarsie Indians' name for Columbia
Heights.

Book 4. <u>The Myth of the Pierced Rock</u>. Translated
by Louise Bogan. Elements of Indian legend are
fused with occult learning. Pierced Rock is on
the Gaspe peninsula.

1963

724. Johann Wolfgang von Goethe. <u>Elective</u>

Affinities. Trans. Elizabeth Mayer and
Louise Bogan. Intro. by Victor Lange.
Chicago: Henry Regnery Company, 1963.
Reprinted in Gateway Edition from Regnery
Gateway, 1988.

Goethe's famous novel of two couples' intertwined
associations destined for tragedy.

1964

725. The Journal of Jules Renard. Trans. Louise
     Bogan and Elizabeth Roget. New York: George
     Braziller, 1964.

Selections from Renard's journal dealing with his
bitter memories of boyhood, his writing, other
famous French writers and actors, his civil and
domestic activities, and his loving relationship
with his wife.

1971

726. Johann Wolfgang von Goethe. Sorrows of Young
     Werther and Novella. Trans. by Elizabeth
     Mayer and Louise Bogan. Poems translated by
     W. H. Auden. Foreword by W. H. Auden. New
     York: Random House, 1971. Republished by
     Vintage Books in New York, 1973.

Influential novel of impulsive young man's suicide
over unrequited love and novella of a second
youth's attainment of self-knowledge.

G. POEMS ON RECORDS AND TAPES

This section contains records and tapes of Louise Bogan reading her poems. Many of the original recordings were made at the Library of Congress, beginning in 1948 and ending in 1969. A complete listing of these records and tapes may be found in the bibliography section of <u>Louise Bogan: A Woman's Words</u> by William Jay Smith.

Records

727. <u>Poets Reading Their Own Poems</u>. Library of Congress Recording Laboratory PL2 (1953).

The subject of this series is twentieth-century poetry in English, with contemporary poets reading their own works. The series of 31 recordings was originated by Louise Bogan as Poetry Consultant of the Library of Congress in 1946. This record also includes Paul Engle, Marianne Moore, and Alan Tate. Bogan reads "The Sleeping Fury," "The Alchemist," "Henceforth from the Mind," "The Daemon," "Last Hill in a Vista," and "The Mark."

728. <u>Louise Bogan Read from Her Own Works</u>. Yale Series of Recorded Poets. Decca Records DL 9132 (1961). Reissued by Carillon Records YP 308 (1961). Jacket notes by Harold Bloom are reprinted in <u>Critical Essays on Louise Bogan</u>. Ed. Martha Collins. Boston: G. K. Hall, 1984. pp. 84-87. (Entry 823)

The text of the poems read on the record is included. Among the poems read are: "Medusa," "The Romantic," "Statue and Birds," "The Alchemist," "Men Loved Wholly Beyond Wisdom," "Women," "Division," "The Crossed Apple," "Fiend's Weather," "Old Countryside," "Summer Wish," "Henceforth, from the Mind," "Man Alone," "The Sleeping Fury," "M., Singing," "Putting to Sea," "Spirit's Song," "Kept," "Variation on a Sentence," "The Dream," "Come, Sleep . . .," "March

195

Twilight," "July Dawn," "The Meeting," "The Young
Mage," and "Song for the Last Act."

729. <u>Poets for Peace</u>. Spoken Arts SA 990 (1968).
     Recorded Nov. 12, 1967, in Town Hall, New
     York. Slipcase notes by Paul Kresh.

Also reading from their own works at this antiwar
rally were: Daniel Berrigan, Richard Eberhart,
Abbie Huston Evans, Paul Goodman, Barbara Howes,
Stanley Kunitz, Robert Lowell, Arthur Miller,
Anais Nin, Bink Noll, W. D. Snodgrass, Mark Van
Doren, John Hall Wheelock, Richard Wilbur,
Marguerite Young, and Ned O'Gorman. Bogan read
"To an Artist, to Take Heart" and "To My Brother."

Tapes

730. Poetry Reading at Academy of American Poets.
     Sound tape reel (1968).

Bogan's new book of poetry is introduced. Her
work is the "poetry of restraint, truth,
integrity, awareness and it is humane." She is
"one of the finest lyric poets of our time."
She reads and comments on the following poems from
<u>Blue Estuaries</u>: "Medusa," "Women," "Animal,
Vegetable, and Mineral," "Question in a Field,"
"The Dream," "Italian Morning," "Roman Fountain,"
"Spirit's Song," "Kept," "After the Persian," "The
Dragonfly," "Night," "St. Christopher," "Winter
Swan," "The Mark," and "Psychiatrist's Song."

731. Poetry Reading at Library of Congress. May
      5, 1969, in Coolidge Auditorium.

The Chancellors of the Academy of American Poets
read their poems in honor of the 50th anniversary
of the Academy. Also reading are Elizabeth
Bishop, Robert Fitzgerald, Robert Lowell, Allen
Tate, and John Hall Wheelock. Bogan reads
"Medusa," "The Crossed Apple," "To My Brother,"
"Cartography," and "Psychiatrist's Song."

732. <u>The Eight-Sided Heart</u>. Watershed Tapes,
     Archive Series C-159 (1984).

This tape was made from earlier recordings in the

Library of Congress collection. Side one
includes: "Women," "Animal, Vegetable and
Mineral," "The Dream," "To Be Sung on the Water,"
Cartography," "March Twilight," "July Dawn,"
"'Come, Sleep . . .,'" "Zone," "To My Brother,"
"The Meeting," "Psychiatrist's Song," and "Song
for the Last Act." Side two includes: "Italian
Morning," "Short Summary," "The Alchemist," "The
Sleeping Fury," "Last Hill in a Vista," "Hypocrite
Swift," "Song for a Slight Voice," "Cassandra,"
"The Mark," "Henceforth, from the Mind," "Single
Sonnet," "Kept," "Medusa," "M., Singing," "Song
for a Lyre," "The Daemon," "Evening in the
Sanitarium," and "Didactic Piece."

733. <u>Spoken Arts Treasury of 100 Modern American
     Poets Reading Their Poems</u>. Spoken Arts, Inc.
     Vol. 6, SA 1045 (1985). Also available on
     record.

Taping done in Manhattan in 1970. "She was still
on the staff of <u>The New Yorker</u> when I approached
her and at first she wanted no readings done, but
she soon came around." Quotation from a letter to
the bibliographer by Arthur Luce Klein, Chairman
of the Board of Spoken Arts. The other poets on
this tape are Babette Deutsch, Lenore Marshall,
Stephen Vincent Benet, and Malcolm Cowley. Bogan
reads "Henceforth, from the Mind," "Italian
Morning," "Baroque Comment" (first time recorded),
"To My Brother," "Song for a Lyre," "To Be Sung on
the Water," and "The Daemon."

H. TALKS AND LECTURES

Louise Bogan gave many talks and lectured on
literature at various colleges and conferences.
The talks annotated here may be found in the
sources listed, but most of the others are
unpublished and are found only in her collected
papers.

734. "Some Notes on Popular and Unpopular Art."
     The Hopwood Lecture at University of
     Michigan, June 2, 1944. Also given at Bard
     College, Feb. 21, 1945. Included in
     APA. (Entry 179)

735. "On the Pleasures of Formal Verse." Talk
     given in opposition to W. C. Willams on Nov.
     5-6, 1948. Published in Quarterly Review of
     Literature 7, No. 3 (1953): 176-185.
     Included in APA under title "Formal Poetry:
     The Pleasures of Formal Verse (1953)."
     148-59. (Entry 240)

736. "Poetry at Its Source." National Institute
     of Arts and Letters. Talk given on Dec. 21,
     1953. Published later in Institute's
     proceedings.

Bogan discusses formal poetry beginning with a
history of the muses. The muse of inspiration is
"still symbolically a link with universal mystery
and with universal love." Poets feel constricted
when their society sets up false and unhuman
standards to which they are expected to conform.
Victorian propriety forced W. B. Yeats' revolt.
"Poets once more were attracted to the ageless
simplicity, the realism and authority of folk-song
and story." Formal poetry expresses symbolically
our minds, senses and intuition and rhythmically
our breath and heart.

737. Talk to Phi Beta Kappa and University
     Research Club of the University of Vermont.
     March 18, 1958. Review published in the
     Burlington *Free Press* March 19, 1958.

Miss Bogan discusses writing poetry, which is "a
pattern of sound in which the poet shares his
experience with the reader." There is a trend
toward formalism in modern poetry. "No one can
ever expect to earn their living from it."

738. "A Mystical Poet." Talk given at
     Bicentennial Celebration of Amherst,
     Massachusetts, 23 Oct. 1959. Included in
     APA. (Entry 238)

739. What Makes a Writer?" Talk given at New
     York University, March 18, 196?. Published
     in part in *Journey Around My Room* by Ruth
     Limmer, pp. 119-21.

"A writer's power is based on . . . talent . . .
which is a gift," not on love of writing or
intellectual ability. "The adolescent writer-to-
be finds himself or herself *compelled* to write."
The young writer is a voracious reader who is
intoxicated with words. A writer needs talent and
technique. "A writer's power is . . . based upon
his intuition and his emotions." For a poet,
inspiration comes and goes, so the poet must
remain open. The usual lifetime progress of a
lyric poet is "apprenticeship, a period of full
flowering, and a gradual decline in creative
energies."

740. "The Role of the Poetry Journal." Paper read
     at the National Poetry Festival at the
     Library of Congress, 22 Oct. 1962. Printed
     in Government Document No. 103. Recorded
     on Library of Congress tape LWO 3868, Reel 1.

Harriet Monroe began the "pamphleteering for a
neglected art with her journal, *Poetry: A Magazine
of Verse*. In her first issue she stated that
poetry should be written, be printed, be
circulated, and be read." The contributors in the
first issue were E. A. Robinson, Vachel Lindsay,
Edgar Lee Masters, Carl Sandburg, and Robert

Frost. The Imagists appeared in the second issue
in Nov. 1912. The poetry journal provided a link
between British and American poets. The important
functions of the poetry journal are to reject the
false, threadbare, and sentimental; and to bring
back the lost and neglected. Avant-gardism and
provincialism must be guarded against, including
the regionalism of the 1930's, as well as the
disguised mutual admiration society and
pornography. The poetry journal should provide a
showcase for the young and be supported by
patrons. The editor must be above materialism.
Poetry journals should be preserved for the
future.

741. "What the Women Said." Lecture at Bennington
     College, Oct. 1962. Printed in <u>Journey</u>
     <u>Around My Room</u> by Ruth Limmer. pp. 134-158.

The subject is the "achievement of certain
remarkable women writers, who were not poets, but
novelists, critics and (dreadful word) feminists."
Women must be their own muses and make their own
artistic place in spite of the shifts of history.
Bogan reads quotations for or against female
nature and artistic powers from Byron, Shaw, Lewis
Mumford, Robert Graves, and Homer.

Absolute male domination has not existed in an
unbroken line throughout history. The periods of
humiliation included the beginning of the
Christian period, but changed in the Middle Ages
when women began to assert themselves in the
Reformation. British feminists reacted to the
strictures against women of the Victorian Age.
Their struggles are documented in their novels.
Dorothy Richardson, the first writer to introduce
stream of consciousness into novels, was a
feminist who did not believe that "men have been
continuously out to conquer, subdue and enslave
women."

Virginia Woolf, though an excellent critic of
English women writers, had lapses in her own
novels. She was convinced of the "unbreakable
historic dominance of men." Simone de Beauvoir
carried on this argument, and found that the vast
leisure women now enjoy gives them time to be
"chatterers and scribblers." De Beauvoir also has
contempt for the intuitive side of women's nature
that "complements the virtues of the male." But

Bogan counters "in women's deportment . . . the brutal, rough, swaggering masculinized gesture never . . . works." Women may break through taboos of subject matter, but still should avoid surrealism and shocking language.

Rules for women in literature: Do not lie, do not whine, do not "attitudinize as a femme fatale or little girl," and do not "stamp a tiny foot at the universe." The love sonnet sequence could stand a period of rest. Women, like men, should still ask the universal questions and tell great stories in poetry and song. They are companions and complement each other.

742. "Is Kindness Killing the Arts?" Panel Discussion at the MacDowell Colony, Peterborough, New Hampshire, 24 Aug. 1963. Participants: Louise Bogan, Meyer Shapiro, and Virgil Tompson.

Transcription by the Colony extracts two remarks by Bogan.

743. Homage to Archibald MacLeish. The Academy of American Poets, 1966.

The speakers include Louise Bogan, Allen Tate, Stanley Burnshaw, William Meredith, and Archibald MacLeish reading his own poems. Bogan reads a MacLeish poem "Men," that has haunted her because of its ancient intensity in a primordial sense.

744. "The Making of an Anthology." National Children's Book Week 50th Anniversary. Library of Congress, 17-18 Nov. 1969. On Library of Congress tape LWO 5854.

This is a panel discussing which poems to include in a children's anthology. Participants are Louise Bogan, William Jay Smith, William H. Cole, and moderator J. V. Cunningham. Bogan states it is necessary to choose poems that stretch children's minds and open up their horizons. The poems must have a natural rhythm children can feel when they are read to. She reads from her and Smith's anthology, <u>The Golden Journey</u>, "Ferry Me Across the Water" by Cristina Rossetti, "The

Midnight Skaters" by Edmund Blunden, and her poem,
"M., Singing."

I. MISCELLANEA

This section lists several miscellaneous items
including introductions to books; letters to the
editor; collections of juvenilia, papers and
letters; and poems put to music.

Introductions

745. Introduction to <u>Green Mansions</u> by W. H.
Hudson. New York: Harper & Brothers, 1951.
pp. v-xi.

W. H. Hudson's book was popular among Americans
because he wrote from his heritage as a
Connecticut Yankee. He also had the eye of a
naturalist and a style "remarkable for its
simplicity." His heroine Rima may have been
mystical, but she was still human. He mingles
humor and realism with fantasy in his allegory.
In this work and Hudson's latter essays, "he based
his vision . . . squarely upon living and
eternally contemporary facts."

746. Introduction to <u>Sentimental Education: The
Story of a Young Man</u> by Gustave Flaubert.
New York: New Directions, 1957. pp. vii-xiv.

Reprint of "Sentimental Education Today" in SC
223-30 and APA 131-136 with minor changes in the
first and second paragraph and an additional
paragraph inserted at the end of the introduction
beginning "Within the prevalent atmosphere of
fiasco, bafflement and fraud . . . ." This
section describes Flaubert's impressionism.

747. Foreword to <u>The Scarlet Letter: A Romance</u> by
Nathaniel Hawthorne. New York: Libra, 1960.
pp. ix-xiv. Reprinted in APA 206-210.
(Entry 243)

748. Introduction to <u>A Cookbook for Poor Poets</u>
     <u>(and Others)</u> by Ann Rogers. New York:
     Charles Scribner's Sons, 1966. p. vii.

"This book will be devoted to sitting-down meals,
however humble." Poets and other who are out of
funds usually eat standing up on the run. These
recipes appeal to all the senses and are offered
"with warm sympathy" from Miss Rogers.

749. "Afterword" with Josephine Shaefer to
     A Writer's Diary. Ed. Leonard Woolf. New
     York: Signet, 1968. New American Library
     Edition.

This selective collection of diary entries by
Virginia Woolf includes most of her comments on
her new works in progress, some examples of her of
her diary used for other literary purposes, and a
few instances of "the raw materials of her art."
Her process of creation begins with her elation at
the idea of a book, continues through the hard
work of writing and rewriting, and ends with her
exhaustion and depression previous to its
publication. Leonard Woolf's arrangement of
material is visible.

Letters to The Editor

750. "Miss Dudley Defended." <u>The New Republic</u> 73
     (11 Jan. 1933): 246.

Letter defending <u>Forgotten Frontiers</u>, a book on
American letters in general and Theodore Dreiser
in particular from a snobbish review by Granville
Hicks.

On reviewing books Bogan states, "Whatever the
book's faults, it is not to be dismissed by a wave
of a reviewer's hand. And I have yet to see a
volume in print that deserves a reviewer's sneer."

751. "Freud and Marx." <u>The New Republic</u> 86 (8
     Apr. 1936): 251-52.

Letter in response to Malcolm Cowley's review of
<u>The Destructive Element: A Study of Modern Writers</u>
<u>and Beliefs</u> by Stephen Spender and Cowley's reply.

Bogan takes issue with Cowley's review and
maintains that Auden's fundamental ideas on
Marxism as a social phemonenon and psychoanalysis
as a treatment are important. Cowley responds
that the relationship between Freud and Marx
should be studied further and petulantly
concludes, "As for psychoanalysis as a method of
curing individual neuroses, I advance no opinion,
never having been psychoanalyzed except by
unfriendly book reviewers."

752. Letter. New Republic 95 (30 March 1938):
     225.

Entire text of letter correction of phrase quoted
in review by Miss Borgenicht of Auden's Starting
Point should be the "intolerable neural itch,' not
"neutral itch."

753. Reply to "Letter to Editor" by John Crowe
     Ransom. Nation 153 (20 Sept. 1941): 263-64.
     (Entry 676)

Bogan's review of The New Criticism brought forth
this response by Ransom who "expected that in the
Nation the book would fall into the hands of a
reviewer who would examine its argument instead of
into those of a lady looking for literature and
images." He made several other insulting remarks.

Bogan's reply: "May I say that after having
reviewed books for eighteen years and lived for
forty-four, without ever having been called a
lady, a four-flusher, a three-flusher, a
Southerner or (implicitly a fool) Mr. Ransom's
pure truculence in calling me all these things
makes me laugh very much?"

754. "On the Brooks-MacLeish Thesis." Partisan
     Review 9, No. 1 (Jan.-Feb. 1942): 41-42.

In response to Van Wyck Brooks' theory of modern
literature, Bogan criticizes him as an "offical
critic functioning on the behalf of an offical
literature." He attempts to fit all literature
into his preconceived "ultimately moral pattern."
But American literature will survive in spite of
him.

755. Letter in reply to Jacques Barzun's letter
     objecting to essay "Time of the Assassins."
     <u>Nation</u> 158 (27 May 1944): 635. (Entry 182)

Bogan says her sources "conflate the police novel
and detective story" in opposition to Barzun's
remarks.

Collections of Juvenilia, Letters, Papers, and Books

756. Juvenilia published in <u>The Jabberwock</u>, the
     publication of Girls' Latin School from
     1911-1915.

Essays, stories, and poems published in the
monthly magazine of Girls' Latin School. Louise
Bogan was an associate editor her last year of
school. The library containing the publications
is in the Boston Latin Academy.

757. "The Louise Bogan Papers." Amherst College,
     Amherst, Mass.

Eleven boxes of poetry and prose, including
translations, short stories, articles, book
reviews, lecture notes, and journals, and
newspaper clippings from 1930 to 1970.

758. The Henry W. and Albert A. Berg Collection,
     The New York Public Library.

Forty folders of letters and postcards to Kathryn
Italia Iff Lanz (2 folders), Alfred Kazin, Katie
Louchheim (5 folders), Elizabeth Mayer (6
folders), Howard Moss, May Sarton (24 folders),
Frances Steloff, Kay Steele, and Ruth Witt-
Diamant. Photographs, translations of Ernest
Junger's "Zinnia," and Hans Carossa "Goethe's
Influence Now" with Elizabeth Mayer.

759. Cornell University. New York.

Collection of letters and other papers.

760. The Houghton Library, Harvard University,

Cambridge, Mass.

Letters and postcards to W. S. Braithwaite, Witter Brynner, Robert Lowell, and Bradley Phillips.

761. Library of Congress. Washington, D. C.

Manuscripts listed in Louise Bogan: A Woman's Words by William Jay Smith, include letters, memoranda, postcards, talks, as well as records and tapes. Also collected are newspaper clippings, manuscript of Works in the Humanities, Library of Congress Information Bulletins, lists of awards, etc.

762. Lockwood Memorial Library of the University of Buffalo, New York.

Manuscripts of poems.

763. Newberry Library, Chicago, Ill.

Letters to Morton Zabel.

764. Western College for Women. Oxford, Ohio.

Collection of Louise Bogan's books.

Poems Put to Music

765. Barber, Samuel. Musical setting of "To Be Sung on the Water." New York: G. Schirmer, 1969. Octavo No. 11644.

Music dedicated to Florence Kimball, and written for 4-part a cappella chorus of mixed voices.

766. Benson, Warren. "Five Lyrics of Louise Bogan: for Mezzo Soprano and Flute." Bryn Mawr, Pa.: Theodore Presser, 1984.

Benson, who had met Bogan at the MacDowell Colony in 1963, notes, "Louise Bogan is acknowledged as one of the great lyricists of our time." His settings for these poems, in which the lyrics are not included, are "straightforward and vulnerable,

taking their cue from the elegance of the texts."
The poems the music is based on are: "My Voice Not
Being Proud," "The Alchemist," "Juan's Song,"
"Fifteenth Farewell," and "Knowledge."

J. UNCOLLECTED POEMS

The following poems, originally published in various journals, do not appear in any of Louise Bogan's collections of poetry. These poems are listed in alphabetical order.

767. "The Betrothal of King Cophetua." <u>Boston University Beacon</u>, Apr. 1916, 298. Reprinted in <u>Anthology of Boston University Poetry</u>. New York: Colony Press, 1931. p. 36.

768. "A Carol." <u>Boston University Beacon</u>, Christmas 1915, 210.

769. "The Catalpa Tree." <u>Voices</u> 164 (Sept.-Dec. 1951): 8-9.

770. "Consolations of Religion; by a Reincarnationist." <u>New Yorker</u> 2 (22 May 1926): 56.

771. "Elders." <u>Poetry</u> 20, No. 5 (Aug. 1922): 248 (under title "Beginning and End").

772. "Empty Lyrics: Plain, Fancy." <u>Nation</u> 147 (10 Dec. 1939): 625 (under title "Five Parodies").

773. "The Engine." <u>New Yorker</u> 6 (3 Jan. 1931): 21.

774. "For an Old Dance." <u>New Yorker</u> 5 (1 Feb. 1930): 17. Reprinted in <u>New Yorker Book of Verse 1925-1935</u>. New York: Harcourt, Brace, 1935. p. 52.

775. "Gift." New Yorker 8 (28 May 1931): 20.

776. "Hidden." New Yorker 11 (115 Feb. 1936): 20.

777. "Imitation of a Novel (or a Prose Poem) by
     Kay Boyle." Nation 147 (10 Dec. 1938): 624-25
     (under title "Five Parodies").

778. "Imitation of a Poem by Frederick Prokosch."
     Nation 147 (10 Dec. 1938): 625 (under title
     "Five Parodies").

779. "Leavetaking." Poetry 20, No. 5 (Aug. 1922):
     250 (under title "Beginning and End").

780. "New Moon." Nation 145 (7 Aug. 1937): 153.

781. "Old Divinity." New Yorker (14 Dec. 1929):
     35.

782. "Pyrotechnics." Liberator 6, No. 5
     (May 1923): 14. Reprinted in May Days, ed.
     Genevieve Taggard. New York: Boni and
     Liveright, 1925. p. 202.

783. "Resolve." Poetry 20, No. 5 (Aug. 1922):
     248-49 (under title "Beginning and End").

784. "The Stones." Measure 28 (June 1923) 12.

785. "Survival." Measure 9 (Nov. 1921): 5.

786. "To A Dead Lover." Poetry 20, No. 5
     (Aug. 1922): 250-251 (under title "Beginning
     and End").

787. "To Wystan Auden on His Birthday. Shenandoan
     18 (Winter 1967): 43. Alternative lines

composed by Edmund Wilson and Louise Bogan.
(Entry 697)

788. "Trio." _Measure_ 28 (June 1923): 12.

789. "Untitled." _Poetry_ 51 (Oct. 1937): 3.

790. "The Young Wife." _Others_ 4 (Dec. 1917):
     11-13.

K. POETRY IN ANTHOLOGIES

The following entries from selected anthologies
were chosen to illustrate the poems by Louise
Bogan which have been included in popular
anthologies published from 1929 until 1990.

791. <u>Women's Poetry Today</u>. Ed. Lewis Worthington
     Smith. New York: G. Solly & Co., 1929.
     pp. 6-7

"Cassandra." Biographical note and poem. "Her
sensitive mind and sharp eye . . . have produced
some very crisp and unforgettable pictures." The
two short poems most read in public are "Women"
and "Decoration."

792. <u>The New Poetry</u>. Eds. Harriet Monroe and
     Alice Corbin Henderson. New York: Macmillan,
     1932. pp. 46-49.

Poems include" "The Crossed Apple," "Old
Countryside," "Cassandra," "Song," "Song for a
Slight Voice," "The Romantic," "The Mark," and
"Come Break with Time."

793. <u>Modern American Poetry</u>. Ed. Louis
     Untermeyer. New York, Harcourt, Brace, 1936.
     pp. 553-57.

Brief biography and review of <u>Body of this Death</u>
and <u>Dark Summer</u>. Poems included are "Medusa,"
"Women," "Decoration," "Statue and Birds," "The
Alchemist," "Simple Autumnal," "Come, Break with
Time," and "Cassandra."

794. <u>A Little Treasury of Modern Poetry</u>. Ed.
     Oscar Williams. New York: C. Scribner's
     Sons, 1946.

Portrait of Louise Bogan, p. 637. Poems include:
"Men Loved Wholly Beyond Wisdom," p. 338; "Putting
to Sea," p. 472; "The Sleeping Fury," p. 490; and
"The Dream," p. 493.

795. New Poems by American Poets. Ed. Rolfe
     Humphries. New York: Ballantine Books, 1954.
     pp. 20-23.

After a brief biography, the following poems are
included: "After the Persian I," "After the
Persian II, III, IV," "After the Persian V,"
"Train Tune," and "Song for the Last Act."

796. The Modern Poets: An American-British
     Anthology. 2nd ed. Eds. John Malcolm and
     Bill Reid. New York: McGraw Hill, 1970.
     pp. 42-45.

After a portrait and brief biography, these two
poems are included: "Women" and "Evening in the
Sanitarium."

797. Maine Lines. Ed. Richard Aldridge.
     Philadelphia: Lippincott, 1970. pp. 17-26.

This selection contains brief comments on Maine,
especially the Casco Bay area, by Louise Bogan.
Her book Blue Estuaries "has images in it which
refer to the Maine coast." Poems included are:
"Knowledge," "Late," "Fiend's Weather," "Old
Countryside," "Question in a Field," "The Crows,"
and "Train Tune."

798. What the Poem Means: Summaries of 1000 Poems.
     Eds. Harry Brown and John Milstead.
     Glenview, Illinois: Scott, Foresman, 1970.
     pp. 16-17.

Two of Bogan's poems are summarized with the
editors' theories of their main themes and
important images noted. In "The Dream" a woman,
through a dream, comes to a reconciliation with
her suppressed sexual nature. "Women" describes
that "provident trait of women by which, in
fearing to produce 'wilderness' by making a
mistake, they actually deprive themselves and are

thus improvident."

799. The Riverside Anthology of Literature.   Ed.
     Douglas Hunt.   Boston: Houghton Mifflin,
     1988.

This anthology contains Bogan's poems, criticism,
and a translation. A biography on p. 2120 states:
"Her work as poet, critic, translator and
philosopher of art is receiving increasing
attention." The poems, on pages 998-1001, are:
"Come, Break with Time," "The Dragonfly," "The
Dream," "The Engine," "Evening in the Sanitarium,"
"Medusa," "To My Brother," and "Zone."   Her
criticism on Emily Dickinson is on p. 680; Edna
St. Vincent Millay, pp. 971-72; and e. e.
cummings, pp. 987-89. Her translation of "Castle
of my Heart" is on p. 680.

800. The Bedford Introduction to Literature.
     2nd ed. Ed. Michael Meyer. Boston: Bedford
     Books of St. Martin's Press, 1990.

Poems included are "Dark Summer," p. 759 and
"Dragonfly," p. 596. Bogan's essay "On Formal
Poetry," is on p. 642.

II. WORKS ABOUT LOUISE BOGAN

A. BOOKS ABOUT LOUISE BOGAN AND REVIEWS

The four complete books written about Louise Bogan
and her work, as well as listings of selected
reviews of these books, are included in this
section.

801. Ridgeway, Jacqueline. LOUISE BOGAN. Boston:
Twayne Publishers, 1984.

Bogan's lyrics "fulfilled her psychological need
to express the inexpressible through the formal
components of meter and stanza" with symbols and
imagery that welled up from her unconscious. In
the first two chapters, Ridgeway discusses Bogan's
poetic form and the poets from the metaphysical
tradition who influenced her. She organizes
Bogan's biography around a chronological
discussion of her poetry, analyzing many of the
poems from her five books of poetry. One chapter
is devoted to Bogan's short stories and another to
her critics. The critical reviews from The New
Yorker, other criticism, translations, and
journals writings are not discussed.

802. CRITICAL ESSAYS ON LOUISE BOGAN. Ed. Martha
Collins. Boston: G. K. Hall, 1984.

This collection of 35 critical essays on Bogan's
poetry is arranged in chronological order. Except
for five original essays written for this volume
by Bogan scholars Deborah Pope, Ruth Limmer, Diane
Wood Middlebrook, Carol Moldaw, and Sandra
Cookson, most of the essays are reviews reprinted
from other sources and written by Bogan's
illustrious contemporaries such as Yvor Winters,
Theodore Roethke, W. H. Auden, and Marianne Moore.
Louise Bogan's 1939 reply to the Partisan Review

215

questionnaire "The Situation in American Writing:
Seven Questions" is also included, as is the
posthumous tribute by William Jay Smith, "Louise
Bogan: A Woman's Words." In her generous
introduction, Collins discusses Bogan's previous
neglect, when she was considered a poet's poet,
and the revived interest in her work in the 1980s.
She also includes biographical material and
comments on critical reactions to Bogan's poetry.

Reviews of CRITICAL ESSAYS ON LOUISE BOGAN.

803. Bowles, Gloria. "The Pursuit of Perfection."
     Women's Review of Books (July 1985): 8-9.

Bowles announces the birth of a full-blown Bogan
criticism in her review of Critical Essays. She
also discusses Louise Bogan by Jacqueline
Ridgeway, Louise Bogan: A Portrait by Elizabeth
Frank, and A Separate Vision: Isolation in
Contemporary Women's Poetry by Deborah Pope.

804. Guimond, James K. "Poetry: 1900 to the
     1940s." American Literary Scholarship. Ed.
     J. Albert Robbins. Durham, North Carolina:
     Duke University Press, 1984. pp. 341-44.

Many of the reprints of the reviews are mentioned
and the original essays are discussed
individually.

805. Frank, Elizabeth. LOUISE BOGAN: A PORTRAIT.
     New York: Alfred A. Knopf, 1985.

Bogan's life, according to Auden's eulogy at her
funeral, was a "struggle to wrest beauty and joy
out of dark places." This sympathetic biography
discusses the dark places as well as the beauty in
the poems, and the infrequent moments of joy in
Bogan's often bitter existence. Bogan's life is
arranged into five periods of greater and lesser
poetic creativity. The major portion of the book
focuses on her experiences while writing her first
three books of poetry. Most of the biographical
information comes from letters, journals, and
criticism from Bogan's contemporaries. Frank

explores Bogan's literary and personal friendships
with Edmund Wilson, Rolfe Humphries, Morton Zabel,
and May Sarton. She describes Bogan's second
marriage to Raymond Holden and mentions her brief
love affair with Theodore Roethke, which later
ripened into a lasting friendship.

Frank discusses the poems in Body of this Death,
Dark Summer, and Sleeping Fury in thematic
clusters and quotes contemporary reviews. She
includes Bogan's 13 stories published in The New
Yorker in the 1930s, as well as other unpublished
stories and prose pieces. Frank theorizes that
Bogan's psychiatric treatment during her first two
hospitalizations helped cure her neuroses, but
helped kill her creativity. "With the publication
of Sleeping Fury [in 1937] her most productive
days as a poet were over." During the 1930s she
became estranged from many of her literary friends
over their politically-influenced writings. Her
energies subsequently went into her criticism,
especially the 38 years of reviews as poetry
critic for The New Yorker, her teaching, and her
literary honors, which included being the
consultant in Poetry to the Library of Congress in
1945-46.

Bogan's life in the later sad years became more
and more constricted. She stopped writing
completely when she resigned from her position on
The New Yorker in September 1969, a year before
her death from a coronary occlusion on February 4,
1970.

Reviews of LOUISE BOGAN: A PORTRAIT.

806. Bawer, Bruce. "Louise Bogan's Angry
     Solitude." New Criterion 3, No. 9 (May
     1985): 23-31.

807. Bernard, April. "Arresting, But Not
     Arrested." Nation 240, No. 7 (23 Feb. 1985):
     215-17.

808. Breslin, James E. American Literature 58,
     No. 1 (March 1986): 121-22.

809. Carr, Virginia Spencer. _America_ 152 (31
     Aug.-7 Sept. 1985): 106-8.

810. Carruth, Hayden. "Poetry and Excess."
     Sewanee Review 94 (1986): 127-31.

811. Gross, John. _New York Times_ (15 Feb. 1985):
     C32.

812. Hadas, Rachel. "The Eyes in Hiding."
     Partisan Review 53 (1986): 297-300.

813. Hirsch, Wendy. "Intimate Formalities."
     American Scholar 55 (1986): 275-79.

814. Howard, Richard. "Yelling Fiend, Soft
     Child." _New Republic_ 92, No. 12 (25 Mar.
     1985): 34, 36-37.

815. Maxwell, William. "Louise Bogan's Story."
     New Yorker 61 (29 July 1985): 73-76.

816. Ostriker, Alice. "Innocence of Heart and
     Violence of Feeling." _New York Times Book
     Review_ (3 Mar. 1985): 1, 30.

817. Pollitt, Katha. "Sleeping Fury." _Yale
     Review_ 74 (1985): 596-602.

818. Wheeler, Elizabeth. _Los Angeles Times Book
     Review_ (31 Mar. 1985): 1, 15.

819. Bowles, Gloria. _LOUISE BOGAN'S AESTHETIC OF
     LIMITATION_. Bloomington: Indiana University
     Press, 1987. (Entry 870)

In this feminist interpretation, Bogan's aesthetic
of limitation was "demanded by her temperament and
her age, which was lying in wait to condemn the
woman poet for her sentimentality, her lack of
range. . . ." That Bogan stopped writing poetry

at 40 was inevitable, given her quest for
perfection and her major themes. Bogan "absorbed
the stylistic lessons of modernism and used [its]
techniques . . . in the themes of love, madness,
and art derived from her life as an American
woman."

Bogan scholars will find the discussion of her
first three books of poety valuable. Body of this
Death, Bogan's "most immediate volume" is a young
woman's response to the first failure of love
"with its themes of chastity, imprisonment and
self-destructiveness." This poetry is a bridge
between female tradition and modernist influence.
The poems in Dark Summer, her "most difficult
book," show her "sado-masochistic manifestations
of love" and the inevitability of the passage of
time in the "ironic voice of an older woman."
Sleeping Fury is her "most consciously
psychological work" in which she confronts her
twin demons of failure in love and conflict with
her mother. Bogan wrote few new poems, with the
splendid exception of "After the Persian," after
this 1937 publication. The contemporary reader
finds Bogan's poems obscure because of her
combination of compact form and female subject.

Reviews of LOUISE BOGAN'S AESTHETIC OF LIMITATION

820. Osbourne, Karen Lee. "At Poetry's
     Crossroads." Women's Review of Books 5, No.
     8 (May 1988): 17-18.

821. Schendler, Sylvan. American Literature 60,
     No. 2 (May 1988): 314.

B. GENERAL CRITICISM

This section contains essays and parts of books
which deal principally with Louise Bogan's poetry
and her personal experiences. A few authors refer
to her criticism. The entries are arranged in
chronological order. Reprints of these works are
also mentioned.

1954

822. Olsen, Elder. "Louise Bogan and Leonie
Adams." Chicago Review 8 (Fall 1954): 70-87.
Reprinted in Critical Essays on Louise Bogan.
Ed. Martha Collins. Boston: G. K. Hall,
1984. pp. 71-84.

Because both poets have recently published poetry
collections, Olsen can review each poet's overall
work and compare their writing. Miss Bogan's
principal character in her poems is a woman,
"sensitive, passionate, sensuous . . . strong-
willed, intelligent, but emotional rather than
intellectual." The course of her love is never
tragic or epic; she is a suffering human in
ordinary, often New England settings. There is a
similar context in which many of her poems take
place, and the overall tone is apprehension. The
reader cannot clearly understand the events the
poems describe, but knows they are scenes from an
ongoing drama. Her metaphors and images are
clear; her style is "generally plain, terse, bare
to the point of austerity. . . ." The remainder
of the article is devoted to Léonie Adams who, in
contrast, is a poet of "the calm and gentle
emotions."

1958

823. Bloom, Harold. "Louise Bogan" from jacket
notes on record Louise Bogan Reads from Her
Own Works. Yale Series of Recorded Poets.
Decca Record, DL 9132, 1958. Reprinted in
Critical Essays on Louise Bogan. Ed. Martha

Collins.   Boston: G. K. Hall, 1984.
pp. 84-87. (Entry 728)

Although Bogan is "usually categorized as a
metaphysical poet . . . she is a Romantic in her
rhetoric and attitudes." She tends toward the
visionary in the tradition of Blake and Yeats, as
there is no resolution in her poems as well. The
sequence of the poems read on the record leads
toward "a delicate and tentative balance."
"Medusa" introduces Bogan's "landscape of
desolation." "Men Loved Wholly Beyond Wisdom" is
"a gnomic parable" and "The Crossed Apple" is
about freedom and the necessity of choice.
"Summer Wish," her most ambitious poem, is a
Yeatsian dialogue between the passionate soul and
the observant soul. "Henceforth from the Mind"
shows the "necessity of resignation" to some
permanent sense of loss. "Song for the Last Act"
rounds off a "life of humanistic craftsmanship."

1960

824. Roethke, Theodore.   "The Poetry of Louise
     Bogan: The Work of a True Inheritor." 1960
     Hopwood Lecture at the University of
     Michigan. Published in Michigan Alumni
     Review (Autumn 1960): 13-20. Reprinted in
     Critical Quarterly 3 (Summer 1961): 142-50
     and in Michigan Quarterly Review 246-51. Also
     reprinted in On the Poet and His Craft:
     Selected Prose of Theodore Roethke. Ed.
     Ralph J. Mills, Jr. Seattle: University of
     Washington Press, 1965. pp. 133-48. Also in
     To the Young Writer: Hopwood Lecture, Second
     Series. Ed. A. L. Bader. Ann Arbor:
     University of Michigan Press, 1965.
     pp. 122-35.

Bogan, unlike other women poets, "writes out of
the severest lyrical tradition in English." "The
word order is usually direct . . . the music rich
and subtle . . . and the subject invariably given
its due and no more." Her subject ranges are
wider both geographically and emotionally than
many lyric poets. One of her central themes is
the moment when thing are frozen in time, found in
"Decoration," the early poem dropped after Dark
Summer and printed in full here, as well as in
"Statue and Birds," and "Medusa." Time can be her
adversary as seen in "Come, Break with Time." Her

other important theme is "love, passion, its
complexities, its tensions, its betrayals."

Her obliquity in never stating the experience
directly in the poem is "both Puritan and
feminine" and "brings [her] close to Emily
Dickinson and Marianne Moore." A poet of the
final prespective, her masterpiece is "Henceforth,
from the Mind," a "poem that could be set beside
the best work of the Elizabethans." Bogan is "one
of the true inheritors . . . whose work will stay
in the language as long as the language survives."

1970

825. Ramsey, Paul. "Louise Bogan." Iowa Review
     1, No. 3 (1970): 116-24. Reprinted in
     Critical Essays on Louise Bogan. Ed. Martha
     Collins. Boston: G. K. Hall, 1984.
     pp. 119-28.

"Louise Bogan is a great lyric poet." Her rhythms
and her talent in ending poems are unique. Her
meter, diction, image, and thought come from
sixteenth-century English tradition. She writes
about emotion and the struggle between restraint
and passion. Even though "Henceforth, from the
Mind" has a poor second stanza, its two last
stanzas contain "one of the most perfectly
modulated analogies in English poetry." Love
comes deeply and darkly in dreams and grief in
"The Dream" and "The Sleeping Fury." Perhaps her
greatest poem is "Song for the Last Act," which
was "probably influenced" by Sara Teasdale.

826. Smith, William Jay. "A Woman's Words."
     Lecture given at the Library of Congress 4
     May, 1970. Reprinted in The Streaks of the
     Tulip: Selected Criticism by William Jay
     Smith. New York: Seymour Lawrence-Delacorte,
     1972. pp. 31-56. Also in Critical Essays on
     Louise Bogan. Ed. Martha Collins. Boston:
     G. K. Hall, 1984. pp. 101-118. (Entries 992
     and 1020)

Smith's tribute begins with the full text of
William Maxwell's eulogy to Louise Bogan printed
in The New Yorker and a poem written to her by
Daniel Hoffman, "A Sonnet (Remembering Louise
Bogan)." Although she disliked any personal

reference, Smith discusses various conversations
and correspondence that went on between them. He
mentions their collaboration on The Golden
Journey, an anthology for children. He shows her
early influences by comparing a poem by Alice
Meynell to Bogan's "Dark Summer," and quotes at
length from her friend Léonie Adams on the same
subject. He also quotes from Bogan's essay "The
Heart and the Lyre" and her lecture "What the
Women Said" on the role of a woman poet. That she
was "almost a musical instrument" is seen in her
poetry, especially "Musician" and "To Be Sung on
the Water," both quoted here. Smith also reads
from her essay "Journey Around My Room," and ends
his memorial lecture with the poem on poetry,
"Henceforth, from the Mind."

1975

827. Kaplan, Cora. Salt and Bitter and Good:
     Three Centuries of English and American Women
     Poets. New York: Paddington Press Ltd.,
     1975. pp. 273-74.

Bogan is "perhaps the most talented" woman poet of
her generation and "one of the most influential
poet-critics of the last 40 years." She isolated
herself from the politics of the 30s and from most
other women poets of her time. Along with H. D.,
Bogan was "among the first women to use the
concept of the female unconscious in poetry." She
spent her entire life struggling to be "an
independent, but outgoing woman and an artist," in
a social climate which was "hardly encouraging to
women on their own."

1976

828. Sarton, May. "Louise Bogan." A World of
     Light: Portraits and Celebrations. New
     York: Norton, 1976. pp. 215-35.

Sarton reminisces about her relationship with
Bogan, her friend and mentor, beginning in 1937
with Sarton's correspondence after reading The
Sleeping Fury and continuing by letter until 1953
when the two women finally met at Bogan's
apartment in New York City. They became good
friends and collaborated on translations of
Valéry's poems. Sarton tells about several
episodes with Bogan, including the time when a

horse bumped into the car in a New York street
market, reminding them of the terrible horse in
"The Dream," and Sarton's New Hampshire house
warming which was almost destroyed by too many
martinis. Sarton never got close to Bogan because
the older woman needed detachment to "provide her
with survival from her demons." Sarton doubts
about Bogan's admiration for her poetry seemed
proven when Bogan slighted the younger poet's work
in The New Yorker reviews.

1977

829. Bowles, Gloria. "Louise Bogan: To Be (or Not
     to Be?) Woman Poet." Women's Studies 5
     (1977): 131-35.

Modern feminist writers rely on support from their
colleagues, but the women poets of the 30s and
40s, including Bogan, "were in competition with
each other." Craftsmanship, considered a
masculine quality, competed with feminine
emotions. Bogan's poetry shows "ambivalence and
contradiction in regard to her womanhood." Bogan
"supported her mad need to write poetry by writing
criticism on poetry." The personal poems Bogan
left out of her collected works need to be revived
and read with her letters to understand these
conflicts.

830. Frank, Elizabeth Perlmutter. "A Doll's
     Heart: The Girl in the Poetry of Edna St.
     Vincent Millay and Louise Bogan." Twentieth
     Century Literature 23 (May 1977): 157-79.
     Reprinted in Critical Essays on Louise Bogan.
     Ed. Martha Collins. Boston: G. K. Hall,
     1984. 128-49.

Edna Millay and Bogan, who emulated Millay's work
in her first published poems of the early 1920s,
both used the persona of "The Girl," a flapper who
moves from innocence to sophistication, usually in
a sexual rite of passage. While Bogan's lyrics
were serious, Millay's were superficial. Bogan's
"Girl" grew into a mature woman, while Millay's
remained an adolescent.

831. Ridgeway, Jacqueline. "The Necessity of Form
     to the Poetry of Louise Bogan." Women's

Studies 5 (1977): 137-49. From the first
chapter of Ridgeway's dissertation, "The
Poetry of Louise Bogan." University of
California at Riverside, 1977. (Entry 985)

Bogan's use of form arises from her internal
struggle with will and authority. This conflict
stems from the strictures of her conventional
lower middle class Catholic upbringing, as well as
her acceptance of the prevailing societal views on
women artists as being "somehow less than men."
Especially important in her poetry is the conflict
between the sexes, which can be resolved only when
her persona chooses freedom and loneliness over
self-destructive love. "Because she herself
unconsciously represented some of the strictures
her spirit rebelled against, only form and symbol
can express the tight concentrated emotion of the
unconscious struggling with the conscious." She
uses form to express these conflicts in "A Tale,"
"Song," "Fifteenth Farewell," "Sonnet,"
"'Come, Sleep . . .'" and "Little Lobelia's Song."

                        1978

832. Goldfern, R. Phyllis. "Words She Always
     Knew: A Consideration of Louise Bogan and her
     Poetry." Moving Out 7, No. 2 (1978): 73-77.

On the occasion of the paperback reissue of
Bogan's final work, The Blue Estuaries, Goldfern
reflects on why the public has ignored Bogan's
poetry. It takes courage to read her work because
the poetry states that we must bear the
unbearable, and that "we cannot even congratulate
ourselves for the valiancy of the effort."
However, writing the poems took greater courage
because of Bogan's "uncompromising integrity" in
her work. Included in the discussion of several
poems is "Exhortation," which is "the most deeply
bitter of her poems."

833. Swafford, Russell Anne and Paul Ramsey. "The
     influence of Sara Teasdale on Louise Bogan."
     CEA Critic 41, No. 4 (1981): 7-12.

The intent of the essay is to "illuminate some of
the workings of [Bogan's] emulation of Sara
Teasdale." Both poets' works show "romanticism
constrained within classic form and balance." The

authors maintain that Teasdale's "Alchemy" (1915)
and Bogan's "The Alchemist" (1923) are "very close
in subject matter and handling," and that
Teasdale's "Spring Rain" (1917) and Bogan's "Old
Countryside" (1919) both have the same organizing
idea. They consider Bogan's "Song for the Last
Act" to be her "most extensive emulation of
Teasdale."

1980

834. Moore, Patrick. "Symbol, Mask, and Meter in
     the Poetry of Louise Bogan." <u>Gender and
     Literary Voice</u>. Ed. Janet Todd. Vol. 1 of
     <u>Women and Literature</u>. New York: Holmes &
     Meier, 1980. pp. 67-80.

Bogan's "true feelings are blurred by symbol,
distanced by masks, muted by form." Her thematic
and stylistic effects show in the contrast between
her free verse which illustrates "fluidity and
freedom" and her "rigidly objectified" formal
verse which symbolizes "a separation from the
oneness and unity of experience and of love." The
obtuseness of her poems also results "from the
pressures male society placed upon her." Her
later poems, often written in free verse, are more
relaxed and accessible.

835. Rovit, Earl. "Our Lady-Poets of the 20's."
     <u>Southern Review</u> 16 (1980): 65-68.

In this somewhat patronizing defense of Teasdale,
Millay, Wylie, Amy Lowell, Marianne Moore, Babette
Deutsch, and Bogan, Rovit suggests that these
women "display a debilitating dichotomy between
their intellectual confidence and their sense of
emotional vulnerabliity." He also attempts to
incorporate these poets' lives into the Cinderella
legend.

When he states that Bogan, like the others, shy
away from fiction, using her journals "which brood
with loving mordancy over her childhood" as
"evidence that she may very well have suppressed
an authentic fiction imagination," Rovits
overlooks Bogan's 13 published short stories.

1981

836. Kumin, Maxine.   "'Stamping a Tiny Foot
     Against God': Some American Women Poets
     Writing between the Two Wars." _Quarterly_
     Journal of the Library of Congress 39, No. 1
     (Winter 1981): 48-61.

Kumin compares and comments upon the influences of
Amy Lowell, H. D., Sara Teasdale, Edna Millay,
Marianne Moore, Muriel Rukeyser, and Louise Bogan
in the 1920s and 30s. The title quotation from
Roethke denigrates them all, except for Bogan who
shares his distaste for most women poets. In
ironic contrast to Bogan's definition of the chief
asset of women's poetry being female lyricism,
Bogan herself wrote "spare and unsentimental
lyrics in the manner of Ben Jonson." Bogan
trivializes other women's lives in the poems
"Evening in the Sanitarium" and "Short Summary."

                    1982

837. Frank, Elizabeth Perlmutter.   "Putting to Sea
     (Louise Bogan in 1936)." _Grand Street_ 2
     (1982): 131-44.

The year 1936 marked a turning point in Bogan's
life. She had faced and overcome the problems
with her mother and her former husband, Raymond
Holden. That she was able to forgive her mother
is shown in the poem "Sleeping Fury." She could
even deal with Holden's inability to tell the
truth, evidenced by the unpublished poem, "The
Lie." Bogan said that her long poem, "Putting to
Sea" "summed up the Holden suffering, endured so
long, but now, at last completely over." She
could now enjoy "ordinary satisfaction in her work
and in her association with people," such as a
brief affair with Theodore Roethke and her
continuing friendships with Edmund Wilson and
Rolfe Humphries.

838. Pais, Sarah Via.   "Shapes of the Feminine
     Experience in Art." _Women: the Arts and the_
     1920s in Paris and New York. Ed. Kenneth W.
     Wheeler and Catharine R. Stimpson. New
     Brunswick: Transaction Books, 1982.
     pp. 49-55.

"Sonnet," the last poem from Bogan's first
collection, is misinterpreted in this essay on the

artistic contributions of women in New York and
Paris in the 20s. The entrapment in the poem
comes from a lover, not from society. Although
Bogan was one of "the first generation of American
women to openly share a commitment to the
enterprise of art," she stayed firmly within the
constraints of the male-dominated society.

1983

839. Peterson, Douglas L. "The Poetry of Louise
     Bogan." Southern Review 19. No. 1 (Winter
     1983): 73-87.

Bogan's formalist poetry, with the "rhythmical
technicalities of traditional prosody," contrasts
with the modern poetry of her contemporaries and
shows the influence of the "English Renaissance
plain stylists." Stoicism appears in her
"renunciation and practiced indifference in
dealing with loss and betrayal." Her later poems
show a preoccupation with death and time. Bogan's
style and subjects have a "limiting sameness."

1984

840. Cookson, Sandra. "The Repressed Becomes the
     Poem: Landscape and Quest in Two Poems by
     Louise Bogan." Critical Essays on Louise
     Bogan. Ed. Martha Collins. Boston: G. K.
     Hall, 1984. pp. 194-203.

Cookson compares the early poem "Putting to Sea"
and the late poem "The Psychiatrist's Song" with
their similar themes of sexual passion and
jealousy, their setting off on an ocean voyage,
and their dialogue between two voices. In the 30
years between writing these poems, Bogan has
achieved a "psychic equilibrium." She now
controls the rudder of the boat that steers
towards the shore, as she controls her own life.

841. Limmer, Ruth. "Circumscriptions." Critical
     Essays on Louise Bogan. Ed. Martha Collins.
     Boston: G. K. Hall, 1984. pp. 166-74.

If Bogan had permitted herself the poetic license
she permitted men, would she have written more
poetry? She required that women's poetry be
anonymous, dignified, not harsh or coarse, and

expecially not confessional. She wrote little
poetry in her last two decades perhaps because of
her self-imposed limitations.

842. Middlebrook, Diane Wood. "The Problem of the
     Woman Artist: Louise Bogan, 'The Alchemist.'"
     Critical Essays on Louise Bogan. Ed. Martha
     Collins. Boston: G. H. Hall, 1985.
     pp. 174-80.

"In her life Bogan never conquered the ambivalence
toward the woman artist that colored her cultural
milieu." In her poetry men's intellectual power
is symbolized by "breath," while women's
physicality is "flesh," illustrated in the poems
discussed here: "The Alchemist," "Cassandra," and
"Fifteenth Farewell."

843. Moldaw, Carol. "Form, Feeling, and Nature:
     Aspects of Harmony in the Poetry of Louise
     Bogan." Critical Essays on Louise Bogan.
     Ed. Martha Collins. Boston: G. K. Hall,
     1985. pp. 180-94.

Moldaw provides close readings of the images,
sounds, and rhythms in the poems "Sub Contra,"
"Baroque Comment," "Night," and "Song for a Lyre"
to prove her assertion that "the correlation
between the rhythmical nature of the aesthetic and
natural worlds and the human psyche is at the
heart of Bogan's poetry."

844. Pope, Deborah. "Music in the Granite Hill:
     The Poetry of Louise Bogan." A Separate
     Vision: Isolation in Contemporary Women's
     Poetry. Baton Rouge: Louisiana State
     University Press, 1984. Reprinted in
     Critical Essays on Louise Bogan. Ed. Martha
     Collins. Boston: G. K. Hall, 1984.
     pp. 149-66.

Pope limits her discussion of Bogan's poetry to
her first collection, Body of This Death, a study
of female isolation "caused by an inner paralysis
of the will and selfhood," which lays the
foundation for all of her subsequent work. The
arrangement of the poems in this collection
reflects the way Bogan dealt with paralysis.

Poems from the beginning of the book: "The
Frightened Man," "Betrothed," and "Words for
Departure," show the failure of escape through
another person. Women's inability to love is the
theme of the central poems: "Men Loved Wholly
Beyond Wisdom" and "Women." Determination for
positive action and responsibility characterize
most of the remaining poems, especially "Last Hill
in a Vista," which advocates throwing off the
constraints of convention.

1985

845. Novak, Michael Paul. "Love and Influence:
     Louise Bogan, Rolfe Humphries and Theodore
     Roethke." Kenyon Review 7, No. 3 (Summer
     1985): 19-20.

Humphries and Bogan gave Roethke "tempered
encouragement and tough advice." They provided
examples of literary incorruptibility for the
"success-driven" Roethke. Bogan also introduced
her lover from an early brief affair and longtime
friend to the importance of the unconscious in
poetry. Her criticism helped him improve his
work.

846. De Shazer, Mary K. "'My Scourge, My Sister':
     The Elusive Muse of Louise Bogan." Coming to
     Light: American Women Poets in the Twentieth
     Century. Ed. Diane Middlebrook and Marilyn
     Yalom. Ann Arbor: The University of Michigan
     Press, 1985. Revised and reprinted in
     Inspiring Women Reimaging the Muse. New
     York: The Pergamon Press, 1986. pp. 45-66.

De Shazer uses Bogan's poems to attempt to prove
feminist theories concerning women's artistic
silences and their struggles to write poetry in a
male-dominated world, where a woman poet must be
her own muse. She shows Bogan's conflict between
her need to write poetry and her fear of exposing
her private life, symbolized in several poems,
including: "The Daemon," "Cassandra," "Medusa,"
and "The Sleeping Fury," in which the demonic, but
also benevolent muse torments the speaker, but
won't allow her to be silent. De Shazer replaces
the mythological Furies with the Maenads in her
discussion of "The Sleeping Fury."

1986

847. Muller, John. "The Light and Wisdom of the
     Dark: Aging and the Language of Desire in the
     Texts of Louise Bogan." Memory and Desire:
     Aging-Literature-Psychoanalysis. Ed.
     Kathleen Woodward and Murray M. Schwartz.
     Bloomington: Indiana University Press, 1986.
     pp. 76-96.

In this difficult essay, Muller deals with
Lancanian theory on light and desire as evidenced
in Bogan's poetry, letters, and journals. Muller
argues "light and its associated objects have a
distinctive function in Bogan's texts, a
particularity deriving from the nature of her
desire as lured to the gaze of the other." He
defines the other for Bogan in a progression which
begins with her personal other, her mother; and
continues with the framework of order provided by
the other, the objects in the Gardners' orderly
house; and leads to the symbolic other, Bogan's
reading. The subsequent others are the men in
Bogan's life, her husbands and lovers. But the
most important "Other" for Bogan remains her
poetry. As an example of the relationship between
light and the other, Muller refers to the
childhood occasion when her mother's infidelities
affected her so much that the child Louise lost
her sight for a few days. The ultimate "Other" is
death, personified in Bogan's last poem, "The
Demon Lover."

1987

848. Drake, William. "The Passion of Friendship."
     The First Wave: Women Poets in America
     1915-1945. New York: Macmillan, 1987.
     pp. 258-265.

Drake discusses two decades of friendship between
Louise Bogan and May Sarton and finds that Bogan,
perhaps because of the struggle with her mother,
could not enter into a deeply felt friendship for
the younger emotionally demonstrative poet. Bogan
worked within the defensive lines for women set
down by men, while Sarton found empowerment in a
woman-centered atmosphere. Each woman's
sensibility is reflected in her poetry, with
Bogan's small output tightly controlled, and
Sarton's prodigious output expansive and

emotional.

849. Schechter, Ruth Lisa.   "Louise Bogan: A
     Reminiscence."   _Croton Review_ 10
     (Spring/Summer 1987): 30-33.

In this reminiscence about Bogan's poetry·workshop
at New York University in the 1960s, she is
described as "a mature, oval-faced woman . . . who
spoke in perfect syntax" and "whose patience with
students was unique." She taught control and
discipline and set formidable, challenging
standards. She emphasized organization in writing
poetry. Schechter includes the text of several
postcards she received from Bogan, as well as a
description of Bogan's apartment.

C. BRIEF MENTIONS

Selected brief, but important references to Louise
Bogan's work and life are contained in this
section. The selections are arranged
chronologically with reprints noted.

1929

850. Wilson, Edmund. I Thought of Daisy. New
     York: Farrar, Straus and Young, 1929. p. 8.
     Reprinted London: W. H. Allen, 1952 and New
     York: Farrar, Straus and Young, 1953.

In this novel Wilson describes Bogan's poetry
reading technique, although Rita Cavanaugh, the
character who is reading, is not otherwise based
on Louise Bogan. "When she read at all [it was]
as if her poems had been compositions which she
had never seen before, poems written by some other
person and by someone of whom she disapproved."

1932

851. Deutsch, Babette. "The Ghostly Member."
     Poetry in Our Time. New York: Holt, 1932.
     pp. 238-9. Reprinted New York: Doubleday,
     1952 and 1963. pp. 265-267.

"Miss Bogan's themes are the reasons of the heart
that reason does not know, the eternal strangeness
of time in its periods and its passage, the
curious power of art." Her lyric poems come from
the spirit; her few images are fit, her muse is
strong and fine. The savage world is controlled
by the heart.

1938

852. Nevins, Allan. "American Civilization:
     1922-1938." Saturday Review of Literature.
     18 (22 Oct. 1938): 4. Review of America Now:
     An Inquiry into Civilizations in the United
     States by Thirty-six Americans. Ed. Harold

E. Stearns. New York: Charles Scribner's
Sons, 1938. (Entry 690)

The book as a whole supports an "introverted
culture" and isolationism in most aspects.
"Louise Bogan thinks American poetry . . . has
dropped to a low ebb of spiritual strength, the
vitalizing influence of Pound and T. S. Eliot
having run out."

853. Ritchey, John. "Poetry, the Rediscovery of
     Words." Christian Science Monitor Magazine
     Section (4 May 1938): 5.

Robert Frost and John Hall Wheelock are the most
important men poets; Ruth Pitter and Louise Bogan
the most important women poets now that Edna St.
Vincent Millay's new book, Conversation at
Midnight, has been critically reviled. "If one
were to look for an example of the better kinds of
poetry being written at present by women, one
might turn with satisfaction to Miss Louise Bogan.
Never a prolific poet, her latest book is a slim
but arresting volume entitled The Sleeping Fury."

                    1941

854. Cowley, Malcolm. "Marginalia." New Republic
     104 (7 July 1941): 25.

Cowley and Bogan discuss the bitterness that poets
of this age seem to feel toward one another.
Louise Bogan suggests in jest a column in The New
Republic where poets can attack each other and
Cowley thinks this is an excellent suggestion even
though Auden preaches that love has more strength
than hate.

                    1959

855. Mead, Margaret. An Anthropologist at Work:
     The Writings of Ruth Benedict. Boston:
     Houghton Mifflin, 1959. pp. 77, 88, 90.
     (Entry 999)

Benedict's Feb. 29 and 30 diary entries mention
Bogan's poetry reading and traveling: "Louise was
a lovely figure . . . [she] read with an accent of
disdain, very becoming," and "Louise may be abroad
with Maidie while we are. She isn't happy, but

that would be a miracle. She's one of the most
lovable beings." Mead states that she wrote the
poem, "For a Proud Lady," for Louise Bogan.

1961

856. Simon, John. "Are You Literate About Modern
     Poetry?" Vogue 138, No. 8 (1 Nov. 1961):
     178.

"Louise Bogan is possibly the best American woman
poet writing in a field that includes strong
contenders." In her poems such as "Cassandra,"
(quoted in part here) "a feminine sensibility is
wedded . . . to a masculine firmness." Her poems
are examples of "pure, supple, slightly devious
lyricism."

1971

857. Wilson, Edmund. Upstate. New York: Farrar,
Straus and Girous, 1971. p. 154.

Wilson's 1957 journal entry written at Stone
House, his Talcottville, New York, residence
describes the inscriptions on the windows which
his guests have written with a diamond-tipped
pencil. "Louise Bogan in Helen's bedroom
[writes]: The landscape where I lie . . ."

1974

858. Stauffer, Donald Barlow. "Pound, Eliot, and
     the Imagists." A Short History of American
     Poetry. New York: Dutton, 1974. pp. 285-89.

"[Bogan's] tightly constructed, carefully tuned
lyrics treat sexual passion, death, and the
passage of time with a combination of intellectual
brilliance and sensuality." Compared with Elinor
Wylie and Léonie Adams, all three were influenced
by metaphysical poets, especially Donne in their
"attention to craftsmanship, to precision in
language, and . . . carefully constructed
conceits."

1976

859. Parini, Jay. "The Poet as Apprentice."
     Antaeus 23 (1976): 153-169. Reprinted as
     Chapter 2 in Theodore Roethke: An American

<u>Romantic</u>. Amherst: University of
Massachusetts, 1979. pp. 17-29.

Rolfe Humphries, Roethke's first mentor,
introduced him to Louise Bogan "whose poems the
younger poet had loved for several years." She
became his "most personal counselor, extending her
solitude from his poems to his life in general."
Parini quotes from her letter criticizing
Roethke's poem, "Open House," in which she
suggested he "open up." In other letters she
warned him against abstract diction and writing
political poetry. Parini speculates that Bogan
didn't understand Roethke's mental state when she
"attempted to jolt him out of his depression."

860. Pinsky, Robert. "Descriptions: Bogan,
     O'Hara." <u>The Situation of Modern Poetry:</u>
     <u>Contemporary Poetry and its Traditions</u>.
     Princeton, New Jersey: Princeton University
     Press, 1976. pp. 97-104.

Pinsky discusses Bogan's poem "Simple Autumnal" as
a description of grief, "a modern poem as well as
a traditional sonnet about grief and time." This
poem brings that "Romantic and modernist formula
to bear upon the older formula of the autumnal
lament." Pinsky also discusses Frank O'Hara's
"Poem." In both poems "the vivid, insensate
physical world serves to embody the painful stress
between time as it is, objectively and subjective
[to] human demands."

                           1978

861. Duffy, Bernard. "The Poem of the Act of the
     Avant-Garde Mind." <u>Poetry in America:</u>
     <u>Expression and Its Values in the Times of</u>
     <u>Bryant, Whitman and Pound</u>. Durham, North
     Carolina: Duke University Press, 1978.
     pp. 256-57.

Bogan's poetry of personal desolation continued
the American lyric revival in contexts of
"passion, aspiration, remorse, and exhortation as
whole sources of the poetic itself." Also
predominant in her poetry are stark loneliness and
isolation in poems with "an avant-garde extremity
of feeling."

Her criticism suggested, however, that writers

need not insist on a "stubborn avant-gardism" and
she also stressed the parallels between twentieth-
century American poetry and French Symbolist and
post-Symbolist writing.

1979

862. Brown, Ashley. "Allen Tate: A Poet on
     Poetry, 1924-1944." Poetry 135, No. 2
     (Nov. 1979): 106-7.

Tate promoted Bogan in his criticism, pairing her
almost always with Léonie Adams. Brown quotes
from Tate's essay "American Poetry Since 1920" his
comments on Body of This Death, "a slight but
almost perfect exhibit, [which] announced the most
accomplished woman poet of the time. . . ." Tate
undoubtedly advanced both poets' reputations all
the way to the Bollingen Prize which they
eventually shared.

863. Janeway, Elizabeth. "Women's Literature."
     Harvard Guide to Contemporary American
     Writing. Ed. Daniel Hoffman. Cambridge,
     Massachusetts: Belknap Press, 1979.

In a discussion of the role of romantic passion in
women's poetry, Janeway states "committing the act
of poetry is held to turn a woman into a fabulous
monster." "Louise Bogan puts the intenser forms
of female experience into mythic figures, under
the names of 'Medusa' or 'Cassandra' or 'The
Sleeping Fury,' while still assuring us that this
'wilderness' is not to be found in [ordinary]
women. . . ." "A woman's consciousness cannot
speak fully and openly" in its own form. Other
poems which use this mythic mask are "Tears in
Sleep" and "The Dream." Magic and enchantment
appear in "The Crossed Apple."

1980

864. Gallagher, Tess. "Poem: Time-The Pen in the
     Hands of Time." American Poetry Review 9,
     No. 4 (Jul.-Aug. 1980): 6-12.

"American poets . . . are exceptionally good at
talking about poetry," but they don't say enough
about the sense of time in poems. The author and
her graduate students explore five poets and their

work on time, beginning with Louise Bogan's poem
"Come Break with Time." A student discusses
Bogan's poems in her paper, especially "Train
Tune" which goes back through time in a train
rhythm.

865. Hartman, Charles O. <u>Free Verse: An Essay on
     Prosody</u>. Princeton, New Jersey: Princeton
     University Press, 1980. pp. 61-63.

In a discussion of counterpoint as a prosodic mode
in "The Cupola," Hartman finds that passion rises
in the last stanza of the poem. The conclusion is
shocking after the meditative opening of the first
six lines. "In the context of the whole poem, we
interpret the surprise as a sudden passion in the
speaking voice."

1981

866. Ellman, Mary. "The Moving I." <u>Sewanee
     Review</u> 89, No. 3 (Summer 1981): 457-58.

Ellman discusses forms of recent biographies,
mentioning Ruth Limmer's "excellent notion in
putting together a mosaic of autobiographical
prose and verse." "The material is a little
strained and affected" in its organization around
the poem "Train Tune." Louise Bogan seldom felt
happiness or joy. She paid for her nature in
loneliness and depression. "God bless her, her
intelligence was too fine."

867. Halpern, Daniel. "The Pursuit of Suffering."
     <u>Antaeus</u> 40/41 (Winter/Spring 1981): 438-39.

We want suffering in our poetry; it is more
popular than happy love. Ambivalence towards love
comes out in the romantic love vocabulary where
"passion means suffering." In Bogan's poem, "Song
for the Last Act," the loved one is absent and
only his presence, which has been memorized,
survives. The narrator has the "Other" by heart.
Compared to other poems, death functions as a
final romantic obstacle. "In this poem the memory
is frozen, fixed and offers little chance of
alteration."

1982

868. Walker, Cheryl. <u>The Nightingale's Burden</u>.
     Bloomington, Indiana: Indiana University
     Press, 1982. p. 149

In 19th century poetry the nightingale tradition
was the theme that the real forbidden lover is the
world or worldly powers. It suggests the "deeply
revolutionary consequences of indulging one's
desire for power." Several late poems by Louise
Bogan show similarities to poems by 19th century
poetesses on this theme, including "Henceforth,
from the Mind," "I Saw Eternity," "Dragonfly," and
"Kept."   Secret sorrow and the forbidden lover
archetype, prominent in the 20s and 30s, appear in
"Masked Woman's Song," representing a "mythical
female figure, perhaps Justice."

869.   Monteiro, George. "'A Way Out of
       Something': Robert Frost's Emily Dickinson."
       <u>The Centennial Review</u> 27 (1983): 192-203.

Monteiro quotes from a conversation he had with
Frost in connection with the Emily Dickinson panel
discussion organized by Amherst College to
celebrate Amherst's bicentennial in 1959. Frost,
in spite of his well-known interest in Dickinson
and his importance as an American poet, was not
asked to join the panel, which consisted of Louise
Bogan, Archibald MacLeish, and Richard Wilbur.
Miffed at being left out, Frost described the
panel's participants: "Louise does not know as
much as she thinks she knows [about Dickinson],
Archie doesn't know too much, [Richard Wilbur] a
college man here isn't interested in Emily at
all."

                         1987

870. Bowles, Gloria. "Two Poets in an
     Apartment." Quotation from <u>Louise Bogan's
     Aesthetics of Limitation</u> in <u>New York Times
     Book Review</u>, 15 Nov. 1987, 51. (Entry 819)

May Sarton describes Louise Bogan's apartment on
her first visit as a "civilized human room, filled
with the light of a sensitized, bitter, lucid
mind." "The habitation reflected . . . the tone,
the hidden music . . . of a woman living alone."

871. Fraser, John. "Discourse and Authority."
     <u>University of Toronto Quarterly</u> 56, No. 3
     (Spring 1987): 426, 427-429.

In a discussion of meaning in discourse, Fraser
quotes the last 12 lines of "Exhortation" to prove
it is a bitter poem. He also comments on
"Solitary Observation Brought Back from a Sojourn
in Hell" as illustrating how discourse connects
with nature when the title is longer than the
poem.

1988

872. Bawer, Bruce. "Léonie Adams, Poet."
      <u>New Criterion</u> 7, No. 2 (Oct. 1988): 21-26.

Louise Bogan was a longtime friend of Adams with
whom she was often compared, and to whom she
partially dedicated <u>High Falcon</u>, and with whom she
shared the Bollingen Prize. Bogan commented about
Adams' poetry: "She has moments of cousinship with
Webster and Tourneur, with Vaughan and Traherne."
Bogan also said Adams' later poetry is so charged
with meaning that "it sometimes slips out of
syntax in the manner of the late Mallarmé."

873. Fowlie, Wallace. "Remembering Léonie Adams."
     <u>New Criterion</u> 7, No. 2 (Oct. 1988): 16-20.

Léonie Adams' and Louise Bogan's names were often
joined. These two friends' work had been
recognized about the same time. In a description
of the two poets discussing Mallarmé's sonnet
"M'introduire dans ton Historie," they analyzed
the lines, often repeating them by memory.

1989

874. Hall, Donald. "Death to the Death of Poetry:
     A Response to the Elegists." <u>Harper's</u> 279
     (Sept. 1989): 72-76.

In an article contradicting the doomsayers of the
death of poetry, Hall states that the greatest
falling off of reviewing books of poetry is in <u>The
New Yorker</u>, which once regularly published Louise
Bogan's essays on "Verse." Poetry needs to be
reviewed. Poetry readings don't take the place of
reviewers who "occupy continual soapboxes and

promote developing standards [and] . . . provide
sensors to report from the confusing plentitude of
the field." Helen Vendler is more inclined to
write about translations or poets who are safely
dead. Men or women like Louise Bogan, Conrad
Aiken, and Malcolm Cowley practiced literary
journalism to make their livings. Their
successors now meet classes "MWF." "People with
tenure don't need to write book reports."

D. REVIEWS OF LOUISE BOGAN'S POETRY

These reviews span 46 years, beginning with reviews of single poems and continuing through the publication of all of her books of poetry. Included are reviews that contribute important information on each collection. Omitted are reviews that simply list each book's publication with few comments, except for those briefly noted in The New Yorker. The books of poetry reviewed are listed chronologically, with the individual reviews of each book listed alphabetically by author or title. Reprints of the reviews are also included.

875. "The Poems of the Month Selected by William Stanley Braithwaite." Bookman 55 (May 1922): 259. (Entry 21)

Louise Bogan's "Women" from The Measure is a sharp and acid portrait of the feminine sex. The merciless exposure of paradox in women's nature acts like an acid and eats up all the former sentiment of women.

876. "The Poems of the Month Selected by Genevieve Taggard." Bookman 58, No. 2 (Oct. 1923): 197-98. (Entry 26)

"Nothing else this month has such style" as Louise Bogan's poem "Chanson un Peu Naïve," which is quoted in full in this review. Although it is difficult to analyze a good poem that is especially interesting to craftsman, in this lyric's first four lines "a nice balance between the rise and fall of common speech, and the movement of the strict stanza, contribute part of the quality."

Reviews of BODY OF THIS DEATH, 1923.

877. "Briefer Mention." Dial 76 (March 1924):
     289.

Miss Bogan "gives the impression of being an
inexpert craftsman striving fitfully and
inchoately to express that which defies
expression."

878. Douglas, A. Donald. "Body of This Death."
     New Republic 37 (5 Dec. 1923): 20, 22

Miss Bogan's first book of poems sings one song
over and over, "under a multiple dazzle of title
and imagery." Her range is narrow, but intense
and unforgettable. The images may be obscure, but
they have an "austere and perdurable beauty"
illustrated in "A Tale." This book "unlocks the
luminous abyss of pain."

879. Fletcher, John Gould. "Minor Poetry."
     Freeman 8 (5 Mar. 1924): 622.

"The minor poet, like the poor, is always with
us." Miss Bogan's work "betrays close study of
Donne, Miss Lowell, and H. D." Her craftsmanship
"conceals an emptiness of thought that is
positively painful."

880. Jones, Llewellyn. First Impressions: Essays
     on Poetry, Criticism and Prose. New York:
     Knopf, 1925. pp. 118-22. Reprinted in
     Critical Essays on Louise Bogan. Ed. Martha
     Collins. Boston: G. K. Hall, 1984.
     pp. 27-29.

Bogan's poetry is a struggle against the
limitations placed on women and a cry "for
something compelling." Her diction and rhythm are
austere. She has learned from E. A. Robinson and
Yeats. Some of her poems are difficult because
she is writing about her inner experiences in
dream imagery, as in the poem "A Tale."

881. Kreymborg, Alfred. A History of American
     Poetry: Our Singing Strength. New York:
     Tudor Publishing Company, 1934. pp. 550-552.

Bogan is a metaphysical poet who owes something
to Elinor Wylie. Her primary concern is a woman
bereft of love. "Fire and wisdom have gone into
the composition of these lyrics."

882. Nicholl, Louise Townsend. "Miss Bogan's
     Book." Measure 32 (Oct. 1923): 15-19.

"There is no doubt she is one of the best American
poets. . ." She should take up prose and write
the kind of novels Viola Meynell writes. Nicholl
quotes in full "Chanson un Peu Naive," "Memory,"
"Women," "Decoration" (left out of subsequent
collections), "The Alchemist," and "Fifteenth
Farewell." Bogan puts into her poems the
"individual and typical psychology of women, of
men, and of their relationships."

883. Tate, Allen. "American Poetry Since 1920."
     Reviews of Allen Tate 1924-1944. Eds. Ashley
     Brown and Frances Neel Cheney. Baton Rouge
     and London: Louisiana State University Press,
     1983. p. 83.

"Miss Bogan's Body of this Death, a slight but
almost perfect exhibit, announced the most
accomplished woman poet of the time. "[She] had
succeeded in reducing a sharp sense of peripheral
sensations to which women are peculiarly
sensitive, to form." However Léonie Adams' (whose
work is also reviewed) range is "considerably
richer than Miss Bogan's."

884. Van Doren, Mark. Nation 108 (31 Oct. 1923):
     494. Reprinted in Critical Essays on Louise
     Bogan. Ed. Martha Collins. Boston: G. K.
     Hall, 1984. pp. 29-31.

A poet rarely achieves so much pure poetry in so
few pages. "Under a diversity of forms Miss Bogan
has expressed herself with an almost awful
singleness." Because of the concentrated images,
it is difficult to describe the poems. Van Doren
quotes "The Alchemist," which "alone would
establish excellence in her art." Although
sometimes her poems are too personal to be
meaningful to others, the volume "may be a
classic."

885. Wolf, Robert L. "Impassioned Austerity."
     Poetry 23, No. 6 (March 1924): 335-38.

Bogan's work is the "love experience of a modern
woman." Her poems suffer from constriction and
"terrible intensity," and she needs to "deliver
herself more loosely and luxuriously to her art."
She is difficult because she has too much to say.

Reviews of DARK SUMMER 1929

886. Engels, Vincent. "A Memorable Poetry Year."
     The Commonweal 7 (13 Nov. 1929): 52-53.

"Old Countryside" is one of the best poems of
1929, even though the rest of the collection of
"hard-bitten verses is not always the easiest kind
of reading." Miss Bogan has two voices, seen in
"Summer Wish," "one implacable, the other
proclaiming the detachment that comes . . . from
nature."

887. Gorman, Herbert. "Some Interesting Winter
     Books." Century 120, No. 1 (Winter 1930):
     157-58.

There is no one in America who can compare with
Louise Bogan, nor who is "more suggestive of the
finished French artist." Gorman quotes "The
Romantic" to give "proof of her self-discipline
and exactness of phraseology."

888. Gregory, Horace. "Louise Bogan's Lyric
     Crystals." New York Evening Post,
     23 Nov. 1929.

In a review that also discusses Merrill Moore,
Gregory finds Bogan a representative of the right
wing of politics, "long associated with The
Measure group." Her limitations are similar to
those of Elinor Wylie. She "has mastered a cool,
inflexible technique" in concentrating her world
into "brief crystalline lyric forms."

889. Jones, Llewellyn. "Miss Bogan's Poems:
     Beauty Thru Conflict." Chicago Post,

18 Oct. 1929.

Jones assumes Body of This Death is out of print
because this book has so many poems taken from it.
He compares Bogan to Yeats in that she has come
through her earlier disillusionment and
romanticism. Her poetry is a "record of difficult
living." He quotes "The Alchemist" to show her
inability to "take things on easy terms."

890. S. M. New Yorker 5 (7 Dec. 1929): 163.

Two collections of poems, Dark Summer by Louise
Bogan and High Falcon by Léonie Adams, "recall in
some ways the finely etched work of Emily
Dickinson." The two young poets resemble each
other stangely in that "they both write
exceedingly well, frequently in the same mood, and
their defects of attenuation of thought and
intricacy of phrase" are the same. Each book,
however, "contains many lyrics of unusual beauty."

891. New York Times Book Review (24 Nov. 1929):
     37.

"Miss Bogan's poetry has in it the breath of the
forests and the beauty of the sea," perhaps coming
from her Maine background (although she was the
granddaughter of a sea captain, not the daughter
as mistakenly stated here). "Portrait" is perhaps
"a little overwrought," and "Simple Autumnal"
departs from the Italian model in the sextet.

892. Taylor, Parker. "Five Contemporary Poets."
     The New World Monthly 413 (Feb. 1930): 159.

Taylor distains a "squeamish attitude" toward
criticizing poets and proceeds to pan the work of
each poet, including Bogan, in this article. He
fails to "find any ultimate value" in her new
volume of poems with a "metaphysical tendency."

893. Untermeyer, Louis. "In a Gold Stain."
     Saturday Review (1 Feb. 1930): 692.
     Reprinted in Critical Essays on Louise Bogan.
     Ed. Martha Collins. Boston: G. K. Hall,
     1984. pp. 36-37.

This poetry is "almost perfect of its kind." It
is as "exquisite in content as it is in format."
"Its quality lifts it high above the merely
adequate writing published in such qualities by
women in these so literate states." She deals
with reality and "the secret behind appearance."
"Cassandra," quoted here, illustrates her vision
and her "unusually exact economy."

894. Walton, Edna Lou. "Verse Delicate and
     Mature." Nation 129 (4 Dec. 1929): 682-84.
     Reprinted in Critical Essays on Louise Bogan.
     Ed. Martha Collins. Boston: G. K. Hall,
     1984. pp. 37-38.

"No other poet in America has a more inevitable
sense of the exact word to be employed." Miss
Bogan examines the warfare between heart and mind,
without finding respite in the passionate
interludes of the poems from the first volume.
She is "one of the true poets" who is an excellent
technician "with an extremely sensitive approach
to [her] physical world. . . ."

895. Winters, Yvor. New Republic 60
     (16 Oct. 1929): 247-48. Reprinted in
     Critical Essays on Louise Bogan. Ed. Martha
     Collins. Boston: G. K. Hall, 1984.
     pp. 31-34.

Miss Bogan has progressed from being influenced by
E. A. Robinson into a more purely lyrical mode
that culminates in "The Mark," "Come, Break with
Time," and "Simple Autumnal." Her technical
limitations include free verse and an inability to
write a developed long poem. Her style, not the
complexity of her ideas, provides the poems'
complexity. Her subject matter is limited, but
"it would take only a turn, a flicker to transform
her into a major poet." "She is beyond any doubt
one of the principal ornaments of contemporary
American poetry."

896. Zabel, Morton Dauwen. "The Flower of the
     Mind." Poetry 35 (Dec. 1929): 158-62.
     Reprinted in Critical Essays on Louise Bogan.
     Ed. Martha Collins. Boston: G. K. Hall,
     1984. pp. 34-36.

"She has brought her verse to a state of ripe
completeness. . . ." Since her artistry depends
upon reduction, the two long poems "The Flume" and
"Summer Wish" are not her best. The lyrics show
her delicate imagery. The symbols derive from her
experience. "By her fine craftsmanship and sure
judgment, she has made herself a master of her
art."

Reviews of SLEEPING FURY, 1937.

897. Benet, William Rose. "Contemporary Poetry."
     Saturday Review 15, No. 26 (24 Apr. 1937):
     22.

"Louise Bogan stands in the forefront of American
women poets. . . ." Hers is an "aristocratic art
with a slight Celtic flavor."

898. "Briefly Noted." New Yorker 13
     (11 Dec. 1937): 118.

"A collection of concise lyrics by the poetry
reviewer of The New Yorker."

899. Davidson, Eugene. "Poetry Defined and
     Redefined." Yale Review 26 (Summer 1937):
     819-20.

Bogan's poems "have a delicacy that is rare in
modern poetry." She is occasionally "bitter and
reticent."

900. Ford, Ford Madox. "Flame in Stone." Poetry
     50 (June 1937): 158-61. Reprinted in
     Critical Essays on Louise Bogan. Ed. Martha
     Collins. Boston, G. K. Hall. pp. 45-47.

Denying that he is a poetry critic, Ford says he
knows Miss Bogan's work is authentic because of
his feeling when reading her "bitter but beautiful
words." Her place should be with Herbert and
Donne.

901. Holmes, John. "Poetry Now." Boston Evening

Reviews of Books of Poetry   249

"The most distinguished poet to issue a new book
this spring is undoubtedly Louise Bogan." A
darkness runs through her effortlessly simple
poems. Holmes quotes her New Yorker review on
Roethke's Trial Balances to show her critical
abilities.

902. Lechliter, Ruth. New York Herald Tribune
     Books, 30 May 1937, 2. Reprinted in Critical
     Essays on Louise Bogan. Ed. Martha Collins.
     Boston: G. K. Hall, 1984. pp. 43-45.

"Miss Bogan has achieved a mastery of form rare in
the realm of modern poetry," art resembling that
of a sculptor which captures "the terrible (but
corruptible) vitality and beauty of the living in
deathless marble." Her poem "Sonnet" is one of
the "most flawlessly formed and motivated sonnets"
of our day. She continues to be indebted to the
metaphysical masters of form, Herbert, Donne and
Vaughan. The title poem recalls the earlier poem,
"Medusa." "Putting to Sea" has similar themes and
images as those in D. H. Lawrence's poem, "The
Ship of Death." However Lawrence comes from the
school of poets that bases its ideas on the
concept of Becoming, while Bogan belongs to the
metaphysicians who believe in a permanent Being.

903. Rexroth, Kenneth. San Francisco Chronicle,
     25 July 1937, 4D. Reprinted in Critical
     Essays on Louise Bogan. Ed. Martha Collins.
     Boston: G. K. Hall, 1984. pp. 40-41.

After her first book which "concerned itself with
the conflicts arising from . . . the old war of
flesh and spirit, translated into a critical
disillusion," this latest book has found her
mature in wisdom and mellowing. "The Fury has
found time to rest." The conquests of militant
femininity were bitter, while the conflicts on a
higher plane, within Bogan's personality, were
mirrored in Bogan's best earlier poems. "Perhaps
she will rise again and wake to this struggle."

904. Tate, Allen. "R. P. Blackmur and Others."
     Southern Review 3 (Summer 1937): 190-92.

Reprinted in <u>The Poetry Reviews of Allen Tate</u>
<u>1924-1944</u>. Eds. Ashley Brown and Frances
Neel Cheney. Baton Rouge and London:
Louisiana State University Press, 1983.
p. 184.

Miss Bogan improves with each book she publishes.
Three or four poems in this collection have no
superior within her purpose or range (except for
her peer Léonie Adams). "Miss Bogan is a
craftsman in the masculine mode." She "reaches
the height of her talent in 'Henceforth, from the
Mind,' surely one of the finest lyrics of our
times." This poem and "The Mark" "entitle her to
the consideration of the coming age." But "The
Sleeping Fury" and "Hypocrite Swift" are both
failures.

905. Walton, Edna Lou. "Henceforth from the
     Mind." <u>Nation</u> 144 (24 Apr. 1937): 88.

"The conflict between emotional intensity and an
intellectual analysis almost equally violent. .
. is in these poems resolved." Betrayal is her
theme. Her poetry is distinguished by its wisdom.

906. Zabel, Morton Dauwen. "Lyric Authority."
     <u>New Republic</u> 90 (5 May 1937): 391-92.
     Reprinted in <u>Critical Essays on Louise Bogan</u>.
     Ed. Martha Collins. Boston: G. K. Hall,
     1948. pp. 48-49.

Miss Bogan's example of lyric discipline is
necessary in an age when public and proletarian
verse is in fashion. Her finest poems may be
compared to those of Yeats and Rilke, neither of
whom allowed themselves to be dictated to by
poetic fashion. She has "kept to the hardest line
of integrity a poet can follow," her own self-
criticism.

Reviews of <u>POEMS AND NEW POEMS</u>, 1941.

907. "Briefly Noted." <u>New Yorker</u> 17
     (25 Oct. 1941): 92.

"A selection from earlier volumes by <u>The New</u>

<u>Yorker's</u> poetry reviewer, with seventeen
additional poems, several of them light in tone,
but not in substance." The book is distinguished
for her "beautiful, exact, and heart-rending
language."

908. Auden, W. H. "The Rewards of Patience."
     <u>Partisan Review</u> 9 (Jul.-Aug. 1942): 336-340.

In an age when poets write like journalists to
please public taste, Miss Bogan's poetry
"represents a victory over the Collective Self and
over the Private Self." Her development from the
early "catharsis of resentment" poems shows growth
beyond a personal system of myth. By her lifelong
self-discipline, she has achieved wisdom and
technical mastery, as well as an objectivity about
personal experience.

909. Benet, William Rose.   "Three Women Poets."
     <u>Saturday Review of Literature</u> 25, No. 17
     (25 Apr. 1942): 22-23.

Miss Bogan is "one of the most accomplished of the
older women poets still with us." Her limitations
are difficulty of understanding and intensely
personal poetry. Her "Celtic magic of language
has somehow blended with the tartness of New
England."

910. Colum, Mary. <u>New York Times</u> 30 Nov. 1941.

"What a good thing if Miss Bogan could get out of
the mood and the mold." Colum refers to Bogan's
habit of concocting sonnets "that sound as if they
could have been written by other poets such as
Elinor Wylie or Leonie Adams." Bogan's difference
is her "Celtic turn" influenced by Yeats. "The
craftsmanship is exquisite, but it is the poetry
of self-absorption. . . ."

Replies to review in "Letters to the Editor" by
David Morton and Rolfe Humphries, <u>New York Times</u>,
14 Dec. 1941.

Humphries states: "Bogan has published exactly
seven sonnets. . . ." Her poems are not like
those of Yeats, Léonie Adams or Elinor Wylie.

Reply to Humphries' letter by Mary Colum, <u>New York Times</u>, 28 Dec. 1941.

"Bogan must begin to get out of the Yeats mold. . . for at present she is saturated with him."

911. Cowley, Malcolm. <u>New Republic</u> 105
     (10 Nov. 1941): 625. Reprinted in <u>Critical Essays on Louise Bogan</u>. Ed. Martha Collins.
     Boston: G. K. Hall. pp. 58-59.

Bogan's real subject is poetry itself. Her type of poetry is "terrifyingly difficult to write." She has "added a dozen or more [poems] to our small stock of memorable lyrics." Cowley hopes that Bogan will relax and write more "carelessly."

912. Daniels, Earl. "Civilized-Barbaric-Honest."
     <u>Voices</u> 108 (Winter 1941): 54-57.

"Miss Bogan is our most civilized poet," writing in a "mature and cultivated way," but she will never be a popular poet. This new book, which could have included more poems, shows the "frugality of the poet's talent." (Charles Henri Ford's book, <u>The Overturned Plate</u> is "barbaric," and George Zabriskie's <u>Mind's Geography</u> is "honest.")

913. Deutsch, Babette. <u>New York Herald Tribune</u>
     Books, 28 Dec. 1941, 8. Reprinted in
     <u>Critical Essays on Louise Bogan</u>. Ed. Martha Collins. Boston: G. K. Hall, 1984.
     pp. 57-60.

Although the new poems in the present collection do not "exceed or equal" any of her earlier poems, they do show that Miss Bogan has not changed her work according to current fashion. The two strains that influence her work, the metaphysical and the modern woman, can also be found in the poems of Léonie Adams and Elinor Wylie. Many of her poems are about music or are written to be sung.

914. Kunitz, Stanley. "Pentagons and

Pomegranates." Poetry 60 (Apr. 1942): 40-43.
Reprinted as "Land of Dust and Flame" in
A Kind of Order, a Kind of Folly by Stanley
Kunitz. Boston: Little, Brown, 1975,
pp. 194-97. Also reprinted in Critical
Essays on Louise Bogan. Ed. Martha Collins.
Boston: G. K. Hall, 1984. pp. 63-66.

Miss Bogan's poetry cannot be reviewed with
generalized criticism of women's poetry because
she is not careless of words and the rhythmic
pattern. To her, subject matter is not all. She
has respect for her art and capacity for self-
disdain. But, except for "The Dream" and "The
Daemon," her new poems are "less consummately
organized than before." There should be more
poems like "Hyprocrite Swift" and "Kept."

915. Moore, Marianne. "Compactness Compacted."
     Nation 153 (15 Nov. 1941): 486. Reprinted in
     Predilections by Marianne Moore. New York:
     Viking, 1955. pp. 130-33. Also reprinted in
     Critical Essays on Louise Bogan. Ed. Martha
     Collins. Boston: G. K. Hall, 1984.
     pp. 61-63.

Bogan uses a kind of forged rhetoric that
nevertheless seems inevitable. She is a workman
who refuses to be deceived; her work is not
mannered. Her poems "let the sound [of others]
come forth unhindered," including Auden in
"Evening in the Sanitarium," Hopkins in
"Fuernacht," Yeats in "Betrothed," and W. C.
Williams in "Zone." In her poems are "medicines
for mortal rage and immortal injury."

916. Moses, W. R. "Louise Bogan: Poems and New
     Poems." Accent 2 (Winter 1942): 120-21.

Although Bogan's subjects are similar to those of
Edna St. Vincent Millay and Elinor Wylie, there
are differences in detail, diction, and meter in
her favor. Her limitations have to do with "the
strength of [strong primary emotion] and the
object or situation to which they attach." The
new poems are "a scattered lot."

Reviews of <u>COLLECTED POEMS 1923-1953</u>, 1954.

917. Adams, Léonie. "All Has Been Translated into
     Treasure." <u>Poetry</u> 85 (Dec. 1954): 165-69.
     Reprinted in <u>Critical Essays on Louise Bogan</u>.
     Boston: G. K. Hall, 1984. pp. 68-71.

Things that were said about <u>Body of This Death</u> in
1923, are still "being said with perfect soundness
in 1954." She refused to be deluded then and now.
"Small ironic portraits" and epigrams are still
found, as well as acceptance in some of the last
lyrics, especially "Song for the Last Act."
"Henceforth, from the Mind" is "surely one of the
perfect lyrics of the period." The virtues of her
writing might "well delimit the classic form of
the short lyric. . . ." Bogan seems to write only
when compelled "by the strong experience of the
private person."

918. Ciardi, John. "Two Nuns and a Strolling
     Player." <u>Nation</u> 178 (22 May 1954): 445-46.
     Reprinted in <u>Critical Essays on Louise Bogan</u>.
     Boston: G. K. Hall, 1984. pp. 66-67.

"Miss Wylie, Miss Adams and Miss Bogan were surely
sisters in the same aesthetic convent [whose]
sisterhood insisted on wearing its chastity belts
on the outside. . . ." "Miss Bogan began in
beauty, but she has aged to magnificence. . . ."
In her later poems "she comes out of timelessness
into time" and has wrestled with the more
difficult demon.

919. Eberhart, Richard. <u>New York Times Book
     Review</u>, 30 May 1954, 6. Reprinted in
     <u>Critical Essays on Louise Bogan</u>. Boston:
     G. K. Hall, 1984. pp. 67-68.

"When compulsion and style meet we have a strong,
inimitable Bogan poem." She writes in traditional
verse forms, about forceful emotions. She
struggles to "confront naked realities at their
source." Her universal poems include "My Voice
Not Being Proud." In the pure lyric category is
"Song for a Slight Voice." Her reviews for <u>The
New Yorker</u> have developed to a "fine point of
critical interest and sagacity."

920. Flaccus, Kimball. "Daughters of Whitman and
     Donne." Voices 155 (Sept.-Dec. 1954): 49-51.

If Edna Millay is a "daughter" of Walt Whitman,
then Louise Bogan and Léonie Adams might be termed
"daughters" of John Donne. They both "possess
fine, almost precious talents, and great technical
skill within strictly limited and condensed forms,
in a minor key." They are less American in their
selection of poetic themes than Edna Millay.

921. Jones, Llewellyn. "Poets in Epitome."
     Universalist Leader (Jan. 1948): 8-9.

"This poet digests hard iron" in the creative
process. It is possible to divide the poems into
three categories: "confrontations, observations of
inevitabilities, and expressions of dissent." She
has a very healthy, well-developed sense of humor.

922. Meredith, William. The Hudson Review 7,
     No. 4 (Winter 1955): 601.

In a comparison with Rolfe Humphries, the reviewer
finds both their works "span and reflect the same
period . . . and have certain points of fashion in
common . . . ." Her "purity of taste" and wit
save her. In this collection the poems that are
least successful "fail by a kind of
calculatedness."

923. New Yorker 30 (8 May 1954): 148.

"Note: The Noonday Press has collected Louise
Bogan's Collected Poems, many of which were first
printed in this magazine."

924. Redman, Ben Ray. "Precise Images." Saturday
     Review of Literature 37, No. 7 (3 July 1954):
     119. 126.

Since Louise Bogan's first book of poetry was
published, "she has practiced her art gravely and
discreetly, with controlled passion and steady
devotion." "She is mistress of precise images. .
. and a musician" in her metaphysical poetry.

925. Rexroth, Kenneth.   "Among the Best Women
     Poets Writing Now in America."   New York
     Herald Tribune Book Review, 4 July 1954, 5.

Except for Marianne Moore, the three best American
poets are Babette Deutsch, Léonie Adams, and
Louise Bogan, although there is a world of
difference between them. Bogan's work causes
considerable problems for the reviewer. The
hyperesthesia, or trance state common in early
twentieth century poets is evident in her work,
but she deals with life honestly.

926. Sinha, Krishna Nandan.   "The Poetry of Louise
     Bogan."   Thought (23 July 1960): 13-14.

The reviewer incorrectly states this is Bogan's
first collection of poems which had been published
previously only in magazines. He finds her a more
satisfying "woman-poet" than others like Edith
Sitwell, Marianne Moore, etc. "She has the
piercing and uncanny insight of a wise and tender
woman." Death and love in the manner of Yeats and
Donne are her great themes. She writes of the
natural world which "she records like a sensitive
instrument."

927. Whittemore, Reed.   "The Principles of Louise
     Bogan and Yvor Winters."   Sewanee Review 63
     (Winter, 1955): 161-68.

Verbal discipline is what these poets are known
for. Mr. Winters' and Miss Bogan's poetry is an
"exercise in, or a demonstration of principle."
Their passion in poetry is rhetoric itself. Their
poetry is placed in the 16th or 17th century (or
perhaps 18th century) and has been praised by the
critic Tate for being in that time. In most of
their poems, the style is more noteworthy than the
substance. An example is Bogan's poem "Kept" in
which the technique supercedes the message of
putting away childish things.

Reviews of BLUE ESTUARIES, POEMS 1923-1968, 1968.
Also reviews of paperback edition published by
Ecco Press in 1977.

928. Carruth, Hayden. "A Balance Exactly Struck."
     Poetry 114, No. 5 (Aug. 1969)) 330-31.

Approximately 25 of her poems "may be the best of
their kind in English literature." She writes
with "a passionate austerity, a subtle balance,
and . . . perfect poetic attention, far beyond
technique . . . ." Poems where the intact poetic
experience is found include "Women" and "To My
Brother."

929. "Dorian, Donna. "Knowledge Puffeth Up."
     Parnassus 12-13 (Spring-Winter 1985):
     144-159.

This review of the paperback edition of Blue
Estuaries, published in 1977 by the Ecco Press,
states that the psychological motivation for
Bogan's poems came from her complex relationship
with her mother. Dorian uses material from
Frank's biography, Louise Bogan: A Portrait, to
show how the poems derive from the life. The
first poem, "A Tale," shows Bogan beginning her
journey into self-awareness. "Medusa" is a
statement of the complexities of the mother and
daughter relationship which is severed when the
child begins to feel sexual desire. "Cassandra,"
a "truncated sonnet," is the voice of the female
poet. In "The Sleeping Fury," Bogan makes peace
with her personal demons, her mother, and her
muse.

930. French, Robert. Concerning Poetry 2, No. 1
     (Spring 1969): 96-99.

"Style cannot compensate for lack of human
interest." Miss Bogan's craftmanship is apparent
throughout these few poems from her 45 years of
poetic creation. The reviewer admires her poems,
but does not like them because he misses the sound
of the human voice. Her poems are "almost always
conscious of their art," and many times the reader
does not know what they are about.

931. Heyden, William. "The Distance from Our
     Eyes." Prairie Schooner 43, No. 3
     (Fall 1969): 323-26.

In this "cold, comforting book," Miss Bogan forces
her readers to look at what life is really like.
It is a "portrait of a remarkable sensibility."
Her greatest strength is compression in this
poetry of meditation.

932. Meredith, William. <u>New York Times Book</u>
     Review, 13 Oct. 1968, 4. Reprinted in
     <u>Critical Essays on Louise Bogan</u>. Ed. Martha
     Collins. Boston: G. K. Hall, 1984.
     pp. 96-98.

Louise Bogan is "one of the best women poets
alive." But what does it mean to be a woman
artist in a man's culture? Bogan's answer is
correct: "I am an observant and feeling human
being." Her diction stems from the "severest
lyrical tradition in English." Her language is
"as supple as it is accurate." Her reputation has
lagged behind a career of "stubborn, individual
excellence."

933. Mills, Ralph. "In the Lyric Poetry
     Tradition." <u>Chicago Sun-Times Book Week</u>,
     9 Sept. 1968.

Bogan has placed herself "squarely in a line of
descent from some of the great Renaissance lyric
poets." She resembles Robert Graves in her
formalism and love themes. She "maintains a
fundamental attitude of self-reliance. . . ." She
integrates natural phenomena with innner life in
poems such as "Putting to Sea" and mythic,
dreamlike, hallucinatory visions in "Medusa" and
other poems.

934. Park, Clara Claibourne. "Poetry, Penetrable
     and Impenetrable." <u>Nation </u>3 (3 Sept. 1977):
     182-86.

Park presumes that the Ecco publishers have
reissued Bogan's poetry because of the new "clout
of Women's Studies" even though her "combination
of formal music and delicacy of feeling . . .
wouldn't get by the publisher in poems written by
a man." Park finds Ashbery an "impenetrable
gamesman" and Stanley Plumly an "all too
penetrable journeyman," while Bogan is an

"impenetrable sibyl." Bogan writes only of "the perennial landscape of the heart" with the "great beautiful generalizing words." Her "desire for personal privacy makes her poetry as a whole unsuccessful."

E. REVIEWS OF BOGAN'S OTHER BOOKS.

These reviews present the most valuable reviews of
Bogan's work, excluding her poetry, from the
sources available. The entries are arranged by
date of publication of her works, with the
individual reviews listed alphabetically.
Reviews of her survey of American literature, her
two books of collected criticism, her
collaborations on an anthology and translations,
her collected letters, and her "autobiography" are
included here.

Reviews of <u>ACHIEVEMENT IN AMERICAN POETRY</u> 1951

935. "Briefly Noted." <u>New Yorker</u> 28
     (22 Mar. 1952): 134.

Bogan has "very nearly brought off" a detailed
history of American poetry over the past half
century. "She has a great many wise and moving
things to say." "Many of her capsule criticisms
are just and penetrating--the deflating of Robert
Frost's nostalgia" for example. The anthology "of
fresh and sensitively chosen selections
supplements and illustrates the text.

936. "Feidelson, Charles. <u>American Quarterly</u> 4,
     No. 3 (Fall 1954): 272.

Miss Bogan's book is the most unsatisfactory of
the current surveys of modern American poetry
because of the "strange segregation of the
illustrative poems into a sort of anthology at the
end" and because her "all-too-impressionistic
critical method is given free rein . . . ." The
uncertainty of purpose in this study is obvious.

937. Fitts, Dudley. "Fifty Years of Promise and
     Fulfillment." <u>New York Times Book Review</u>,

25 Nov. 1951, 28.

In this review of the first three books in the
Regnery projected six-volume series, 20th Century
Literature in America, Fitts finds there are
problems with all three books attempting to
compress "a formidable amount of information into
[a] small compass." However, Bogan manages to do
a great deal of satisfactory talking about her
facts. She provides "sustained passages of true
criticism" and "rather breathless sketches" which
might have been developed further if the end of
the book had not been devoted to a "thoroughly
inconclusive anthology of poetry."

938. Fjelde, Rolf. New Republic 126
     (3 Mar. 1952): 21.

In a comparison of surveys of American poetry, the
reviewer finds "Louise Bogan's study of
contemporary poetry the most satisfying, a nicely
drawn history. . . ." The poems in the anthology
"sometimes appear as unrepresentational as they
are unhackneyed."

939. Fuller, Dorothy V. Arizona Quarterly 8,
     No. 1 (Spring 1952): 93-94.

Miss Bogan has the wide knowledge to "present the
background, the problems, the achievements of
American poetry over half a century," but she does
not "present the main trends clearly and draw
sound conclusions [from them]." She tends toward
sweeping generalization, especially in her
emphasis on Pound and Eliot, and the foreign
writers Lorca and Rilke. She does not give enough
emphasis to contemporary young poets, but she does
give the reader an idea of the complexity of the
period.

940. Lechlitner, Ruth. "Shifting Currents in
     Poetry. New York Herald Tribune Book Review,
     16 Dec. 1951, 9.

This survey, "intended as a history of
contemporary poetry," succeeds because of Louise
Bogan's "intelligent, lucid, and detached critical
approach."

941. "Poetic Half-Century." <u>Newsweek</u>,
       3 Dec. 1951, 96-97.

"Despite her cool and detached tone, her selection
[of poems] gives an impression of almost blinding
brilliance in American poetry" which she connects
to its European sources. She contributes to <u>The
New Yorker</u> "almost the only sustained criticism of
modern poetry that the general reader can follow."

942. Spiller, Robert. <u>American Literature</u> 25,
       No. 2 (March 1953): 117-18.

This book differs from other reviews of American
literature during the first half of the century in
that Miss Bogan, "poet and critic of note," writes
a personal essay, not an objective history. Her
assessment of foreign poets' influence makes it
more an essay on modern poetry. Its thesis is
"that T. S. Eliot discovered an aesthetic which
successfully resolved the confusions of modern
industrial man and made his experience once more
available to poetic insight."

943. Untermeyer, Louis. "About Trends in Poetry."
       <u>Saturday Review of Literature</u> 35, No. 5
       (2 Feb. 1952): 21, 37, 38.

Miss Bogan "measures achievement strictly in terms
of the breakthrough of a modern esthetic," without
considering social context. She helps her reader
understand the "influence of various mediums and
significant forms" in American poetry, including
symbolist prose and verse. She recognizes the
important part played by the little magazines and
the Imagists. Her appreciations of Yeats, Pound,
and Eliot are "eminently precise." She analyzes
with perception "the experimental talents of Hart
Crane and the midwestern poets, but even her
praise of Frost seems "unnecessarily niggling."
The 30-page anthology is a "queer collection."

Reviews of <u>SELECTED CRITICISM</u> 1950

944. Coxe, Louis O. "High, Healthy,
       Invigorating." <u>Poetry</u> 87, No. 6
       (March 1956): 370-72.

These pieces are too compact and too general, and
too many contemporary authors are included. But
Bogan's "perception is right in her insight into
the poetic predicament of moderns from Hopkins to
Karl Shapiro," even though she dares to question
the "total virtue of Wallace Stevens . . . and
plays the delicate iconoclast . . . with Virginia
Woolf." The reader should be glad to listen to
Miss Bogan's "rare civilized voice."

945. Emmet, Paul. "Among the New Books." San
     Francisco Chronicle (9 Oct. 1955): 20.

Miss Bogan "brings to this volume the technical
knowledge of a fellow-craftsman, the insight of a
sympathetic intelligence, and a journalist's
clarity and conciseness." She uses the
comparative approach to criticism which "traces
influence, compares and contrasts, and attempts to
place each poet into his proper context."
However, "the essays are too short and fragmented
and sometimes repetitive."

946. "The Exact Impression." Times Literary
     Supplement, 16 May, 1958.

Miss Bogan should be read as an example of
civilized integrity on both sides of the Atlantic.
Her work as a reviewer has the strengths of a
quick first impression rather than reasoned
judgment. She is often mistaken about a work's
scale and importance. She deals with flaws of the
famous moderns, Pound, Joyce, and Eliot, as well
as their successes.

947. Mayne, Richard. "Far But Not Wee."
     New Statesman (22 Mar. 1948): 383-84.

This book "proclaims a genuine and most discerning
critic, very American, very feminine, and very
understanding. . . ." Her only notable fault is
"the tendency to round off an article with
slightly after-dinner compliments."

948. Moore, Marianne. Poetry London-New York 1,
     No. 1 (Mar.-Apr. 1956): 36-39. Reprinted in
     A Marianne Moore Reader. New York: The

Viking Press, 1961. pp. 229-232.

"This writing has fiber." "With an eye to virtues
rather than defects, Miss Bogan does not
overburden. . . ." Her two necessary capacities
are "instinctiveness" and "coming to terms with
oneself." Henry James, Ezra Pound, and W. H.
Auden are "especially well-observed." It is a
fascinating book, abounding in insight, as well as
mastery of material and associative creative
insight that "treats everyone fairly."

949. Rexroth, Kenneth. "A Poet's Critical
     Essays." New York Herald Tribune
     (5 Feb. 1958)

One of the most esteemed poets in America, Miss
Bogan's "sure and deft intelligence and
considerable profundity" is reflected in her
critical essays, in which there is no trace of
that "fraudulent blight on American letters, the
Higher Criticism." Every review is compact with
sense and sensibility. The reviewer disagrees
with Bogan's contentions that La Farge had such
great influence on American poets and that the
avant-garde in poetry is over. He also is
surprised that William Carlos Williams is not
mentioned.

950. Untermeyer, Jean Starr. "A Seasoning of
     Wit." Saturday Review of Literature 38,
     No. 52 (24 Dec. 1955): 24.

Miss Bogan's essays come from "the living center
of the culture she has inherited and cherished and
to which she has contributed." She can pack a
great deal of information into a short space.
Grouping critiques of one author is a worthy
device that could have been used more uniformly.
Her wit seasons her essays, and her analogies "to
painting and music are particularly apt, as is her
discussion of the hazards of translating poetry."

Reviews of ELECTIVE AFFINITIES 1963

951. Auden, W. H. New York Times Book Review,
     18 Oct. 1964, 6.

This is the only readable translation of Goethe's
"romantic portrayal of 18th century high society."

952. Bauke, Jospeh P. "Disastrous Liaisons."
     Saturday Review (4 Jan. 1964): 82-83.

This new translation achieves "presence and
modernity" in the hands of its translators. "It
is ingenious in its handling of the difficult
prose of the older Goethe."

Reviews of THE JOURNAL OF JULES RENARD 1964

953. Bliven, Naomi. "Books: Renard the Fox." New
     Yorker 41 (12 June 1965): 153-55.

Although the book is abridged, the translation is
excellent. Renard's style, reproduced marvelously
by the translators, is "crisp, witty, and shrewd."

954. Bree, Germaine. Saturday Review of
     Literature 47 (7 Nov. 1964): 38, 43.

Renard's editors "very carefully and briefly
recall his honorable literary career." The
choices they make from the original 1200-page
journal lose some of the "full flavor of an
individual life," but the selection is judicious
and the translation apt. . . ." Bogan's
introduction and Roget's short biographical page
give just the insight that can make the journal
come alive for the reader."

955. Cosey, Florence. "Renard Explored."
     Christian Science Monitor (19 Nov. 1964): 10.

Although a translation is long overdue, it is
surprising to find the "swearwords missing or
diminished . . . and the professional writing . .
. transmuted into college English" in this
version. Too much emphasis is placed on the idler
side of Renard, so that the "English-language
reader will wonder legitimately how such a lazy
dreamer could be killed off by overwork."

956. Klein, R. H.   "Writers from the Interiors."
     Harper's 229 (Oct. 1964): 132-33.

"Jules Renard's Journal has finally been expertly
translated and edited." Renard's transformation
from country squire to "earthly boulevardier" is
fascinating to watch. "It is a pleasure" to have
his epigrams and short character sketches in
English.

957. O'Brien, Justin.   "A Cynic's Mask, a Love of
     Nature, a Gift of Phrase." New York Times
     Book Review (1 Nov. 1964): 4.

"In presenting Renard's Journal to American
readers, [the editors] wisely chose what is most
likely to interest us. . . ." The selections
contain "almost every example of the acute
observation of nature and gift for making unusual
comparisons" that produced Renard's Histories
Naturelles of 1896.

958. Wescott, Glenway.   "Le Carrot-Top." New York
     Herald Tribune Book Week 27 Dec. 1964, 1, 8.

This new first English translation is a cultural
event of importance. The editors have handled the
text discreetly, and have been ruthless in their
cutting, "but this lively selection ought to send
readers scampering to the original."

Reviews of THE GOLDEN JOURNEY 1965

959. Dalgliesh, Alice.   Saturday Review of
     Literature 49 (22 Jan. 1966): 46.

With its title taken from "The Golden Journey to
Samarkand," this book "has something for everyone,
from the most familiar poems to those not so well
known. A good collection compiled by two poets."

960. Dickey, James.   "The Language of Poetry."
     New York Times Book Review (7 Nov. 1965): 6.

This book "may well be the best general anthology
of poems for young people ever compiled." The

anthologists expect children to be "capable of
rising to good poems" which is the correct
attitude for them to take. "The poems could have
been selected only by poets as distinguished as
these two."

961. Jackson, Katherine Gauss. Harper's 231
     (Dec. 1965): 137.

"A delightful anthology for the young of all ages
selected by two distinguished contemporary
American poets."

962. Maxwell, Emily. "Briefly Noted." New Yorker
     41 (4 Dec. 1965): 238.

This anthology is "an invaluable collection of
lyric poems, nonsense verse, and ballads." The
poems, ranging from "Edmund Waller to Edmund
Wilson . . . have in common their purity of
sound."

963. Rich, Adrienne. "Six Anthologies." Poetry
     108, No. 5 (Aug. 1966): 334.

Rich and her two children liked The Golden Journey
because it is "well-balanced between classics and
odd, rather inspired choices" such as Lawrence's
"Bavarian Gentians," W. C. Williams' "The Dance,"
and Dylan Thomas' "Johnny Crack."

Reviews of A POET'S ALPHABET 1971

964. "A Poet's Alphabet: Reflections on the
     Literary Art and Vocation." Choice 8, No. 1
     (Mar. 1971): 62.

This is a "virtually complete collection of the
criticism of the late Louise Bogan arranged in a
convenient alphabetical order and ranging from
American literature through Yeats." Bogan has
"the penetrating intelligence of the best academic
minds without their narrowmindedness." She shows
courage of judgment with wisdom, grace, wit,
humor, and writes in classic language. This book

belongs on every literate person's shelf.

965. Morris, Harry. "Poets and Critics, Critics
     and Poets." <u>Sewanee Review</u> 80, No. 4
     (Oct.-Dec. 1972): 627-29.

This book is "a delight to read." Miss Bogan's
critical generosity stands out, but not at the
expense of truth. The reviewer would prefer a
chronological arrangement of writers rather than
alphabetical, so he could follow Miss Bogan's
development as a critic. He also misses the
original source of the reviews. Her most
important service for letters is her "constant
approval of the significant literary movements on
the continent and her vigorous support of
translation as a means of making available [the
literature of European countries,] Greece, and the
Orient."

966. <u>New Yorker</u> 46 (7 Nov. 1970) 184.

"Note: . . . McGraw-Hill has published <u>A Poet's
Alphabet: Reflections on the Literary Art and
Vocation</u>, a collection of criticism by Louise
Bogan, edited by Robert Phelps and Ruth Limmer.
Most of the essays were first published in these
pages."

Reviews of <u>WHAT THE WOMAN LIVED</u> 1973

967. Bell, Pearl K. "Writers and Writing: A Woman
     of Letters." <u>The New Leader</u>, 4 Feb. 1974,
     23-24.

This collection "ranks with the letters of Keats,
Henry James and Rilke." Bogan's letters, "tossed
off with breath-taking facility," cover a
"staggering range of topics and happenings." Her
letters to such literary friends as Edmund Wilson,
Rolfe Humphries, and William Maxwell, illustrate
her ability to write "at the top of her forte" to
men, while her letters to women, such as May
Sarton, are strained.

968. "Briefly Noted." <u>New Yorker</u> 49

(12 Nov. 1973): 219.

"The range of these letters is all the way from persons and places . . . through aesthetic appraisals put down at the moment of their forming . . . to the weather in the soul." Miss Bogan "could be terribly funny" about both friends and sometime enemies. She was extremely candid about her personal life in these letters, admirably introduced and edited by Ruth Limmer.

969. Grumbach, Doris. New Republic 169 (1 Dec. 1973): 33.

These letters cover 50 years of correspondence with "every important poet and critic of her time." Bogan was "herself a fine lyric poet, [who] is extraordinarily humble when she speaks of her own work and was, apparently as gentle to the work of others." She felt alternately affection and hostility for The New Republic.

970. Harrison, Barbara Grizzuti. "A Troubled Peace." Ms. 3, No. 5 (Nov. 1974): 40, 46, 93, 94, 96.

"These are the letters of a woman too reticent and austere ever to become a cult figure." "Her sanity and her dignity inform and ennoble . . . this remarkable book." She was unable to grasp completely the irony of her situation as a former housewife who still had to make time to do her writing even when "her hero-husband worship" was over. Her letters reveal her to be "essentially a religious ecstatic with a great deal of good common earthly sense."

971. Kennedy, Eileen. Best Sellers 33, No. 17 (1 Dec. 1973): 399.

The letters "trace the growth of a poet's mind and character." The book is a "treasure house" of Bogan's relationships with other poets and literary friends, but it lacks a chronological account of Bogan's life.

972. Louchheim, Katie. "True Inheritor."

Atlantic 233, No. 2 (Feb. 1974): 90-91.

"She was the most gracefully lucid, learned, and
unprogrammatic critic of her generation." The
letters fill in the background of Bogan's
deliberate aloneness and give a brief description
of her work, especially her isolation from the
various political and social trends of the 20s and
30s. The quotations from letters to friends Rolfe
Humphries and Theodore Roethke show her literary
relationships to these men. The letters contain
all that is important about her, "including her
intellectual powers, her depressions, her taste
for the good life . . . her incorruptibility,
[and] her conspiratorial heritage." The title
should have been, What the Woman Lived Through.

973. Mitford, Nancy. "Through a Poet's Private
     Voice into her Life." New York Times Book
     Review, 16 Dec. 1973, 1-2.

That Louise Bogan's options as a woman writer were
limited comes through her letters which form a
kind of informal biography. Unfortunately the
"simplest facts of her life" are not made clear.
Why are there no letters to members of her family
in this collection which includes mainly letters
to her literary friends?

Reply to the Milford review by Herman G. Weinberg
and Frederick Feinstein in New York Times Book
Review, 13 Jan. 1954, 34.

Reviews of JOURNEY AROUND MY ROOM: THE
AUTOBIOGRAPHY OF LOUISE BOGAN, A MOSAIC 1981

974. Kinzie, Mary. "Two Lives." American Poetry
     Review 10, No. 2 (Mar.-Apr. 1981): 20-21.

In this review, which also discusses Straw for the
Fire: From the Notebooks of Theodore Roethke 1943-
1936, Kinzie contrasts Bogan's independent mature
writing with Roethke's adolescent displays. His
character comes across as "coy, undisciplined and
predatory," while Bogan's is "vivid, direct and
passionate." Each life is "compulsive and
touching." Bogan was obsessed by her mother and
Roethke by his father. Bogan's letters succeed

because she wrote them to "amuse, to inform, to
craft without falsehood or self-consciousness."
Roethke's fail because he "attempted to sound like
the great ones in their greatest moments."

975. Leithauser, Brad. "Portrait of a
      Temperament." Washington Post Book World
      (18 Jan. 1981): 4, 10.

Although the book is not actually an
autobiography, bits and pieces from Bogan's
writings are well arranged to form an account of a
life. The most affecting reading is her account
of her return to the old Boston neighborhood where
she lived as a child and her memory of the
problems her family had there. Her poetry,
however, still remains the measure of her
achievement, and much of it now seems "old-
fashioned."

976. Pritchard, William. "Pieces of Private
      Feeling." New York Times Book Review,
      4 Jan. 1981, 4, 25.

How would Louise Bogan, who was so jealous of her
privacy, have reacted to this "mosaic" of her
journals, poems, bits of criticism and letters,
notebook entries and "other fugitive expressions?"
Limmer has reconstructed the life imaginatively.
Quoted at length is Bogan's description of Mrs.
Gardner's orderly house in Ballardville. This
work, "in some of its juxaposition of prose and
poems, helped [the reviewer] to a sharper sense of
how good a poet she could be."

977. Shaw, Robert. "The Life-Saving Process."
      Nation (27 Dec. 1980): 710-12.

Ruth Limmer's imaginative and unobtrusive
assemblage of Bogan's "widely disparate writings
of a personal bent" in this collection "fuse in a
greater unity than one would have thought
possible." It is remarkable, given Bogan's
"intense reticence and the traumatic quality of
her past," that she got as much on paper as she
did. Writing poetry helped her to deal with her
difficult life. Several of her poems, including
"Henceforth, from the Mind," "Song for the Last

Act," "To My Brother," and "Roman Fountain" are
"among the best in English in this country."

978. Tane, Miriam. "A Heart that Speaks."
    <u>Virginia Quarterly</u> 58, No. 1 (1982): 161-65

Limmer's organizing devices of poem, story, and
pictures are "too elaborate [a] format . . . for
one who was so wary of excess." Bogan's words are
"most welcome," even if the confessional mode was
beyond her. The stories "stand with the best of
Bogan's poems," and the reprinted poems with
Bogan's notations are a pleasure.

F. DISSERTATIONS

These nine doctoral dissertations are arranged
alphabetically. Several focus on Louise Bogan
only, while the others discuss other women poets
as well. The annotations for the unpublished
dissertations are taken from Dissertation
Abstracts International, except for those by
Sandra Cookson and Catherine Stearns, which were
read by the bibliographer.

979. Aldrich, Marcia Ann. "Louise Bogan and the
     Crisis of Kinship. Ph.D. diss. University of
     Washington, 1987. Abstract in Dissertation
     Abstracts International 47, (June 1987):
     4387A-4388A.

Louise Bogan attempted to "cast her poetry in the
high modernist mode of impersonality," but her
sources were the relationship between mother and
daughter. She "camouflaged her thematic concerns
into the obscurity" with which the critics have
charged her. Aldrich reconstructs "the writing
situation for women poets in the 1920s and 30s and
[discusses] psychoanalytic poetics based on a fear
of the maternal." Poems such as "Medusa" and
"Women" represent "crises of kinship with the
mother and the feminine lyric."

980. Bowles, Gloria Lee. "Suppression and
     Expression in Poetry by American Women:
     Louise Bogan, Denise Levertov and Adrienne
     Rich." Ph.D. diss. University of
     California, 1976. Abstract in Dissertation
     Abstracts International 37 (Mar. 1977):
     5822A.

Women poets in Bogan's time had to write like men.
Male critics did not understand her poetry because
she wrote about a uniquely feminine experience,
the inability of women to take a balanced attitude

273

toward love.

981. Cookson, Sandra P. "All Has Been Translated
     into Treasure: The Art of Louise Bogan."
     Ph.D. diss. University of Connecticut, 1980.
     Abstract in Dissertation Abstract
     International 41 (Mar. 1981): 4032A.

"The repressed material of her life was her true
poetic raw material." Cookson uses Bogan's
letters and journal to show how Bogan translated
her life into art, in spite of her dislike for
direct autobiographical statement. Her poetry's
formal rhyme, meter, and stanza organized the
irrational elements from her subconscious. The
love poems in her first two books of poetry
contain "the violence that disrupted her attempts
at love." Poems from the third book show the
"process of catharsis of jealousy and rage."

Cookson discusses Bogan's recurring symbol for
female sexuality, the blackened field. Her other
personal symbols, associated with the universal
archetype of the demon mother, are the Fury, the
Medusa, and the wild horse. After Bogan's
psychiatric therapy, the frightening, punishing
women patterned after her mother become sisters,
protectors, and friends.

Close readings of the late voyage and quest poems,
"Putting to Sea," "Song for the Last Act," "After
the Persian," and "Psychiatrist's Song," give
insight into these poems. Especially valuable is
the reference to the allegorical "land of Id," the
evil "unnatural tropical place . . . that is the
habitation of sexual jealousy and hatred."

Bogan's view of other women writers was
traditional as shown in her 1962 Bennington
College lecture, "What the Women Said." She
identified with illustrious male literary figures
such as her friend Edmund Wilson.

982. De Shazer, Mary Kirk. "The Woman Poet and
     Her Muse. Sources and Images of Female
     Creativity in the Poetry of H. D., Louise
     Bogan, May Sarton and Adrienne Rich."
     Ph.D. diss. University of Oregon, 1982.
     Abstract in Dissertation Abstracts

International 43 (1982): 1967A.

The female poet's muse is problemmatical in that
she does not choose a male muse, but an activated
female muse "re-visioned" as a powerful
alternative "self" rather than an externalized
objectified "Other." "The four poets discussed
represent modern woman's exploration of the dual
nature of the female muse, a force perceived as
both demonic and benevolent."

983. Gabelnick, Faith. "Making Connections:
     American Poets on Love." Ph.D. diss.
     American University, 1974. Abstract in
     Dissertation Abstracts International 35
     (1974): 2266A.

Part III in this dissertation on the study of
modern American women poets as "outsiders and part
of a special minority" examines the love
relationship in Blue Estuaries: Poems 1923-1968.
"The lover is encouraged to give up something of
herself in order to bring the other toward love."

984. Pope, Deborah. "The Pattern of Isolation in
     Contemporary American Women's Poetry: Louise
     Bogan, Maxine Kumin, Denise Levertov,
     Adrienne Rich." Ph.D. diss. University of
     Wisconsin, 1977. Abstract in Dissertation
     Abstracts International 40 (Jan. 1980):
     4029A-30A.

Bogan's formal poetry and constricted life form
the basis for a progression from her isolation and
marginality due to women's previous lack of
opportunity to a contemporary acceptance of
women's poetry and varying life styles illustrated
in the lives and work of the three other poets
discussed.

985. Ridgeway, Jacqueline Cecilia. "The Poetry of
     Louise Bogan." Ph.D. diss. University of
     California, 1977. Abstract in Dissertation
     Abstracts International 38 (Dec. 1977):
     3503A-04A. (Entry 831)

The neglect of Bogan's poems is due to the
complexity of their meaning which "involves the

use of traditional form to parallel psychological
structure." Ridgeway analyzes these forms to
determine the meaning of the poems.

986. Sell, Gwendolyn Sorre. "Louise Bogan: 'The
     Discipline of Recognition': Gender and
     Artistic Maturity." Ph.D. diss. Emory
     University, 1988. Abstract in <u>Dissertation
     Abstracts International</u> 49, No. 6
     (Dec. 1988): 1600A.

A feminist study of Bogan's poetry which "avoids
reducing her to a patriarchal cripple." The
culture of her time gave contradictory images of
women which appear in Bogan's criticism, short
stories, and poetry. The poetry records "her
progress as a writer and as a person."

987. Stearns, Catherine M. <u>Poetic Decorum and the
     Problem of Form: Louise Bogan, Marianne
     Moore, and Elizabeth Bishop</u>. Ph.D. diss.
     Brandeis University, 1985. Abstract in
     <u>Dissertation Abstracts International</u> 46
     (Nov. 1983): 1282A. Published Ann Arbor:
     University of Michigan, 1984.

Bogan's subjective, conventional formal poetry is
compared with Moore's objective, unconventional
poetry. Bishop's work syntheses the two qualities
taken from Bogan and Moore, subjectivity and
unconventional form.

The first third of the dissertation focuses on
Bogan's poetry and its influences. The three
poets' mothers all had a tremendous influence on
their work. Bogan's love/hate relationship with
her mother generated her poetry, beginning with
the early poem "Betrothed." Her conception of art
was "a deliverance from the relationship with
[her] mother." The poems "Medusa," "The Flume,"
and "The Sleeping Fury" center on the frightening
mother images, while "The Dream" symbolizes
psychological rebirth. "Bogan's misogyny clearly
stems from her contradictory feelings towards her
mother."

Bogan was "trapped finally in the consequences of
her acceptance of social and literary contraints,"
unlike Moore and Bishop who were able to throw off

these bonds in their poetry.

988. Walker, Cheryl. "The Women's Tradition in
     American Poetry." Ph.D. diss. Brandeis
     University 1973. Abstract in <u>Dissertation</u>
     <u>Abstracts International</u> 34 (1974): A4294-5.

Bogan's work has the passion of the 19th century
and some of its resignation, but it also reflects
modern reticence and control. Walker explores the
"mainstream of American women's poetry to
establish the existence of a women's tradition . .
. from shared experiences." She finds Bogan is
the woman's classical traditional poet. The
tradition breaks down with modern women poets'
recent emphasis on self-realization.

G. BIBLIOGRAPHIES AND BIOGRAPHIES

This section contains selected bibliographies of
Louise Bogan's works and biographies, as well as
articles about her in reference books. Only
entries of special interest containing important
information on Bogan are included. They are
arranged chronologically.

1930

989. "Louise Bogan." Wilson Bulletin for
Librarians 4, No. 7 (March 1930): 310.

Brief background on Louise Bogan's birthplace,
parents, education, and places of residence,
including the "small farm in upper eastern New
York" where she "lives with her husband Raymond
Holden, himself a poet of distinction." This
biography also lists her publications and
criticism.

1960

990. Nyren, Dorothy, ed. A Library of Literary
Criticism. New York: Frederick Ungar
Publishing Co., 1960. pp. 66-69.
Reprinted in 4th ed, 1969. Eds. Dorothy
Nyren Curley and Maurice Kramer.

Excerpts from reviewers of Miss Bogan's books of
poetry, arranged chronologically. The authors of
the reviews include Mark Van Doren, Babette
Deutsch, Ford Madox Ford, Malcolm Cowley, John
Ciardi, Kenneth Rexroth, Léonie Adams, Marianne
Moore, and Reed Whittemore.

1969

991. Gregory, Horace, and Marya Zaturenska. A
History of American Poetry 1910-1940. New
York: Gordian Press, 1969. pp. 276-280.

Although Bogan shared the weakness of immaturity
with other women poets of the early 20s, her
poetry was more literate and less personal. In
1923, the height of metaphysical poetry, she held
closely to tight phrasing, using a "hammer and
chisel" to write her lyrics. "A fierce, almost
frightening rhetoric, unguarded love, and
passionate sentiment sometimes overwhelms" her
verse, especially in later phases. Her work
echoes Millay. In "M., Singing," she has
"probably written her least pretentious lyric."

1971

992. Smith, William Jay. Louise Bogan: A Woman's
     Words. Memorial lecture delivered at the
     Library of Congress, May 4, 1970, published
     with the bibliography compiled by the
     Reference Department of the Library of
     Congress. Washington: Library of Congress,
     1971. 81 pages. (Entries 826 and 1021)

The bibliography lists Bogan materials in the
collections of the Library of Congress and
concentrates on Bogan's individual poems and
articles not reprinted in Bogan's books,
particulary those in The New Yorker, excluding any
works about her and her books.

1976

993. Couchman, Jane. "Louise Bogan: A
     Bibliography of Primary and Secondary
     Sources, 1915-1975," Part I Bulletin of
     Bibliography 33, No. 2 (Feb.-Mar. 1976):
     73-77, 104. Part II Bulletin of Bibliography
     33, No. 3 (Apr.-June 1976): 111-26, 147.
     Part III Bulletin of Bibliography 32, No. 3
     [sic] (July-Sept. 1976): 178-81.

This bibliography, compiled principally from 1969-
72 with some updating, begins with a chronology.
Works by Bogan include poems, essays,
miscellaneous short works, and New Yorker reviews
and essays, as well as author anthologies and
translations. Works about Bogan are arranged into
books, parts of books, periodical articles,
reviews and obituaries. Couchman's bibliography
is unannotated and she omits any entries published
in William Jay Smith's 1971 Library of Congress
bibliography.

1979

994. <u>American Women Writers</u>. Eds. Theodora Graham
      and Lina Mainiero. New York: Frederick
      Unger, 1979. pp. 183-86.

This brief essay emphasizes Bogan's formal poetry,
a "consciously controlled lyric form with a
restraint and precision which contained passionate
feeling." The subjects are love, loss, grief,
mutability, the struggle of the free mind,
marriage, and dreams.

1980

995. Perlmutter, Elizabeth [Frank]. "Louise
      Bogan." <u>Notable American Women: The Modern
      Period</u>, Vol. 4. Eds. Barbara Sicherman et
      al. Cambridge: Harvard University Press,
      1980. pp. 88-90.

"With major gifts she forged a perfect minor
mode." Perlmutter, later Frank, the author of the
1985 biography, <u>Louise Bogan, A Portrait</u>,
describes Bogan's life, beginning with her unhappy
childhood, her limited classical education in
Boston, her early "elegant prose," and her two
unhappy marriages. The chronology continues with
Bogan's Guggenheim Fellowship, her 30 years of
writing poetry criticism for <u>The New Yorker</u> and
her many honors. Bogan faced depression and lack
of money "with courage, humor, and an extreme
devotion to responsibility." Her five books of
poetry follow "the severe tradition of the
seventeenth century lyric." Her poetry was
"nourished by the technical discoveries and
spiritual concerns of . . . Hopkins, Yeats, Eliot,
and Auden."

1982

996. Jaskoski, Helen. "Louise Bogan." <u>Critical
      Survey of Poetry</u>, Vol. 1. Ed. Frank N.
      Magill. Englewood Cliffs, New Jersey: Salem
      Press, 1982. pp. 230-39.

The article begins with a list of Bogan's works
and achievements, continues with a brief
biography, and ends with a lengthy discussion of
her poems. Jaskoski's unusual analyses differ
from other critics' readings. For example she

considers the speaker in the late poem "Little
Lobelia " to be a "piteous helpless, inarticulate
. . . infant addressing its mother," instead of
the author's suppressed poetic inspiration making
itself felt, which is the usual interpretation.
Jaskoski notes Bogan's emphasis on women in her
poems and her acknowledgement of women's poetic
contribution, even if she did "inherit . . . the
Victorian and Romantic view that applied to the
dichotomies of emotion and intellect to woman and
man, respectively."

1986

997. Wilson, Robert A. "Louise Bogan: A
     Bibliographical Checklist." American Book
     Collector 7, No. 9 (1986): 31-36.

Wilson divides his chronologically arranged
checklist of 25 first editions of Bogan's writings
into primary (first book) and secondary
publications (first appearance in books by
others). He describes each book's binding and
stamping colors and notes Bogan's contributions in
the secondary publications.

998. Schloss, Carol. "Louise Bogan 1897-1970."
     Dictionary of Literary Biography, American
     Poets, 1880-1945, Vol. 45. Detroit: Gale
     Research Co., 1986. pp. 52-59.

This biography, illustrated with pictures of Bogan
at different stages in her life, stresses Bogan's
reputation as "one of America's finest lyric
poets" and describes various influences on her
poetry. Her first two books were influenced by
Yeats and her third by Rilke. Her major themes,
"the destructiveness of romantic attachment and
the need for private sources of strength and
grace," pervade all her collections. Poets and
critics, including Frost, Auden, Roethke, and
Winters, praised her poetry. But "if it was as a
poet Bogan made her reputation, it was as a critic
she made her living." After 1937 Bogan's poetry
output decreased, but her literary reputation
grew, leading to many literary awards, speeches,
and teaching positions. Her last years "were
lived in a kind of secular monasticism."

H. BOOKS AND POEMS DEDICATED TO LOUISE BOGAN

This section contains listings of books dedicated to Louise Bogan and poems written for her. These are listed in chronological order.

999. Mead, Margaret. "For a Proud Lady." <u>Measure</u> 2 (June 1925): 16. (Entry 855)

Poem written for Louise Bogan when she was working with Mead at the Museum of Natural History.

1000. Adams, Leonie. <u>High Falcon and Other Poems</u>. New York: The John Day Co., 1929.

Book dedicated to Louise Bogan and Raymond Holden.

1001. Maxwell, William. <u>The Folded Leaf</u>. New York: Harper & Brothers, 1945.

Book dedicated to Louise Bogan.

1002. Morgan, Robin, et al. <u>Poems by Seven</u>. New York: Voyages Press, 1959.

Book of poetry by seven different poets, limited to 500 copies, dedicated on last page "for Louise Bogan."

1003. Sarton, May. "Elegy (for Louise Bogan)." <u>A Durable Fire: New Poems by May Sarton</u>. New York: W. S. Norton & Co., Inc., 1972. p. 66.

Poem of mourning written six days after Bogan's death.

I. AWARDS AND APPOINTMENTS

Listed chronologically in this section are notices
of Louise Bogan's honors, including literary
awards, fellowships, appointments, and an honorary
doctorate.

1004. "The John Reed Memorial Prize." _Poetry_ 37,
     No. 2 (Nov. 1930): 104-5.

This prize of $100 is awarded as a tribute to the
"high distinction" of Miss Bogan's work in _Poetry_
and her first two volumes.

1005. "Louise Bogan Gets Poetry Chair." _New York_
     Times, 8 July 1945, 11.

Miss Bogan is appointed to the Library of Congress
Chair of Poetry, succeeding Robert Penn Warren.
She will hold the post for one year. She was
awarded Guggenheim Fellowships in 1933 and 1937.

1006. "Louise Bogan Wins Poetry Prize." _New York_
     Times, 28 July 1948, 21.

Miss Bogan was named winner of the Harriet Monroe
Poetry Award for 1948 of $500 by the University of
Chicago.

1007. "14 Win Admission to Arts Institute." _New_
     York Times, 8 Feb. 1952, 18.

Louise Bogan, one of 14 whose works are
"considered most likely to win a permanent place
in American culture," has won election to the
National Institute of Arts and Letters in the
department of literature. She won the Helen Haire
Levinson Memorial Prize from _Poetry_ magazine in
1937, among other prizes.

1008. "Bollingen Award to New York Poets." <u>New
      York Times</u>, 10 Jan. 1955, 16. (Portrait)

Miss Bogan shares $1,000 Bolligen Prize in Poetry
of the Yale Library with Léonie Adams. Bogan was
selected for her <u>Collected Poems 1922-1953</u>. The
first winner was Ezra Pound in 1948.

1009. "Miss Hobby is Speaker." <u>New York Times</u>,
      5 June 1956, 132.

Honorary degree is conferred on Miss Bogan, poet
and literary critic, at Western College's 101
commencement in Oxford, Ohio.

1010. "Brandeis Lists Awards." <u>New York Times</u>, 11
      Feb. 1962, 21.

The 1962 Creative Arts Medals are awarded to
Louise Bogan, poet; S. N. Behrman, playwright;
Alexander Calder, sculptor; and Edgar Varese,
composer. The awards and the $1,500 grants are
for "a lifetime of outstanding artistic creation."
They will be presented at a reception March 18 in
New York.

1011. "Five 'Distinguished' Senior American
      Writers get $10,000 apiece from the National
      Endowment for the Arts." <u>New York Times</u>,
      6 July 1967, 40. (Portrait)

Miss Bogan, along with Malcolm Cowley, Kenneth
Patchen, Yvor Winters, and John Crowe Ransom, have
been given these awards, the first ever "to honor
writers who have not heretofore received all the
recognition due them." Miss Carolyn Kizer,
director of literary programs, calls Bogan
"probably the finest American lyric poet alive,"
although she is best known at this time for her
<u>New Yorker</u> poetry reviews.

1012. "Academy of Arts Adds Louise Bogan."
      <u>New York Times</u>, 10 Dec. 1968, 53.

Miss Bogan fills the vacancy left by the death of
Carl Sandburg in the American Academy of Arts and
Sciences, considered to be the nation's highest

honor society of the arts, which has 50 members
selected from the 250 members of the National
Institute of Arts and Sciences. She will be
inducted May 1969.

J. MEMORIAL SPEECHES AND OBITUARIES

The following selected speeches and obituaries are arranged in alphabetical order by speaker, author, or publication title. Many other obituaries not listed here simply repeated the information found in The New York Times review.

1013. Academy of Arts and Letters Memorial Service. 11 March 1970. Tape of service at Library of Congress.

Speakers: John Wheelock, who read "Henceforth, from the Mind," Leonie Adams, Richard Wilbur, and William Maxwell, who read "Journey Around My Room." Alan Tate, who could not make the service, had a statement read, which also quoted "Henceforth, from the Mind."

1014. Auden, W. H. "Louise Bogan 1897-1970." Proceedings, American Academy of Arts and Letters, National Institute of Arts and Letters. 2nd series, No. 21 (1970): 63-68.

Auden's eulogy on Louise Bogan. Women poets are different from men in that they describe "real events and personal emotional experiences" and are "more tempted than a man to be over-intense in describing them." Louise Bogan was able to guard against this tenseness. Her standards for judging her own work were severe, but she was "the kind of reviewer every writer hopes for. . . ." Her work can be judged by its craftsmanship of uniqueness of perspective. She also produced first-rate translations and had a "deep love and understanding of music" which comes forth in her lyrics. In spite of her difficult life, she was able "to wrest beauty and joy out of dark places." "Henceforth, from the Mind" may be her finest poem.

1015. Ciardi, John. "Manner of Speaking."
      <u>Saturday Review</u> 53 (21 Feb. 1970): 20, 22.

Her true voice was in her poems which speak her
elegy and shall be as immortal as possible in this
transitory world. Her "central quality is the
intensity of her emotion and technical precision."
There is now a sense of completion, "a sadness
that great lives must end, an admiration that
genius can give them such a voice."

1016. Horsely, Carter B. <u>New York Times</u>,
      5 Feb. 1970, 39. (Portrait)

". . . one of the most distinguished lyric poets
in the English language died at her home. . . ."
"With a supple syntax [she] created subtle
structures of delicate, but intense works, . .
rich in passion, robust in irony." Love for her
was a "constant indulgence." Horsely quotes from
"Juan's Song," "Women," and Medusa."

1017. "Louise Bogan 1897-1970." <u>Poetry</u> 116, No. 1
      (Apr. 1970): 58.

The entire notice is the following quotation:

  Words made of breath, these also are undone.
  And greedy sight abolished in its claim.
  Light fails from ruin and from wall the same:
  The loud sound and pure silence fall as one.

1018. Maxwell, William. "Louise Bogan
      (1897-1970)." <u>New Yorker</u> 45
      (14 Feb. 1970): 132. Reprinted as the
      introduction in <u>A Poet's Alphabet</u>.
      New York: McGraw-Hill, 1970. pp. vii-viii.
      (Entry 219)

Miss Bogan served as the poetry critic for <u>The New
Yorker</u> for 38 years. She lived quietly in New
York City, published six volumes of poetry, two of
literary criticism and several distinguished
translations, and received the true literary
honors. Her poems "are not likely to go out of
style" for "in whatever she wrote the line of
truth was exactly superimposed on the line of
feeling."

1019. <u>Newsweek</u> 16 Feb. 1970, 63.

Louise Bogan was one of poetry's leading lights.
"It doesn't come to you on the wings of a dove;
it's something you have to work hard at," she said
of poetry. Even so her "pure direct lines sounded
effortless" as shown in the lines quoted from
"Musician."

1020. Smith, William Jay. "Louise Bogan: A
      Woman's Words." Memorial lecture delivered
      at the Library of Congress, 4 May, 1990.
      (Entries 826 and 992)

1021. <u>Time</u>, 16 Feb. 1970, 63.

Louise Bogan died of a heart attack (rest of
obituary same information as <u>New York Times</u>).

1022. <u>Washington Post</u>, 6 Feb. 1970, C6. Portrait.

Obituary contains the same information as <u>New York
Times</u>.

AUTHOR INDEX

This index lists all authors of books Louise Bogan reviewed, as well as editors, translators, and compilers of these books. Included here too are writers who were subjects of her essays. Authors who wrote about Bogan also appear. The numbers refer to the entries in the bibliography.

Adams, Franklin P. 337
Adams, Léonie 210,
  826, 858, 862, 872,
  883, 891, 904, 910,
  913, 917-18, 920,
  925, 990, 1000, 1008,
  1013
Aeschylus 353, 369,
  553
Aiken, Conrad 303,
  305, 336, 421, 468,
  484, 506, 536, 567
  874
Alberti, Rafael 470
Aldington, Richard
  310, 435, 484
Aldrich, Marcia Ann
  979
Aldridge, Richard 797
Alexander, Lloyd 553
Allen, Donald M. 222
  584
Allen, G. W. 223
Allot, Kenneth 572
Amis, Kingsley 233
Andrade, Jorge Carrera
  487
Angoff, Allan 693
Apollinaire, Guillaume
  159, 203, 284, 544,
  685
Aragon, Louis 484
Aristophanes 592
Arlott, John 521

Armi, Anna Maria 489
Arnheim, Rudolph 513
Ashbery, John 122,
  294, 934
Auden, W. H. 134, 147,
  186-91, 208, 224-26
  244, 309, 311, 316,
  348, 398, 409, 467,
  513, 539, 549, 616,
  623, 626, 633, 660,
  685, 690, 726, 751,
  752, 802-3, 854, 908,
  915, 948, 951, 995,
  998, 1014
Augur, Helen 649
Ault, Norman 532
Auslander, Joseph 305,
  319, 336

Bacon, Leonard 313,
  326, 342
Bacon, Peggy 305, 320,
  321
Barber, Samuel 765
Barker, George 460,
  551
Barnard, Mary 422
Barnes, Djuna 648
Barnes, John S. 478
Barnes, William 547
Barrows, Marjorie 434
Barzun, Jacques 755
Baudelaire 122, 124,
  153, 159, 173, 199,

TITLE INDEX

This index contains titles of Louise Bogan's books, poems, stories, essays, translations, and lectures, all in capital letters. Reviews of the books she wrote and the books written about her follow the individual book title entry. Also listed are titles of books, periodicals, and articles that contain material by and about Louise Bogan. Titles of the books Bogan reviewed in The New Yorker and elsewhere are not included in this index. The numbers refer to the entries in the bibliography.

303